D1447388

THE COLLECTED WORKS OF

ERIC VOEGELIN

VOLUME 28

WHAT IS HISTORY?
AND OTHER LATE
UNPUBLISHED WRITINGS

PROJECTED VOLUMES IN THE SERIES

THE COLLECTED WORKS OF

ERIC VOEGELIN

VOLUME 28

WHAT IS HISTORY?
AND OTHER LATE
UNPUBLISHED WRITINGS

EDITED WITH AN INTRODUCTION BY

THOMAS A. HOLLWECK

AND

PAUL CARINGELLA

LOUISIANA STATE UNIVERSITY PRESS

BATON ROUGE AND LONDON

Designer: Albert Crochet
Typeface: Trump Mediaevel
Typesetter: G & S Typesetters, Inc.
Printer and binder: Thomson-Shore, Inc.

LIBRARY OF CONGRESS CATALOGING-IN-PUBLICATION DATA

Voegelin, Eric, 1901–
    What is history? and other late unpublished writings / edited with
an introduction by Thomas A. Hollweck and Paul Caringella.
        p.   cm. — (The collected works of Eric Voegelin ; v. 28)
    Contains some translations from German.
    Includes bibliographical references.
    Includes index.
    Contents: What is history?—Anxiety and reason—The eclipse of
reality—The moving soul—The beginning and the beyond.
    ISBN 0-8071-1603-3 (alk. paper)
    1. Philosophy. 2. History—Philosophy. 3. Political science—
Philosophy. I. Hollweck, Thomas A. II. Caringella, Paul.
III. Title. IV. Series: Voegelin, Eric, 1901–   Works. 1989 ; v. 28.
B3354.V88   1989 vol. 28
193 s—dc20
[193]   90-35657
                                                             CIP

The editors offer grateful acknowledgment to the Earhart Foundation
and to the Foundation for Faith in Search of Understanding for support
provided at various stages in the preparation of this book for publication.

Contents

Acknowledgments

The editors would like to thank Mrs. Lissy Voegelin for her constant support and her generosity during their work on this volume. Thanks are also due to Mr. Charles Palm and Ms. Linda Bernard of the Hoover Institution Archives for their support and cooperation; to Professor Jürgen Gebhardt and Professor Ellis Sandoz for their helpful advice; to Professor Manfred Henningsen for his assistance in establishing some important factual points; and to Professor Michael P. Morrissey for his valuable suggestions.

Editors' Introduction

What Is History? and Other Late Unpublished Writings contains the most significant pieces of unpublished writing completed by Eric Voegelin in his later years. Spanning the period from the early 1960s to the later 1970s, these selections fill out the body of work Voegelin completed after the publication of the first three volumes of *Order and History* in 1956 and 1957. The volume *Late Unpublished Writings* complements its companion, *Published Essays, 1966–1985*, in initiating the publication of *The Collected Works of Eric Voegelin*. The two volumes conveniently gather together all the studies that surround the two major works of Voegelin's later years, *Anamnesis* (1966) and *The Ecumenic Age* (1974), Volume IV of *Order and History*, and they display in substantial detail the matrix of his philosophy of consciousness, the core of an effort of decades that culminated only in the fifth and final volume of *Order and History*, published posthumously in 1987 as *In Search of Order*.

The publication of this volume and of the *Published Essays, 1966–1985*, edited by Ellis Sandoz, offers the opportunity to establish a context in which the achievement of the two last volumes of *Order and History* will become even more explicit, for it enables the reader to trace much of the genesis of the questions that occupied Voegelin during the years in which the conception of the purpose of his main work was to undergo frequent and perhaps fundamental changes. The nature of these changes was highlighted by the author himself in *The Ecumenic Age* in which he spoke of the break with the original program developed for *Order and History* (Introduction, 1–11) and discussed his use of "Introduction . . . as the form which a philosophy of history has to assume in the present historical situation" (Conclusion, 57–58). Voegelin's frequently cited formulation there of this "new form" of analysis that "had to move backward and forward and sideways, in order to follow empirically the patterns of meaning as they revealed themselves in the self-interpretation of persons and societies in history" (*OH*, IV, 57), if it is to be understood as more than an idiosyncratic style of historical thinking, must be seen against the rich background of the material analyses he gathered in his search for the constants that keep the analysis from losing itself in the multiplicity of historical orders and their symbolizations.

Introduction—Voegelin's term for a new form that "is definitely not a story of meaningful events to be arranged on a time line" (*OH*, IV, 57)—is also the form the editors must adopt in their opening remarks to this volume; for though it is possible to arrange the pieces presented here "on a time line," the reader must always remain aware of the lines connecting those writings with the large body of essays that were actually published during the 1960s and 1970s and with the ongoing, yet constantly changing, project of *Order and History*. There is, for instance, the synoptic table of contents of an earlier plan for the fourth volume of *Order and History*, which is reproduced here in the Appendix. Voegelin projected a vast analytical survey of the emergence of ecumenic civilizations, under the original title *Empire and Christianity*, that was to include all the great civilizations of the ancient world, from Hellas to China, and that was to culminate in a discussion of the "orthodox civilizations" of Byzantium, Islam, and the West. The plan for this massive enterprise, which dates from 1961, was then apparently absorbed into the volume that was to begin with the chapter "What Is History?" which we date around 1963. In 1958, soon after the publication of the first three volumes of *Order and History*, Voegelin had assumed the burdens of a Chair at the University of Munich and was becoming ever more engrossed in the tasks of developing the Institut fuer Politische Wissenschaft, which he had founded there. In a letter written from Munich dated July 21, 1960, to Donald Ellegood, director of the Louisiana State University Press, Voegelin sketched out a plan for Volume IV in which one can recognize the core of the later, fuller synoptic table. The letter is important enough to justify quoting substantial portions.

At last I can give you more precise information about the MS. The whole matter had been held up terribly: (1) by the necessity of working through such outlandish materials as the Chinese and Indian, and (2) by the resistance of the theoretical problem to resolution. Both obstacles have been overcome, and I am proceeding now to write the MS in the order of the chapters. This order will be the following:

Chapter I: Historiogenesis
" II: The Formation of Existence
" III: Empire and Ecumenism
" IV: China and India
" V: Stoicism, Apocalypse, and Gnosis
" VI: Christianity
" VII: The Roman Empire
" VIII: Chronology and Christianity

Large parts are in finished form, and the present work is on the final revision in the order of the chapters, which had been insecure until three months ago.

As soon as the chapters are finished, I shall put them in the mail for you. The first chapters will arrive in about two weeks.

The whole work, as you will see, has gained a different complexion from the earlier volumes due to the fact that now I am not proceeding chronologically with a detailed analysis of materials as in the first three volumes, but by large surveys of the dominant theoretical problems. That procedure has become necessary because several civilizations are treated with regard to the identical problems; and it has become possible as the consequence of an incredible stroke of luck: I have hit on something like a theory of relativity for the field of symbolic forms, and the discovery of the theoretical formula that will cover all forms to whatever civilization they belong has made possible an abbreviation of the whole presentation which I had not dreamt of before, Hence, in spite of the enormous amount of materials covered, Volume IV will not at all be fat.

The discovery also has determined the organization of Volume IV inasmuch as the presentation of the theoretical problems will cover the first two chapters in the enumeration which I have given earlier in this letter, while the great mass of the materials will be covered in the subsequent chapters under the theoretical concept developed in chapters I and II.[1]

The projected volume IV did not, of course, appear anywhere near the date of this letter, nor of the later synopsis, nor of "What Is

1. Eric Voegelin to Donald R. Ellegood, July 21, 1960, in Box 23, Folder 28, Eric Voegelin Papers, Hoover Institution Archives.

History?" but had to wait until 1974 for its publication while un-
dergoing further changes of structure. But clearly the letter speaks
with a sense of exhilaration and a theoretical earnest that is meant
to do more than merely assuage an anxious press director. Voegelin
had indeed made a significant theoretical breakthrough. The nature of this breakthrough can be deduced by looking carefully at
Voegelin's own description of it: "something like a theory of relativity for the field of symbolic forms, and the discovery of the theoretical formula that will cover all forms to whatever civilization
they belong." There can be no doubt that the "theory of relativity
for the field of symbolic forms" is the direct consequence of Voegelin's discovery of the symbolism of "historiogenesis," the full impact of which on the further development of his work Voegelin
describes in the section "The Beginning and the Beyond" of the
introduction to Volume IV (pp. 7–11). With this discovery, the construction of a unilinear history had turned out to be a cosmological
symbolism and a millennial constant in history. The discovery further revealed the persistence of cosmological symbolisms even
when meaningful advances of differentiating consciousness have
occurred, which meant that myth can never be overcome or be disposed of. To do so would be "suspect as a magic operation, motivated by an apocalyptic desire to destroy the cosmos itself" as Voegelin put it in the above-mentioned section (*OH*, IV, 10). The full
implications of this discovery did not become manifest all at once
but took years to ripen into such analyses as that of the mythical
depth of the soul as the equivalent of the divine depth of the cosmos, which we find in the 1970 essay "Equivalences of Experience
and Symbolization in History."[2] But the decisive insight had occurred, and the two opening pieces in this volume testify to the
difficulties involved in resolving the problems that arise from the
discovery of the transcendent unity beyond the pluralism of mythical symbolisms in history.

At this point, the reader must be referred to the initial discussion
of the introductory nature not only of these remarks but of Voege-

2. This essay now appears in Eric Voegelin, *Published Essays, 1966–1985*, ed.
Ellis Sandoz (Baton Rouge, 1990), Vol. XII of *The Collected Works of Eric Voegelin*,
34 vols. projected. It was originally published in *Eternitá e Storia* (Florence, 1970),
215–35, and was reprinted in *Philosophical Studies*, XXVIII (Dublin 1981), 88–103.

lin's own introduction to the *The Ecumenic Age*, for we would give a misleading impression if we were to accord to the first two texts in this volume, "What is History?" and "Anxiety and Reason," a special status in the body of Voegelin's later work. They remained, after all, unpublished, and there are good reasons for that—reasons to be found in the correspondence between Voegelin and the Louisiana State University Press spanning roughly a fifteen-year period. The picture that emerges from Voegelin's letters is that of a scholar trying to organize the wealth of his discoveries into a book while the material stubbornly refuses to be organized into a form that seems to be alien to it. The Press, which showed remarkable patience, wanted a book, perhaps even two or three books; it had every right to expect a continuation of the first three volumes of *Order and History*, and it wanted the project to be brought to a successful conclusion. Voegelin, in turn, had long since realized that the original project would not accommodate the varieties of symbolic orders of which he had become aware. Moreover, it can be argued whether Voegelin was a book author in the commonly used sense. His method consisted rather in working out problems in the form of reflective and meditative essays; only when the problems could be arranged in meaningful clusters would he organize them into a book. Had there not been the excellent relationship between Voegelin and the Press, the project of *Order and History* might well have been abandoned after the first three volumes. On the other hand, the promise of a fourth volume was one the author wanted to keep by all means, and it thus became imperative to organize into a book those materials which did not offer too much resistance to the form and to preface such a volume with a general philosophical introduction in which the project itself could be subjected to a critical analysis. Thus emerged *The Ecumenic Age* with its momentous introduction and, some ten years later, a manuscript for the concluding volume, *In Search of Order*. Neither of these two books, however, contained the full body of Voegelin's published essays and of his writings in manuscript form, and it is questionable if Voegelin would have included the originally planned number of writings in the final volume had he lived to oversee its publication.

"What Is History?"

When, on February 22, 1963, the author wrote to Ellegood that he was contemplating "to make volume 4 the final volume of the whole four," he also announced that he had been able "to solve all the theoretical problems which up to now only turned up on occasion of the work with the materials."[3] In other words, Voegelin finally had the theory that would organize the conclusion to *Order and History*. Among the specific questions that he listed in his letter as "solved" was "the question of 'What is history?'" One can assume that the answer to this question is contained in the text of that title, which opens our volume and which was marked "Chapter 1." There are other reasons for dating "What Is History?" about 1963. First, Manfred Henningsen, now of the University of Hawaii, who was one of Voegelin's first students in Munich and also served as his assistant, reports that, according to his extensive lecture notes, much of the substance and even the language of the chapter was incorporated into Voegelin's lectures on history in Munich in 1961 and 1962. Second, a sizable portion of the chapter seems to have been used for Voegelin's lecture at Grinnell College in the spring of 1963, later published as "Configurations of History" in *The Concept of Order* (Seattle, 1968), the volume that grew out of his and others', notably Toynbee's, lectures at Grinnell during this period. Finally, the chapter seems clearly related to, and practically leads into, "Ewiges Sein in der Zeit," published in 1964 and included in *Anamnesis* in 1966.[4]

As the comprehensive title "What Is History?" indicates, the version of the fourth volume of *Order and History* envisioned in 1963 was to open with an analysis of history as a concept that had, for several reasons, become highly problematic. There was, first of all, the discipline of positivistic historiography, which does not ask questions about its *raison d'être* and which continues to produce

---

3. Voegelin to Ellegood, February 22, 1963, Box 24, Folder 1, Voegelin Papers.

4. "Configurations of History," published now in Voegelin, *Published Essays, 1966–1985,* originally appeared in *Concept of Order,* ed. Paul Kuntz (Seattle, 1968), 23–42. "Ewiges Sein in der Zeit" was first published in *Zeit und Geschichte,* ed. Erich Dinkler (Tuebingen, 1964). It was reprinted in Eric Voegelin, *Anamnesis* (Munich, 1966) and translated as "Eternal Being in Time" in *Anamnesis,* ed. and trans. Gerhart Niemeyer (Notre Dame, 1978). This piece, which closely follows the

studies of whatever appear to be relevant subject matters, using methodologies borrowed from other disciplines. Then there were the progressivist philosophies of history that originated in the eighteenth century and reached their climactic point in the Hegelian system. Their activist transformation into the modern ideological movements resulted in the organized mass murders of the twentieth century committed in the name of history—that is, *one* history of *one* mankind. This process represents the immanentization of the eschatological oneness of the *historia sacra,* and it culminated in the philosophies of history from Condorcet to Spengler. History had become the symbol of rebellion against the old order represented by Church and Empire, dogma and tradition. When, after the death of God, mankind remains, it needs history as that which "we must understand and shape," as Camus put it in his analysis of "historical rebellion." After the apocalyptic catastrophes of the twentieth century, it was precisely historical rebellion that had to be questioned in the name of reality. The questions asked were those of Camus' *L'homme révolté* (1951), of Jaspers' *Ursprung und Ziel der Geschichte* (1949), Löwith's *Meaning in History* (1949), and especially Toynbee's monumental *A Study of History* (1934–1954): Is there a universal history and, if so, what is its meaning? Or, must the concept of a universal history be abandoned and, if so, what happens to the meaning of history? Voegelin had given a preliminary response to these questions in the introduction to *The World of the Polis* (1957) in which he declared squarely: "The program of a universal history valid for all men, when it is thought through, can mean only one of two things: the destruction of Western historical form, and the reduction of Western societies to a compact form of order in which the differentiations of truth through philosophy and revelation are forgotten; or, an assimilation of the societies, in which the leap in being has not broken the cosmological order as thoroughly as in the West, to

detailed outline of a lecture Voegelin prepared for Muenster, dated October 24, 1962, introduced for the first time in his work the Greek term *metaxy*—in German *das Zwischen,* and in English *In-Between.* This term, central to Voegelin's later work, does not yet appear in "What Is History?" though *methexis* (participation) is used and its substance is also represented by the expression "the primary sphere of encounter." (The full *Anamnesis,* in a new translation from the 1966 edition, will form Volume VI of *Collected Works.*)

existence in Western historical form" (*OH*, II, 22). In subsequent essays, such as "Toynbee's History as a Search for Truth" (1961) and "World-Empire and the Unity of Mankind" (1962), Voegelin showed that universality had to be understood as a symbol of the transcendent order of history rather than as a concept nurturing the dream of a mankind that would be capable of political organization because of its common history in time: "The dream of representing universal order through the world of empire has come to its end when the meaning of universal order as the order of history under God has come into view."[5]

This was the status of the problem when Voegelin wrote "What Is History?" The text has difficulties arising from the fact that the question "what is history?" seems to imply that history is an object of external reality to be described with the methods of the sciences of phenomena. In the three propositions about the unknowability of history, which open the text, Voegelin attacks this problem frontally and shows that the propositions are not entirely false, but are not true either, because they are propositions about something that does not exist in the form of objects in the external world. "History is not given as a whole to any human subject with an Archimedic point outside history," writes Voegelin. He continues: "The word *history* has the two meanings of a course of events and of a story telling them." People do not talk about history as an object; they talk about history from within history in the course of telling the story of something other than history: "For it [the double meaning of *history*] seems to point to a univocal phenomenon, to a sort of compactly emergent history preceding the retrospective dissociation into *res gestae* and their story, to situations where history, at the point of its emergence, is experienced not in the past but in the present tense. The remembrance of things past indeed presupposes a present of existence where man

5. "World Empire and the Unity of Mankind," *International Affairs*, XXXVIII (1962), 188. This essay and "Toynbee's History as a Search for Truth," in *The Intent of Toynbee's History*, ed. Edward T. Gargan (Chicago, 1961), 181–98, will be among the essays reprinted in Vol. XI of *Collected Works*. Toynbee responded positively to Voegelin's criticisms in *Reconsiderations* (New York, 1961), 650f, Vol. XII of Toynbee, *A Study of History*, 12 vols. Löwith and Voegelin also carried on an extensive correspondence. Their letters are to be found in Box 24, Folder 4, Voegelin Papers. The most important for the study of history fall between 1944 and 1952.

involved with events senses his passion and action as memorable." Voegelin then calls this area of man's involvement with events "the sphere of involvement or encounter." The entire main part of the text that follows is an elaboration of this understanding of history with its phenomenal objects that are "recognized as historical only through tracing their meaning to the sphere of encounter." Of course, the historian explores phenomenal objects as does any other scientist, but his exploration of phenomena is only one part of what Voegelin calls a "double constitution of history." The other part is "the expressive symbolism of historiography," and the symbolism is the end of a "process leading from the encounter, through the experiences, to their expression." In short, history shares in the givenness of objects while it "constitutes itself in the acts of symbolic expression." Thus, in the final analysis, history is one of humanity's modes of self-interpretation.

Voegelin's subsequent development of the transcendental structure of history and its texture results in the rejection of a universal meaning of history, because that meaning turns out to be "something on which people express opinions, and these expressions of opinion are then part of the reality being examined." This is how Voegelin put the matter in the Grinnell lecture "Configurations of History."[6] But this still leaves open the questions whether the reality examined yields any patterns and, if so, how these patterns are recognized. This precisely is the subject of "What is History?" The importance of this text lies in the careful differentiation of what had been earlier referred to as the "double constitution of history." The patterns that actually emerge are then grouped in what Voegelin calls "the configuration of history," the result of the understanding that history is "the process of eternal being realizing itself in time" and that the structure of history is determined not by the realization of a universal meaning but by the interplay between the meanings expressed and their reflective clarification in the present of existence.

Voegelin, in rejecting a universal meaning of history, re-established the question of meaning as "a subject matter for empirical exploration."

6. Voegelin, "Configurations of History," in *Concept of Order*, ed. Kuntz, 26.

xix

"Anxiety and Reason"

The title is actually the subtitle of the major segment of this text, the whole being designated "Chapter 1" and entitled "Historiogenesis." But the content of this text differs significantly from the three published versions that bear the title "Historiogenesis," *i.e.*, the essay of 1960, the expanded essay printed in 1966 in *Anamnesis*, and the final version, Chapter 1 of *The Ecumenic Age.*[7] The nature of the differences between the present version and the other three lies in the emphasis Voegelin places here on the experiential roots of mytho-speculation, a point that we have tried to emphasize by the choice of the title.

Each time Voegelin treated the question of historiogenesis he introduced it with virtually the same description and analysis of the symbolism. There can be no doubt that its discovery marks a critical juncture in Voegelin's work. *Historiogenesis* is the technical term for a particular type of speculation that occurs in cosmological societies and that links events in pragmatic history with legendary and mythical events leading back to the beginning of the cosmic order. This blend of historiography, mythopoesis, and rational speculation is a complex symbolism that, in Voegelin's words, "displays a curious tenacity of survival, from cosmological societies proper to contemporary Western societies," where it reappears in the various speculations on the origin of history. Voegelin was certain he had discovered, in the form of historiogenesis, "one of the great constants in the search of order from antiquity to the present" (*OH*, IV, 67). With this discovery, Voegelin had also found something that turned out to have far-reaching implications. Besides being a mytho-speculative symbolism on the origin of society, related to theogony, anthropogony, and cosmogony, historiogenesis connects the here and now of pragmatic history with the "mystery of existence out of nothing." The cosmos in which cosmological societies exist is a "groundless" cosmos—that is to say, there is not yet an experience of a transcendent "ground" beyond the cosmos

---

7. "Historiogenesis" was first published in *Philosophisches Jahrbuch*, LXVII (1960), 419–46. It appeared in expanded form in *Anamnesis* (Munich, 1966), 79–116, and in its fullest form as Chapter 1 of Voegelin, *The Ecumenic Age* (Baton Rouge, 1974), 59–114, Vol. IV of Voegelin, *Order and History*, 5 vols.

(itself not an existent thing) that could keep the cosmos from falling, as it were, into the abyss of waste and corruption manifesting itself in the continuous breakdowns of order against which cosmological societies guard through a rich field of rituals. Historiogenesis, too, recognizes the irreversibility of time with which other cosmological symbolisms and their ritual expressions struggle, but its response to the experience of anxiety in a groundless cosmos bears far greater resemblance to medieval and modern theologies and philosophies of history by virtue of its resolute ordering of the records of reigns and events on a single time line. When Voegelin speaks of historiogenesis as a constant, he means precisely the "obsession with unilinear history" that enabled him to call historiogenesis and the modern apocalypses of history equivalent symbolisms created to assuage the anxiety of existence.

Another highly important characteristic of historiogenesis as a constant in the search of order is the result of its concern with irreversible time. What, in historiogenesis, takes on the form of a speculation on the origin of society is the equivalent of the speculation on the *arche* of being in Ionian philosophy and thus is to be understood as an act of reasoning. The fact that historiogenesis is a cosmological "style of truth" tends to obscure this equivalence, but an experience of transcendence, though determining a new "style of truth," does not abolish the search for the ground of things, the process of reasoning. It differentiates the "field of non-existence," but it does not establish a "beyond" that could be regarded as another thing outside man and the cosmos. The tension between existent things and the ground of existence will always be experienced and constitutes the common center of all symbolisms, whether they are mythical, revelatory, philosophical, or expressions of the modern revolt against transcendence. Voegelin states the issue succinctly: "The cosmic sense of existence out of nothing, the waste through time, decline and restoration of order, responsive anxiety, and the search of order have as their common center that clearing in existence to which such terms as *nous*, or *intellectus*, or reason have become associated." Voegelin's subsequent development of ten meanings of Reason as the "clearing in existence" should therefore be read not as a phenomenology of reason in history but as one of the philosopher's most sustained attempts to articulate an area of reality to which the term *field of non-existence* applies in the sense in which it is already symbolized in myth. Ultimately, there is no way out of the "primary experience of the cosmos"; there are only acts of "meditative articulation" of the reality that is already articulated by myth. "The act of contemplation is the philosophic equivalent to ritual in myth," Voegelin concludes, and the differentiation of the cosmic reality through reason must be "actualized through meditation," or else it can become itself a source of disorder, as the phenomenon of modern rationalism shows. Myth and philosophy are equivalent, and yet they are not the same. What makes them equivalent—a point demonstrated in the concluding part of the text, in which Voegelin offers an extensive discussion of the transition from myth to philosophy as it can be seen in Aristotle's *Metaphysics*—can be understood only as long as one recognizes that the primary experience of the cosmos is itself constant. The illusion that the primary experience can be lost or overcome leads to the modern constructions, which Voegelin deals with in "The Eclipse of Reality." Equivalences and constants and the depth of their dimensions became the main concern of Voegelin's late work, whether in the essay "Equivalences of Experience and Symbolization in History" or in the reflections, in Volume V of *Order and History*, on Plato's *Timaeus* and the "superconstant" of the Cosmos and its tension "which becomes luminous in the symbol 'divine'" (*OH*, V, 107). Thus it is justified to speak of "Anxiety and Reason" as a key text that illustrates the meaning of this statement at the beginning of *Order and History:* "The order of history emerges from the history of order."

"The Eclipse of Reality"

The reader may already be familiar with the first part of "The Eclipse of Reality," published in 1970 in a memorial volume for Alfred Schütz edited by Maurice Natanson. The pages on Comte, not published at that time but included here, reprise some of the work done on Comte for the projected "History of Political Ideas" in the 1940s and parallel some of the Comte discussion extracted from the last named work to be placed into *From Enlightenment to Revolution* in 1975. The piece as a whole must be seen in the context of the Candler Lectures that Voegelin delivered at Emory University in 1967 under the title "The Drama of Humanity."[8] The lectures form the outline of a response to the massive critique of modernity that gained its full momentum in the sixties and continues until this day. It must also be noted here that, during the late 1960s and early 1970s, Voegelin seriously contemplated a book under this title in which he intended to deal with the symbols of myth and the constants of human experience from prehistory to modernity by drawing on his already completed writings and by adding a number of further studies. A letter to Charles East, then director of the Louisiana State University Press, specifically excludes *The Drama of Humanity* from *Order and History*, stating that "it will not be a concluding volume for *Order and History*" and that there would not be any commitment at that time to offer the book to the Press. "The reason why is that my work is always hampered by deadlines, and for once in my life I want to write a book in peace."[9] At the time, though, Volume IV was to be the concluding volume of *Order and History* and was to receive the title *In Search of Order.* By 1973, the title *The Ecumenic Age* insinuated itself, and *In Search of Order* was reserved for the concluding Volume V. Voegelin's choice of the phrase "drama of humanity" instead of "drama of man" is crucial to the understanding of the form his respose to the critique of modernity took, as evinced in the formulation "eclipse of reality"; for it is the problem of modernity that it creates such imaginary entities as a *modern man*, a *post-Christian man*, a *man come of age*, a *self*, and countless other such terms of alienation through which *modern man* expresses his condition after he has cut himself off from those areas of reality which are symbolized by myth, philosophy, revelation, and mysticism. In substituting the word *humanity* for *man*, Voegelin acknowledges the changing modes of man's "understanding himself in his relation to God, World and Society."[10] Voegelin writes at the end of the introduction to *The Ecumenic Age:* "The return from symbols which have lost their meaning to the experiences which constitute

8. An unedited transcript of tape recordings of these lectures can be found in Box 74, File 1, Voegelin Papers.
9. Voegelin to Charles East, July 14, 1970, in Box 24, Folder 1, Voegelin Papers.
10. "The Drama of Humanity," unedited transcript of tape recording in Box 74, Folder 1, Voegelin Papers.

meaning is so generally recognizable as the problem of the present that specific references are unnecessary. The great obstacle to this return is the massive block of accumulated symbols, secondary and tertiary, which eclipses the reality of man's existence in the Metaxy. To raise this obstacle and its structure into consciousness, and by its removal to help in the return to the truth of reality as it reveals itself in history, has become the purpose of *Order and History*" (*OH*, IV, 58). Thus Voegelin's response to the ongoing critique of modernity emerges as the constituent that structures the final parts of *Order and History* and helps us place such writings as "The Eclipse of Reality" in the context of the "drama of humanity." The analyses of Sartre, Schiller, Comte, and some of the more recent cases of "the divided self" uncover the representative structures of the disturbances that create the complex called "modernity" to which Voegelin added other examples, which he treated in his essays on Henry James and Hegel, in "The Magic of the Extreme" and in major portions of Volume V of *Order and History*.[11]

"The Moving Soul"

The reader should keep in mind that the text of "The Moving Soul" comes from a typescript of fourteen pages while its description in the Table of Contents of 1969 (see Appendix) allots twenty pages to it[12]—an indication that Voegelin intended to revise and extend it.

11. The reader will see in the Appendix that Voegelin's title "Eclipse of Reality" was to cover the entire last part of the fourth volume of *Order and History* as planned at that time (*ca.* 1970). This part was to include his recently completed essays on Hegel and on Henry James, most of what is published here as "The Eclipse of Reality," as well as other earlier written, still unpublished manuscripts from around the mid-1940s—namely the chapter on Schelling from *The History of Political Ideas* and his study "Nietzsche and Pascal." The Hegel and James pieces appear in Voegelin, *Published Essays, 1966–1985*, and the last two manuscripts mentioned should appear in Voegelin, *Studies in the History of Political Ideas*, Vol. VII, which will be Volume XXVI of Voegelin, *Collected Works*.

12. Voegelin began working on this text during a stay at Notre Dame University in early 1968. He described his efforts, which had culminated in a first draft, in a letter dated March 16, 1968, to his friend Gregor Sebba: "In recent weeks I have concentrated on the problems of time and space in physics. I have been worried for years about the problem how my analysis of time in politics and history would be compatible with the corresponding categories in modern physics. Hence, I have now gone through the consequences of the physicists' assumptions concerning the velocity of light and the manner in which the velocity of the observer affects the experience of physical reality. The result is a series of aporetic propositions which correspond to the Kantian Antinomies for the case of Newtonian physics. I think I

The text is a thought experiment inspired by a remark Henry Margenau had made in *The Nature of Physical Reality* (1950) about the "amusing opportunities for fanciful reflections based on science."[13] In a letter to the Munich historian Fritz Wagner in 1969, Voegelin stated succinctly why he seized the "amusing opportunities":

> I have for quite a while now been attempting to restore and reformulate the connection between Physics and Myth. Last year, during a few quiet weeks in Notre Dame I succeeded in putting together the first draft of an attempt and in the last weeks, during a similar period here at Stanford I was able to reorganize the manuscript. I had barely finished this work when your essay arrived—you can imagine what a delightful coincidence this was for me. My attempt assumes the form of a proof that an image of a physical Cosmos cannot in any way be constructed with the means of theoretical physics. Every such attempt to extrapolate the principles of theoretical physics into the construction of a Cosmos ends up in aporetic propositions. The proof is in principle a revival of Kant's problematic of antinomies. That the Nature of the physicists is a Cosmos cannot be demonstrated by physics but is an assumption of the primary experience of the cosmos which is to be expressed through the symbols of the myth.[14]

Voegelin had sent copies of his paper to Wagner and to, among others, Henry Margenau himself, whose response was polite and

have been able to show that from the assumptions of a physics of relativity with regard to time and space, no empirically verifiable constructs concerning the structure of the physical universe can be derived. The symbolism of a 'universe', and of a spatiotemporal structure of the universe, still is no more than a demythologized version of the myth of the cosmos.—The matter has taken several weeks, but the result is fortunately only 10 pages. I shall use it as an Appendix in the *Drama of Humanity*" (Box 35, Folder 5, Voegelin Papers).

13. Henry Margenau, *The Nature of Physical Reality* (New York, 1950), 151–53.

14. The essay that Wagner had sent to Voegelin, "Neue Diskussionen ueber Newtons Wissenschaftsbegriff" (*Bayerische Akademie der Wissenschaften*, Philosophisch-historische Klasse, Sitzungsberichte: Jahrgang 1968, Heft 4, pp. 1–42), concluded with a quotation from Voegelin's essay "Was ist Natur?" (1965), which Wagner took from *Anamnesis* (Munich, 1966): "The mystery of a cosmos permeated by gods is not done away with through the dissociating of God and world in the experience of transcendence. The impossibility of constructing the world as an innerworldly experiential complex is today a central theme in theoretical physics" (141, translation by the editors; a translation of this essay can also be found in Voegelin, *Anamnesis*, ed. and trans. Niemeyer, 78). This same problem of the appropriate symbolization of the cosmos formed the subject of Voegelin's long concluding paragraph (278f.) to his Harvard Divinity School Ingersoll Lecture on Immortality delivered in 1965, the same year was "Was ist Natur?" (This lecture was published as "Immortality: Experience and Symbol" in *Harvard Theological Review*, LX [1967], 235–79, and is now reprinted in Voegelin, *Published Essays, 1966–1985*.)

Voegelin sent to Wagner, along with "The Moving Soul," his 1948 essay "The whose only criticisms were directed at the paper's strictly technical aspects, as were G. J. Whitrow's.[15] At the same time, Voegelin mentioned in a letter to Manfred Henningsen that "one should view it [the manuscript] in conjunction with the treatise on the 'Equivalences' which I sent you last week. With this the mythical foundation of the areas of the human soul and of the cosmos has been clarified. What remains is a parallel third piece on mysticism." Voegelin concluded the letter by saying: "You see I am systematically working on the organization of the *Drama of Humanity*."[16] If there is one thing one can infer from these remarks, it is that the return to experiences that constitute meaning (mentioned in the discussion of "The Eclipse of Reality") involved, among other things, a major recovery of the standard of knowledge that existed in natural philosophy before the "origins of scientism." This had been a central concern of Voegelin's since his early investigations in the area of the biological foundations of the race-idea.[17]

We should also note that the issues raised in "The Moving Soul" are clearly connected to the passage in *The Ecumenic Age* (201 ff.) in which Voegelin discusses the pseudo-Aristotelian *De Mundo* under the aspect of the concupiscential ecumenic expansions and follows with a lucid analysis of the problem of the perspectival dimensions of reality under the aspect of finiteness and infinity. The extension of those dimensions "toward an 'horizon,' that is toward a border where heaven meets earth, where this world is bounded by the world beyond," is the constant of experience that remains be-

Origins of Scientism" (*Social Research*, XV [1948], 462–94, to be reprinted in Volume XI of Voegelin, *Collected Works*). Wagner's response to Voegelin's letter and the two essays that accompanied it was one of delight (Fritz Wagner to Voegelin, July 22, 1969, in Box 39, Folder 20, Voegelin Papers). Wagner stated that he found Voegelin's "thought experiment" in "The Moving Soul" convincing. He also recognized Voegelin's crucial point that his hypothetical "soul," which had been split off in the experiment from the real soul, still retained "memory." But this was certainly not the "memory" that is Voegelin's *anamnesis*, since Voegelin had deprived this hypothetical "soul" of "existential tension," which constitutes the core of human being. As to "The Origins of Scientism," Wagner bemoaned the fact that he had not had it available while he was working on his Newton piece. He appreciated especially Voegelin's lucid treatment there of the Leibniz-Clarke debate.

15. Margenau's and Whitrow's responses are found in Box 75, Folder 4, Voegelin Papers.

16. Voegelin to Manfred Henningsen, June 27, 1969, in Box 17, Folder 15, Voegelin Papers; translation by the editors.

17. The translations of Voegelin's two books on Race, *Rasse und Staat* (Tuebingen, 1933) and *Die Rassenidee in der Geistesgeschichte* (Berlin, 1933) will be published as Volumes II and III of Voegelin, *Collected Works*.

hind the modern "vulgarian belief" in a "physical universe" and gives rise to types of speculation that can best be classified as science fiction. The "expansion of the astronomical horizon after Galilei" has, in Voegelin's words, become "one of the contributive causes" to this vulgarian belief. It was at that point in his analysis that the author promised, in a footnote, a further elaboration of this problem as a chapter "The Moving Soul" in Volume V of *Order and History*.

"The Beginning and the Beyond: A Meditation on Truth"

This last piece is the most important of Voegelin's unpublished writings. In order to understand its place in Voegelin's work, it may be helpful to remember the remarks Voegelin made in his letter to Manfred Henningsen (cited above) concerning the clarification of the mythical foundations of the two areas of reality represented by the symbols "soul" and "cosmos." What still needed to be clarified were the mythical foundations of the area represented by "mysticism"—that is, the area of "divine reality." "The Beginning and the Beyond" offers at least a partial clarification, which is then continued in "Wisdom and the Magic of the Extreme: A Meditation" (1981) and in substantial sections of Volume V of *In Search of Order*.[18]

What does such a clarification of the mythical foundations of the mystical area of divine reality entail? The answer to this question can only be given in the form of "meditation," and it is no accident that the word *meditation* takes a prominent place in Voegelin's late work, appearing in the titles of the two major writings cited.[19] In

---

18. "Wisdom and the Magic of the Extreme: A Meditation," published in the *Southern Review*, n.s., XVII (1981), 235–87, and in *Eranos Jahrbuch*, XLVI (1981), 341–409, is reprinted in Voegelin, *Published Essays, 1966–1985*.

19. The theme of philosophical meditation was important in Voegelin's work from early on. His unpublished *Herrschaftslehre*, dating from around 1930, which was to be the first part of his systematic *Staatslehre* (see his *Autobiographical Reflections* [Baton Rouge, 1989], 38), begins with a twenty-page analysis of the role of philosophic meditation in determining the core of the person in the works of Saint Augustine, especially *Confessions* XI, in Descartes' *Meditations*, and in Husserl's *Ideen* (Box 53, Folder 5, Voegelin Papers). Voegelin returned to this contrast of meditations—the Augustinian, the Cartesian, and the Husserlian—in the last paragraphs of his 1943 letter to Alfred Schütz, which, in 1966, he placed at the head of his *Anamnesis*, the work that developed his philosophy of consciousness around

the introduction to *The Ecumenic Age*, Voegelin had already announced the directions in which such a meditation on divine reality would have to go. The opening sentence of the present piece follows almost word for word this passage from Volume IV on the experience of divine reality:

> Though divine reality is one, its presence is experienced in the two modes of the Beyond and the Beginning. The Beyond is present in the immediate experience of movements in the psyche; while the presence of the divine Beginning is mediated through the experience of the existence and intelligible structure of things in the cosmos. The two models[20] require two different types of language for their adequate expression. The immediate presence in the movements of the soul requires the revelatory language of consciousness. . . . The presence mediated by the existence and order of things in the cosmos requires the mythical language of a creator-god or Demiurge, of a divine force that creates, sustains, and preserves the order of things.
>
> (*OH*, IV, 17f.)

"The Beginning and the Beyond" represents the meditative exploration of the two modes and the two languages in which they are expressed under the formula *fides quaerens intellectum*.[21]

The occasion for "The Beginning and the Beyond" was the invitation extended to Voegelin to deliver the 1975 Aquinas Lecture at Marquette University in March of that year. The lectures usually lasted sixty to seventy-five minutes. In a letter to a friend, the Austrian art historian Hans Sedlmayr, written in December, 1974, Voegelin said: "The subject is *The Beginning and the Beyond*; I have to

---

the practice of anamnetic meditation, the heart of this philosophy. We note also that one of the small private courses Voegelin offered at his home in Vienna to supplement his meager income during the 1936–1937 school year was entitled "Einfuehrung in die philosophischen Meditation." His pithy two-sentence description of the course must be quoted in full: "In common readings from selected pieces drawn from the Indian Upanishads, from Plato, Plotinus, Augustine, Maimonides, Descartes, et al., the nature of philosophic meditation as the basic form [*Grundform*] of philosophizing will be shown. No kind of prior knowledge is required" (Box 86, Folder 3, Voegelin Papers).

20. The editors suggest that *models* should read *modes*. Perhaps a typographical error slipped by Voegelin and the copy editor of Volume IV of *Order and History*.

21. The most important extended discussion by Voegelin of *fides quaerens intellectum* dates from the time he was working on "The Beginning and the Beyond." This discussion is to be found in his "Response to Professor Altizer's 'A New History and a New but Ancient God?'" in *Journal of the American Academy of Religion*, XLIII (1975), 765–72; reprinted in *Eric Voegelin's Thought*, ed. Ellis Sandoz (Durham, 1982), 189–97. This piece now appears in Voegelin, *Published Essays, 1966–1985*.

make a bit of an effort in order to stand comparison with Gilson and Maritain, who have, among others, given this lecture."[22] Almost exactly a year later, he wrote an apologetic letter to Father Francis C. Wade, S.J., explaining the delay in submitting the manuscript of his lecture for publication. His *apologia* is worth quoting:

> Third, and most important, I hope that you will enjoy this part of my laments, I have been working all the time on the "Beginning and the Beyond," but was held up because I ran into unexpected, and highly theoretical problems, which required time for their analysis. I am through this stage by now and can write continuously for the final form. The Lecture will not become overly long, but treat the problems of language and truth in an entirely new fashion. I have given it now the subtitle: "A Meditation on Truth." The most obstreperous problems concerned the analysis of Meditation and Anselm's *Proslogion*, its relation back to Plato, and forward to Thomas. If I have to say it myself, I now believe the Lecture will become really important and worthy of the opportunity you have offered me.[23]

True to the spirit of the saint, the Aquinas Lecture had become a meditation embracing the universality of experience formed by the tension of existence under God. It had also become, guided by the spirit of this tension, much more than a lecture that could be delivered in an hour or so, even under the illustrious auspices of the Marquette Thomas Aquinas Lectures. Father Wade's gracious and understanding reply was received a few days later.[24]

Voegelin claimed in his letter to Father Wade that he was now able to "treat the problems of language and truth in an entirely new fashion." These were the problems that preoccupied Voegelin at the time, as we can see in his discussions of 1973 that form the last sections of his *Autobiographical Reflections*.[25] For Voegelin's re-

22. Voegelin to Hans Sedlmayr, December 3, 1974, in Box 35, Folder 8, Voegelin Papers, translation by the editors.
23. Voegelin to Francis C. Wade, S.J., December 26, 1975, in Box 81, Folder 5, Voegelin Papers.
24. Father Wade wrote to Voegelin on December 30, 1975: "I am especially pleased to hear that you have liked the thorny problems concerning the analysis of Meditation in Anselm, and I look forward to your solution. And for this reason we can both forget the problem of late publication. After all, I never had much sympathy with the attitude so common in the publishing world—'I don't want a perfect ms., I want one by Wednesday'—that denies excellence in the name of the practical. The Aquinas Lecture Series has always stood for excellence and, to the extent that I have any say about it, the Series will continue along this same line" (Box 81, Folder 5, Voegelin Papers).
25. Voegelin, *Autobiographical Reflections*, cf. especially 72 ff., 108–13.

flections near the time of completing "The Beginning and the Beyond" in 1977, the editors suggest a rereading of the concluding pages of "Remembrance of Things Past" (dated March, 1977), which was his introduction to the 1978 English version of *Anamnesis*.[26] The reader will note there Voegelin's summary statement on "the great breakthrough visions of the prophetic, the philosophic, and the Christian-apostolic type." "Vision" is one of the two or three great themes of Voegelin's meditations of the late 1970s. The best place to begin the study of "vision" in the later Voegelin is in Volume IV, in the chapters "Conquest and Exodus" for Plato, and "The Pauline Vision of the Resurrected" for the Christian vision.[27]

As we noted previously, Voegelin's approach to the complex of the two modes of experience is that of meditation. The language that emerges in the process of meditation is preformed in the Platonic "vision" of the *hyperouranios topos*, the superheavenly region of the *Phaedrus*, the "vision of the Whole of reality, of its structure and movement." The vision of the Whole of reality is in conflict with the mythical vision of a "cosmos full of gods," and it poses problems that require a reformulation of the nature and structure of consciousness. In "The Beginning and the Beyond," Voegelin, through a careful analysis of the Platonic language, lays the groundwork for such a reformulation through which the various conceptual reductions of the structures of consciousness—be they a Cartesian *cogito* or a Hegelian *Bewusstsein*—are overcome. With "The Beginning and the Beyond," Voegelin's work returned to the source that had nurtured all of it throughout a lifetime. It became a mystic philosophy without being mystifying, because it remained always conscious of the tension between the mythical structure of the "Beginning" and its language of things and their order, and the noetic structure of the "Beyond" and its "luminous word"—that is, the language of movement, or process, in which the relation between man and reality is still expressed in the grammar of consciousness-subject and thing-object, but where it is also

26. Voegelin, *Anamnesis*, ed. and trans. Niemeyer, 3–13, cf. especially 11f.
27. Voegelin's most extensive exploration of "vision" is to be found in his "Wisdom and the Magic of the Extreme" meditation, which he must have begun around the time he was completing the final sections on "vision" in "The Beginning and the Beyond."

reflectively understood as a participatory relationship. The two languages, in their manifold manifestations, continue to be the only languages humanity has.

As we said initially, the range of problems explored by Voegelin in the writings contained in this volume does not permit a straightforward discussion of a "development" in Voegelin's thought. We hope to have intimated some of the reasons for this in these introductory remarks. The reader is invited to embark on his own exploratory journey.

THOMAS A. HOLLWECK
PAUL CARINGELLA

Editorial Note on the Texts
Selected for This Volume

This volume of unpublished works is drawn from originals in the collection of Eric Voegelin's papers donated by Mrs. Eric Voegelin to the Hoover Institution on War, Revolution, and Peace at Stanford University. The editors chose for publication only later texts that formed coherent and basically completed wholes. The writings selected showed all the signs of the author's customary care in reworking, even though they did not in all cases evidence the final revisions that would have definitively stamped the author's *imprimatur* on them. The editors scrupulously adhered to the author's texts as he left them; only minor emendations consistent with the author's own history of editing his manuscripts were made. The titles used are the author's own. The texts selected, with their approximate year of completion, are "What Is History?" (1963), "Anxiety and Reason" (1968), "The Eclipse of Reality" (1969), "The Moving Soul" (1969), and "The Beginning and the Beyond" (1977).

These writings came from a shelf in Voegelin's study where he kept the most important of his manuscripts, outlines, notes, photocopies, and other materials for consideration and use in the preparation of the final volumes of *Order and History*. Paul Caringella helped the author rearrange and add to this shelf at the end of the summer of 1979. A few months after Voegelin's death in January, 1985, Caringella discovered the first three pieces that appear in this volume while he was preparing an inventory of the contents of this shelf. In September, 1986, at the initial meeting of the advisory board for *The Collected Works of Eric Voegelin*, Caringella and Thomas Hollweck proposed these three writings, along with the last two, which had been known about and privately circulated earlier, as the basis for a volume of late unpublished writings to complement a volume of Voegelin's later published essays. These two books are now the first two volumes to be published of *The Collected Works of Eric Voegelin.*

Since the first four writings now published here were closely involved in the long period of development of Voegelin's work on *Order and History,* stretching from the publication of the third volume in 1957 to the appearance of the fourth in 1974, the editors have included an appendix that contains three of Voegelin's extended outlines from this period: the first from 1961 for Volume IV still to be entitled *Empire and Christianity,* and the last two, from 1969 and 1971 for the Volume IV which was at that time to be entitled *In Search of Order.*

The editors must now say a few words about the state of the texts selected for this edition.

"What Is History?"

The file entry for this typescript of sixty-eight pages, bearing the author's designation "Chapter 1: What is History?" is dated 1968 in the Hoover Institution Archives' Register for the Papers, but this represents an early attempt at dating. The text used in this volume was one of those found on the shelf mentioned above. It was missing its last four pages, which were located during the organization of the papers in the archives prior to cataloging and microfilming. Variants of the first pages were also found then, but these obviously came from earlier drafts.

"Anxiety and Reason"

The original file folder on Voegelin's shelf in which this text was found bore the title "Anxiety and Reason" on its outside in the author's own handwriting. The text itself begins with the heading: "Chapter 1: Historiogenesis." The only titled section within this text bears the title "Anxiety and Reason." It begins on page 10 of the typescript and continues, without any new headings, to the end on page 80. The title "Anxiety and Reason" also appears as a chapter title in the outlines sent to the LSU Press editors around 1970 (*cf.* Appendix). About two-thirds of the typescript is substantially different in content from Voegelin's published writings, including the three published versions of "Historiogenesis." Wording almost identical to pages near the beginning of the "Historio-genesis" chapter of *The Ecumenic Age* (pp. 59–63, 68–73) can be found on a dozen or so of the typescript's first eighteen pages (pp. 52–63 below) as well as on typescript pages 28 to 32 (pp. 72–75 below). Pages 59 to 65 of the typescript (pp. 94–99 below) correspond closely to much of *The Ecumenic Age* pages 318 to 325—the section of the last chapter that culminates in Voegelin's discussion of the Apocalypse of Abraham. The reader will note that the Apocalypse of Abraham text was also used near the beginning of "What Is History?" (pp. 4–6 below) and that the paragraph of commentary that follows it is very close in wording to the last paragraph of page 324 of *The Ecumenic Age*.

"The Eclipse of Reality"

This is a typescript of seventy pages. The text printed here is clearly the full text from which Voegelin detached its first part (pp. 1–15 of the typescript, pp. 111–21 below) for separate publication under the same title in the memorial volume for Alfred Schütz: *Phenomenology and Social Reality*, ed. Maurice Natanson (The Hague, 1970), 186–94.

"The Moving Soul"

The text printed here is that of a typescript of fourteen pages and represents Voegelin's last revised version dating to 1969. A foot-note in Volume IV of *Order and History* (p. 203) promised a chapter entitled "The Moving Soul" for Volume V. The version used here differs from earlier drafts primarily in its more fully spelled out divisions and headings. One important paragraph (1.4) of Section III, "Conclusions," occurs only in the version printed here.

"The Beginning and the Beyond: A Meditation on Truth"

The typescript and drafts of this text, among the five selected for publication, showed the most signs of a piece still in the process of development, for all its carefully crafted analyses and formula-

tions. The final form of the text does not conform to the order indicated at the end of its first, introductory, section, and while some
seven draft pages exist of a section on Saint Thomas, perhaps intended to begin the whole piece, references to the saint practically
disappear in the text finally worked out, his role apparently being
taken over by Anselm. There also exist earlier draft pages for the
intricate discussions beginning with the section "Being and Intentionality" and leading into the concluding Plato analyses. The editors have included in two footnotes the most important variant
formulations that the author chose not to use but that are still of
great interest to the student of Voegelin's thought. The editors also
discovered in the archives what appears to be a later version of the
last three pages of this text—the concluding section "On Vision"—
and they have used this later version for this volume. The author
apparently intended to go on from this revision, since the editors
also subsequently found a detached page 71 consisting of the few
sentences included in the footnote at the end of the text. Voegelin
seems to have set aside his work on "The Beginning and the Beyond" meditation to concentrate on the analysis of the growth of
the Vision in Plato, published in 1981 as "Wisdom and the Magic of
the Extreme."

WHAT IS HISTORY?
AND OTHER LATE
UNPUBLISHED WRITINGS

1

~~◦❦ ❧◦~~

What Is History?

1. Preliminary Inquiry

An inquiry concerning history has predecessors but no traditions. The reason, well known if not too well understood, is the elusive character of history as an object in the sense in which we speak of things or objects in the external world. In contemporary epistemology and methodology, the various difficulties arising from this source are much discussed. The debate, however, is wanting in theoretical incisiveness inasmuch as the difference between our knowledge of the external world and an experience involving transcendence is not brought to sufficient clarity. Hence, I shall not join the debate but rather summarize the difficulties by means of three propositions, constructed in such a manner that they will recall certain sophistic triads of propositions in which difficulties of the same type have become manifest. These are the three propositions:

1. History, it seems, does not exist—all conduct of man that supposedly weaves the fabric of history can be adequately understood in terms of sociology and psychology.
2. There is a drama of history—but it is unfinished and its meaning therefore is unknowable.
3. There are facts of history, they even can be reasonably well ascertained with regard to phenomenal aspects—but their selection and interpretation is subjective and therefore reflects no more than the historiographer's value judgments.

These propositions will recall, as they are intended to do, certain triads constructed by the Sophists of the fifth century B.C. One of these triads, attributed to Protagoras, concerns the gods:

"What Is History?" was completed in its present form by about 1963. The text used here is found in Box 74, Folder 8, Eric Voegelin Papers, Hoover Institution Archives.

1. It seems that no gods exist.
2. Even if they do exist, they do not care about men.
3. Even if they care, they can be propitiated by gifts.

Another such triad, especially suggestive as a parallel to the propositions concerning history, is preserved by an abstract of Gorgias' *On Being:*

1. Nothing exists.
2. If anything exists, it is incomprehensible.
3. If it is comprehensible, it is incommunicable.

Clearly the sophistic triads have the same general structure as the modern one; and since we are well informed about the genesis of the sophistic paradoxes, they will assist us in understanding the paradoxes concerning history as an object.

The sophistic triads have arisen in the wake of the Parmenidean vision and metaphysics of Being. The truth of Being revealed by the goddess struck its recipient with such force that the world in which we live was reduced to the status of Doxa, of Illusion; Being with a capital *B* became to Parmenides a transcendent object of speculative exploration. In opposition to the Parmenidean experience with its arrogation of true existence to Being as a transcendent object, other thinkers could claim the categories of *object* and *existence* for the things in our world of sense perception, thus arriving at the other extreme of denying reality to transcendent Being. The unresolved conflict between the two extremes of objectification has expressed itself in the construction of the paradoxic triads. The sophistic paradoxes, thus, are due to a chain reaction of theoretical mistakes, which again can be arranged in three propositions:

1. Immanent and transcendent being are treated as if they were objects given to an observer—they become objectified into types of being.
2. According to the preference of the respective thinkers, the categories of object and existence then are rigorously defined to fit one or the other of the two objectified types of being.
3. The categories rigorously fitted to one of the two types of being, finally, are used in propositions respectively concerning the other type.

If this procedure is followed, the result will be the sophistic paradoxes of being. Our modern propositions, denying reality to history as an object, result from the same procedure of transferring rigorously defined categories from the field in which they have originated to another type of being. The triad concerning history thus renews the great conflict of Philosophy versus Sophistic thought.

Once the issue underlying the parallelism of the triads, ancient and modern, is recognized, the philosopher might be inclined to disregard the propositions. He might wish to proceed with his task in the light of his conception of history and let the results speak for themselves. Why should the old quarrel that has been settled by the classic philosophers be resumed? Some contemporary thinkers have indeed adopted this course. Still, it does not commend itself, because in its modern form the ancient quarrel presents a new aspect. In order to clarify this aspect, however, we must penetrate a few steps deeper into the problems of immanence and transcendence.

The sophistic paradoxes have sprung from a chain reaction of theoretical mistakes. The initial mistake, setting off the other ones, was the treatment of immanent and transcendent being as if they were two objects given to an observer. There is no opportunity, however, to make such a mistake as long as there has not occurred an experience of transcendence, and as long as the experience has not been sufficiently articulated to make the tension of immanence-transcendence visible as a structure in the constitution of being. In the compact experience of the cosmos that motivates the symbolism of early civilizations, for instance, this structure cannot become thematic, though it is present in the constitution of being just as much before its discovery as after it. We have stressed that the sophistic paradoxes have arisen in the wake of the Parmenidean vision and metaphysics of Being. Hence, if we want to avoid the mistake of objectivation with any certainty in our own inquiry, it must be traced back to its origin in the experience of transcendence. And not only must it be traced to its root, but an alternative formulation of the problem must be found that will prevent the mistake for the future. In order to meet these conditions, I suggest, as the alternative to the language of immanent and transcendent being, the following statement: Immanence and transcendence are indices that accrue to being when the constitution of being is interpreted in the light of an experience of transcendence. Since, however, this statement will not carry much conviction unless one knows what an experience of transcendence is, and since in our time such knowledge cannot be taken for granted, the presentation of an example will be helpful.

The purpose will be served by the experience of transcendence described in the Apocalypse of Abraham, [Chaps.] 7–8:

> More venerable indeed than all things is fire
> > for many things subject to no one will fall to it. . . .
> More venerable even is water,
> > for it overcomes fire. . . .
> Still I do not call it God,
> > for it is subject to earth. . . .
> Earth do I call more venerable,
> > for it overcomes the nature of water.
> Still I do not call it God,
> > as it is dried up by the sun. . . .
> More venerable than the earth I call the sun;
> > the universe he makes light by his rays.
> Even him I do not call God,
> > as his course is obscured by night and the clouds.
> Yet the moon and the stars I do not call God,
> > because they, in their time, dim their light by night. . . .
> Hear this, Terah, my father,
> > that I announce to you the God, the creator of all,
> > not those that we deem gods!
>
> But where is He?
> And what is He?
> —who reddens the sky,
> who goldens the sun,
> and makes light the moon and the stars?
> —who dries up the earth, in the midst of many waters,
> who put yourself in the world?
> —who sought me out in the confusion of my mind?
>
> May God reveal Himself through Himself!
>
> When thus I spoke to Terah, my father,
> > in the court of my house,
> The voice of a mighty-one fell from heaven
> > in a cloudburst of fire and called:
> > Abraham! Abraham!
>
> I said: Here am I!
> And He said:
> > You seek the God of gods,
> > the Creator,
> > in the mind of your heart.
> > I am He!

4

I have selected this text because it demonstrates not only the *via negativa* as the instrument for describing the experience but also the transition from the compact experience of a cosmos full of gods to the experience of transcendence that differentiates being and endows it with the indices *immanent* and *transcendent.* The mind of the heart is the Aramaic equivalent of the Hellenic psyche or the Augustinian *anima animi.* This mind of the heart in confusion will roam over the realms of being, each claiming its lower or higher divinity, in search of the true God, who is the origin and ground of all being. He reveals Himself, through His word to the heart, as the one who Is. He is the One beyond all realms of being, which through His revelation cease to be a cosmos full of gods and are transformed into a world whose being carries the index *immanent* in relation to the being of the divine source that carries the index *transcendent.* In this Essene document (probably from the first century B.C.) the realms of being are conceived as elemental or stellar, while in Hellenic philosophy they would be conceived rather as inorganic, vegetative, animal, and human (though this characterization needs serious qualifications), but in either case the realms form a hierarchy leading the searching mind upward to the point of transcendence toward the origin of being, toward an *arche,* or first cause. Moreover, when the soul opens (to use the language of Bergson) in an act of transcendence, the beyond of the world is not experienced as an object beyond the world. The text makes admirably clear the tension of the search—of God seeking man, and man seeking God— the mutuality of seeking and finding one another. Not a space beyond space but the search is the site of the meeting between man and the beyond of his heart; and God is present even in the confusion of the heart that precedes the search through the realms of being. The divine Beyond thus is at the same time a divine Within the world. Subtly, the unknown author traces the movement from Within to Beyond as it passes from the confusion of the mind, to the search of the unknown that is present in the search as it was in the confusion, and further on to the call from beyond—until what in the beginning was a disturbance in that part of being called the heart has dissociated into the "Here am I" and "I am He." The experience of transcendence, to summarize, is a movement of the soul, culminating in an act of transcendence in which the divine Within reveals itself as the divine Beyond.

We can now resume the question of immanence and transcendence as indices that accrue to being when the constitution of being is interpreted in the light of an experience of transcendence. The Abraham Apocalypse confines itself strictly to the experience itself. Once such an experience has occurred, however, the question can be asked (though it will not necessarily be asked) whether the divine Within-Beyond experienced in the movement of the soul is not the general structure of being. This question has been asked in Hellenic philosophy and it induced the Platonic conception of the Idea that exists "separately" and at the same time is the form of things in the world. In order to express this general Within-Beyond, Plato has developed the symbol of *methexis*, of participation—things have form insofar as they participate in the idea. This Platonic symbol of *methexis* is the classic case of the constitution of being interpreted in the light of an experience of transcendence. Unfortunately, however, the symbolism is still so close to the objectifying language of the myth that today it will be easily misunderstood as an attempt to constitute transcendent form as an object—an attempt of which Plato is certainly not guilty, as proven by the myth of the Within-Beyond of the idea in the *Timaeus*. If we express the same relationship in our non-mythical language of indices, we may say that the realms of being, as well as the objects within them, are never merely immanent; over their index of immanence there is always superimposed the index of embracing transcendence. If the Platonic symbolism is reformulated in this manner it reveals a crucial insight into the problem of objects and objectivity: Even when, in the climate of secularist epistemology, we believe ourselves to be safe from transcendence and to have immanent objects at hand, the humble object still is never godforsaken but radiates transcendence in its immanent *actus essendi*. The implications of this insight will occupy us further in later chapters. For the present, these reflections will be sufficient to suggest the context into which the issue of the triads must be fitted.

The parallelism of the ancient and modern triads extends only to the improper transfer of categories fashioned for things of the external world to problems of transcendence; it does not extend, within this general class, to the specific problems to which the categories are transferred. The sophistic transfer moves within the structural dimension set by the hierarchy of being—it presupposes the Parmenidean ascent with its distinction of true Being from the Doxa of this world—while the modern transfer moves in the quite different dimension set by the realization of eternal being in time. This is not to say that the two structural dimensions of being have no connection with one another: Transcendent being cannot be present in the realms of being without realizing itself in time, and eternal being cannot realize itself in time without being present in the realms of being. Still, the two dimensions are sufficiently distinct to allow for accentuations that in their turn determine styles of philosophizing. Not without reason will addicts to time characterize Classic philosophy, which through the reception of Aristotle in the Middle Ages also determined the Scholastic style, as static because it accentuates the hierarchy of being and conceives transcendence as an extrapolation of the hierarchy into its beyond. Nevertheless, though we must recognize the Classic style for what it is, we must not fall into the error of recent existentialist thinkers who believe that its characterization as static disposes of Classic and Scholastic metaphysics as obsolete. If Classic philosophy accentuates the hierarchy of being, as well as transcendence towards its beyond, to the neglect of being in time and the problems peculiar to this dimension, the existentialist accent on being in time neglects, with consequences far more destructive, the hierarchy of being and the classic problems peculiar to it. The modern triad concerning history thus has a case of its own. Although the triad in general is sophistic, its specific problems have not been settled by Classic philosophy. Hence, the philosopher must explore its implications if he wants to avoid the risk of falling into sophistic errors himself.

This exploration is of particular importance because the three propositions concerning history are substantially true from a position that conceives of science as an enterprise within the subject-object dichotomy. There is really something problematic about history as an object; and if the propositions express that something only by negatives, they still cannot be set aside as false merely because the thinkers who advance them have asked the wrong questions and given up too early. On the contrary, in order to be safe from elementary criticism, the philosopher must show that he has an object of inquiry, even if it is not an object in the conventional sense of the natural sciences. The objections implied in the propositions impose a discipline: The inquiry must begin with a demonstration of the possibility of its own beginning in spite of the objections. Such discipline does not mean, however, that we now have to engage in extensive exposition of argument and counterargument preliminary to the inquiry itself, for the issue as such—the misuse of the categories *object* and *existence*—is clear, and the challenge will be sufficiently met if an area of experience can be shown that requires categorization in other terms. Moreover, these preliminaries are not truly in the nature of a preface but belong to the inquiry proper, for their subject matter is imposed by the structure of history itself. In fact, by submitting to the discipline we discover the necessary form that an inquiry concerning history must adopt for its beginning. We shall consider the three objections in their order.

The first objection radically denies the existence of history as an object. The denial is substantially justified (the necessary qualifications will be considered presently); there would be no sense in arguing against it. The objection must be countered by drawing on the principle of epistemology that all science is an edifice erected over the pre-scientific knowledge of man. The principle attracts little attention in our time, because the ideological climate of the age favors the idea that the sciences of the external world are coterminous with the area of commonsense knowledge, that they cover the whole field with their methods, so that it seems one can take the principle for granted without much debate. This idea, however, is wrong. The knowledge of man living in his commonsense world extends indeed to far more than the area over which arise the sciences of the external world with their subject-object dichotomy. The classic sciences of ethics and politics, for instance, together with their nucleus in philosophical anthropology, theorize an area of commonsense knowledge that pertains, among other things, to questions of the conduct man is supposed to pursue in the light of his destiny. Since questions of this kind involve the transcendence of man, neither the propositions advanced in the course of their analysis, nor the philosophical concepts developed for fixing the terms of the analysis, will refer to objects in the conventional sense. To this commonsense knowledge, far wider in range than the knowledge of the external world, the philosopher must turn in quest of the subject matter called history—using the term *subject matter* to designate the general class of somethings of which objects are a species. No elaborate search is necessary. Since the objection was radical, the assumption of a subject matter implied in the very act of inquiry will be sufficiently substantiated by the fact that a great number of people in the past were concerned with something they called history and that we, the readers and the author of this book, are concerned with it too. The inquiry into the assumed something, furthermore, need not be motivated by more than the desire to know, by the desire to find out what that something is all about—even if it should prove to be nothing, so that the end of the inquiry would mark the end of an illusion.

The commonsense assumption must meet the second objection that history as an object, if it does exist, is unknowable. The objection certainly has a good case, for the drama of history is indeed unfinished; it continues to be enacted through the philosopher's present and indefinitely into the future. It is not given as a whole to any human subject with an Archimedic point outside history; and as the whole is not an object given to a subject, its meaning is unknown and therefore cannot furnish principles of interpretation even for the part that belongs to the past. The argument is unbreakable. The inquiry, if it is to be undertaken at all, must be conducted inside the object, so that, strictly speaking, there is neither an object nor a subject of cognition. Such conditions may sound preposterous to the fanatics of objects, but the philosopher will insist on clarity precisely with regard to this point in order not to be derailed into easy assumptions concerning the meaning of history.

The third objection provides grim satisfaction inasmuch as it closes the last loophole. If anybody had hoped he could leave the drama of history well alone to pursue its own mysterious ends, if he had hoped he could turn instead to that part of it that safely belongs to the past and seems to be neatly parceled out among the so-called facts of history, he now must learn that the facts, whatever they may be, are no conventional objects and that by their interpretation he would indulge his subjectivity. Again there is no counterargument. On the contrary, the philosopher will want to sharpen the issue: He will consider as miscarried the attempts made by some thinkers to develop a system of values that could serve as objective points of orientation for the selection and interpretation of historical facts; and with particular pleasure will he waive the spurious objectivity offered by social scientists who relate the supposed facts to the values of their respective societies, to the values of the age, or to the values of some dominant creed.

The *tabula* is *rasa* of objects. We have gained the freedom to turn to the world of common sense. A great number of people talk about history; when they use the word in their everyday language, what do they mean by it? From this quarter we expect some light to fall on our search for a beginning.

In common usage, the word *history* has the two meanings of a course of events and of a story telling them. A double meaning is perhaps more than we expected, but at least it is suggestive—assuming it to be more than an accidental equivocation—for it seems to point to a univocal phenomenon, to a sort of compactly emergent history preceding the retrospective dissociation into the *res gestae* and their story, to situations where history, at the point of its emergence, is experienced not in the past but in the present tense. The remembrance of things past indeed presupposes a present of existence where man, involved with events, senses his passion and action as memorable. To this sphere where man is involved with events, to the disturbances in being where man becomes part of events and the events part of human existence, to the units of mutual participation where there is yet no subject or object, where a present is constituted as a past to be remembered in the future, we shall refer as the sphere of involvement or encounter. In this primary sphere of encounter originate the experiences that may pass through various phases of reflective clarification before they culminate in an act of historiography. Obviously, this description of the phenomenon is couched in the same language as the earlier description of an experience of transcendence. At the beginning again there is a something that only can be called a disturbance in being preceding all reflective dissociation; again there follow phases of reflection in which, from an indistinct matrix of involvement, man is released into his search of the meaning that was enclosed in the encounter—in this case, into his search of what is truly memorable about the disturbance—until the movement culminates in an act in which man faces events as the history that occurs to him. This parallelism of formulation, which will appear presently, is not an accident; rather, it indicates the structure of transcendence in history. Before addressing this question, however, the immediate line of analysis must be pursued further.

Some light has fallen indeed on the elusive subject matter, for the equivocation of everyday language, suggestively pointing beyond itself, has revealed an important structure in history. A process has come into view, extending from the encounter, through experiences with several strata of reflection, to the creation of a historiographic symbolism expressing the experiences. A few reflections on this structure will substantially clarify the question, raised by the triad of propositions, of history as an object.

First of all, the insight into this process endows the third objection with a weight much greater than it can derive from its own formulation. There is a better reason than the conventionally discussed subjectivity of value judgments why an inquiry concerning history cannot start from the level of the historiographic subject-object dichotomy. The argument can be presented briefly: The inquiry cannot start from the historical object—*i.e.*, from a manifold of facts objectively given—because events, as well as the traces they have left in the world of sense perception, are not recognizable as historical by phenomenal characteristics, but can be recognized as manifestations of history only through recourse to the sphere of encounter. Nor can the inquiry start from the subject of cognition—*i.e.*, from categories or principles *a priori*—because the categorization of facts is not autonomous; the historiographer will produce no history of anything unless his categorizations express history emergent from encounters. Whether its dependence on the sphere of encounter will make the historiographer's work "subjective" or "objective" is a matter of later exploration, but the insight into this connection definitely disposes of methodological debates about "subjectivity" and "values" conducted without regard to it.

Taking into account the preceding argument we can, second, venture a formulation of the subject-object issue as it appears on the historiographic surface of the process that begins with an encounter. The issue of an object in the conventional sense does indeed exist on this level inasmuch as the historiographer can only reconstruct a memorable event, or a chain of events, by means of the traces they have left in the world of sense perception, be they artifacts or be they of a literary nature. For history, though an expressive symbolism, is not a dream world but is firmly rooted in time, space, and matter; and the historiographer is, after all, a scientist who ascertains given objects. We thus arrive at something like a double constitution of history: On the one hand, the phenomenal objects can be recognized as historical only through tracing their meaning to the sphere of encounter; on the other hand, the phenomena must be explored by methods that, in principle, are the same as those used in other sciences of the external world. The question can be further clarified by applying to historiography the Kantian language of *phenomena* and *noumena,* originally developed for the case of physics. Using this language one might say: History has a phenomenal surface that can be explored by an objectifying science, but the enterprise of science makes sense only as long as the facts ascertained can be related to the noumenal depth of the encounter. This proposition, if it is thought through, shows the point at which the analogy with physics will prove untenable. The natural phenomena envisaged by Kant, it is true, have a noumenal depth, but the ontic underground of the external world is that part of the constitution of being that is hidden from man, so that the manner in which the phenomenon depends on the noumenon is unknown. What is accessible to knowledge is only the definitely constituted surface of phenomena. One might define *given,* therefore, as the *pre-given definiteness of constitution.* This is the sense in which one can speak of objects as given. In history, on the contrary, the noumenal depth of the encounter involves man in the constitution of being; and the process leading from the encounter, through the experiences, to their expression, again involves man in its constitution at every step. In particular, the expressive symbolism of historiography in which the process culminates is not exempt from this structure. As a consequence, the surface of the process does not have *pre-given definiteness of constitution;* it is not *given* at all but constitutes itself in the acts of symbolic expression. Still, we cannot escape the earlier insight that history has a surface that is phenomenal in character; history, if it is not a given object, at least partakes of givenness in one of its strata. The resulting relationship between the two factors of what we have called the double constitution of history can be formulated as follows: The historiographer's work is essentially a part of the expressive surface of history, while the subject-object dichotomy of the phenomenal surface is a secondary stratum within the primary expressive surface. Hence, if a philosophy of history were reduced to a methodology of exploring the phenomenal surface, its essential part would have been abandoned. The course of the analysis thus has confirmed the initial assumption that the equivocation of the term *history* is not an accident: Even on the level of the historiographic dichotomy, univocal history dominates equivocal history and endows it with meaning.

While the three propositions have nothing positive to say about history, while their ontological misconceptions result only in negatives, at least they make abundantly clear the difficulty of finding history as an object. We consider the aporia unbreakable and therefore reject all attempts, characteristic of an age impassioned by the will to power over objects, to evade or ignore, to escape or break it. The aporia must be accepted. If the level of objectified events is secondary, the inquiry must begin the unfolding of its problems from one of the primary encounters. This formulation is deliberately vague. A higher degree of precision at this point would be liable, however unintendedly, to inject a definite conception of history and thereby to compromise the conception that should emerge from the analysis as its result. No further definitions of the terms *history, encounter,* or *event* will be given at this time; the terms are used in a topical sense in order to achieve a preliminary understanding of the issue.

2. Substantive Inquiry

The substantive inquiry concerning history must begin the unfolding of its problems from one of the primary encounters. I shall briefly characterize the field from which the choice must be made:

The encounter involving man with events is the starting point of a process that may culminate in a symbolism expressing concern with history. I shall refer generically to this chain of reflective experiences culminating in a symbolism as *responses* to the encounter. They differ widely with regard to comprehensiveness and intellectual penetration, as well as with regard to the symbolic forms expressing the experiences. Some of the responses have expanded into well-circumscribed symbolisms with such frequency that the types have attracted attention and received names—as, for instance, the symbolic forms of historiogenesis, historiography, or

apocalypse. Other responses have produced forms of no less importance, but because they have occurred infrequently, or are even
unique, they have received no names in common usage, as have the
symbolisms created by Plato or Deutero-Isaiah, or the historical responses contained in the *Puranas* or the *Shu-ching.*

The choice to be made from this field will be guided by the same
commonsense rule that was used in the preliminary inquiry. The
choice must fall not on one of the rarer forms but rather on one
occurring with some frequency. Choosing further among the typi-
cal forms, it will be best to decide for the one that, because of its
massive occurrence, is most readily associated in the commonsense world of our time with historical concern—the form of historiography. Having settled on historiography as the preferred type,
the field must be narrowed to a particular member of the class.
In the face of the immense historiographic literature, this final
choice would be difficult but for the consideration that we are interested not in a piece of historiographic work picked at random, or
perhaps in a recent publication, but only in early encounters where
the expression of discovery is least encumbered with tradition or
obscured by imitation and routine. If this rule of original discovery
were to be applied rigorously, one might even expect the field to
become narrowed down to the one case of the earliest encounter
that has resulted in the writing of history.

In fact, however, the rule cannot be applied rigorously, because it
implies a premise that is in conflict with reality. Only if the encounters that have resulted in the writing of history were lined up
on a single coordinate of time could one of them be determined as
the earliest known. History, however, does not move along a single
line in time but along several parallel lines. The earliest encounters
leading to historiographic form occur, independently of one another, in several societies. Moreover, they occur so close to one another in time that their grouping forms something like a pattern in
history. Because it would be unwise to ignore this pattern, we shall
not insist further on a single encounter as the subject of exploration. The choosing has come to its end; from now on we must surrender to the structure of history and see where its exploration will
lead us.

The earliest encounters resulting in historiographic form occur in three societies: Hellas, Israel, and China, proceeding from west to east. I shall first assemble the relevant data.

1. The first major historiographic work in Hellas, setting aside the logographic antecedents, is the *Historiai* of Herodotus in the fifth century B.C. In a classical tradition, which does not deem it necessary to consider parallel phenomena in other societies, it has merited its author the title of a Father of History. Toward the end of the same century, Thucydides wrote his *Syngraphe*, conventionally known as the *History of the Peloponnesian War*. In the Hellenistic centuries, then, the form unfolded broadly in a massive historiographic literature.

2. The case of Israel is more complicated than the Hellenic one because the histories can neither be ascribed to definite authors nor exactly dated. The biblical narrative in its final form has unknown compilers, editors, and redactors who in their turn have used oral traditions as well as annals and commentaries on annals, superimposing their own form on this body of preformed materials. Leaving aside the vigorous controversies that a structure of such complexity arouses with regard to sources, their authors, and chronology, one can nevertheless recognize a large block of historiographic work—the Deuteronomist history of the Kings—as a unit. Since this history ends with the fall of Jerusalem in 587, one can be sure that its conception lies in the exilic period, in the sixth century B.C., though touches here and there may have been added as late as the fourth century B.C. Within this work are embedded some preformed sources to which one cannot deny the title of historiographic form: The David Memoir (2 Samuel 9 through 1 Kings 2), for instance, can be dated close to the events reported, perhaps still in the tenth century B.C. A second historiographic work of unknown authorship, comprising the books of Chronicles, Ezra, and Nehemiah, was produced at the approximate date of 300 B.C. The Maccabean period finally motivated two histories, which are counted as 1 and 2 Maccabees, written before the capture of Jerusalem by Pompey in 67 B.C. The first was possibly written toward the end of the second century B.C. Beyond Maccabees, with Josephus, Jewish historiography blends into the Hellenistic type.

3. In some respects, the genesis of historiographic form in China resembles the Israelite rather than the Hellenic beginnings. Hellas

had no court or temple annals; historiography was therefore a private enterprise, and the historian hardly had at his disposal sources other than his personal knowledge of events, expanded somewhat by memories of the older generation and by a stock of epic and mythic traditions in general circulation. The historians of Israel could rely not only on a much older and better preserved stock of traditions but, for the time of the Kingdom, on annals and probably extracts from annals. In the same manner, the historians of the Han period could rely, for the pre-imperial period, on a variety of sources, including the documents of the *Shu-ching*. In their present linguistic form, they are hardly older than the eighth century B.C., though they may in part go back at least to the beginning of the Chou dynasty. There were furthermore preserved the libretti of Chou rituals celebrating the victory of the Chou dynasty over the preceding one. And finally, a good deal of Chinese history could be reconstructed from the annals of the several principalities, especially from the *Ch'un-ch'iu*, the annals of the principality of Lu from 772 to 481. To none of these sources, however, would one accord the title of historiography. The Chinese historiographic form proper emerged under the reign of Wu-ti (140–87), when the court historian Ssu-ma T'an and his son Ssu-ma Ch'ien conceived and executed the *Shih-chi*, a record of Chinese history from the early culture heroes to the historians' own time. Again, in the first century A.D., a father-and-son team, Pan Piao (A.D. 3–54) and Pan Ku (A.D. 32–92), produced the *Han-shu*, or *History of the Former Han Dynasty*, thereby setting the style that Chinese historiography was to follow to the end of the empire in 1912.

From the data it appears that historiography is a response to the involvement of man with the event of empire. In Hellas, Israel, and China the early historiographic efforts are connected, directly or indirectly, with the disturbance or destruction of an older order through imperial expansion. In Hellas, the work of Herodotus is a history of the conflict between Asia and Europe, culminating in the Persian attempt to incorporate Hellas into the ecumenic empire of the Achaemenians. The work of Thucydides, then, is concerned with the aftermath of the Persian Wars in Hellas itself, with the growth of the Delian League into an Athenian empire, and with the fatality of its conflict with the Spartan League. The destruction of the Hellenic balance of power among the poleis through the rise of imperial form, as well as the moral dissolution of Hellas through the great *kinesis*, is its theme. The later Hellenistic historians finally move on the scene that is set by the conquest of Alexander, the establishment of the Diadochic empires, and the expansion of Rome. In Israel, the history of the Kingdom begins with the abolition of the older theopolity through the kingship of Saul and the foundation of the Davidic empire, and it ends with the fall of Jerusalem through the expansion of Babylon. The work of the chronicler, then, is motivated by the foundation of the Second Temple after the conquest of Babylon by the Persians. The third spurt of Israelite historiography, finally, is motivated by the Hasmonaean resistance to the Seleucid empire. In China, the historiographic form established by Ssu-ma Ch'ien and the historians of the Former Han dynasty is an official reconstruction of Chinese history from its mythical beginnings, through the Three Royal Dynasties and the agony of the late Chou period, to the abolition of the classic Chinese order by the empire of the Ch'in and Han dynasties.

The aggregate of data puts content into the hitherto empty formulae of encounters and responses. Not everything that happens is an event worth recording; history is discovered as a disturbance of order, caused by the rise and expansion of empire. This may sound like the definition we have been looking for. It would be rash, however, to generalize from the three cases without inspecting them more closely. A few casuistic reflections will prove the issue to be much more complicated.

In the three cases of Hellas, Israel, and China the encounter with empire was, to be sure, experienced as a major disturbance of order and expressed by means of historiography. There can be no doubt about the massive disturbance of order when Athens is destroyed and the freedom of Hellas is at stake, or when Jerusalem is conquered and the Kingdom of Judah is abolished, or when the last Chinese principalities fall to the onslaught of Ch'in. In all known cases, historiography indeed is a response to the encounter with empire. This relation, however, is not reversible—one cannot say that imperial intervention inevitably will cause somebody to write history. There were empires in existence for thousands of years before the period under discussion, and nobody responded to the disturbances they caused with the writing of history. We may say tentatively that an encounter with cosmological empires like the

Mesopotamian or Egyptian, before 1000 B.C., did not have an historiographic sequel, while encounters with multicivilizational or ecumenic empires like the Persian, Macedonian, or Roman did have this remarkable effect. Even with that restriction, however, the relation still is not reversible. When the Persians conquered Mesopotamia, Lydia, and Egypt, none of the conquered Near Eastern societies broke out with the writing of history; only Hellas responded with the Herodotean *History of the Persian Wars.* When Alexander in his turn conquered Persia, no Persian wrote a history of the Macedonian conquest, though his campaigns elicited a rich historiographic literature on the Hellenic side. When the Persians, and after them the Macedonians, expanded into the Indus Valley, the disturbances were of the first magnitude and even precipitated in the foundation of the Maurya empire by Chandragupta; but we would know very little about these events had not Hellenic historians—for instance Arrianus in his *Indika*—left us a certain amount of information. The Indians never responded with historiography to any disturbance of order. Clearly the encounter with an imperial disturbance of order is not sufficient to cause the historiographic response; there also must be men who are able to recognize vicissitudes of this type as historical and therefore worth recording. Apparently the order of man and society must already be conceived in a certain manner if the disturbance of this order by an outburst of power is to be endowed with historical character. If, however, this endowment with the index *history* is shifted from the side of events to the side of man who encounters them, certain questions will inevitably impose themselves—questions such as whether the foundation and expansion of an empire is history only if somebody recognizes it as such or whether it will carry the index in any case. Does India, for instance, have a history though it has never developed historiography? This question must be deferred for later treatment.

For the present, I shall further pursue the question of responsiveness as an independent factor. First, its quantitative aspect should be isolated. In the three cases of Hellas, Israel, and China, a penchant for history is noticeable over long periods preceding its blossoming into actual historiography. Regarding Hellas, we must note the curious fact of a consciousness of history extending back to the Minoan past and even to the migratory movements of the

turn from the third to the second millennium B.C.—a consciousness that in the absence of recording institutions could rely on nothing but oral tradition. With Plato this consciousness crystallized in
the specifically Hellenic conception of a great cycle of civilizational
order beginning with the Minoan foundation and coming to its end
in the philosopher's own time, in the fourth century B.C. In Israel,
if we include Patriarchal history and Abraham's exodus from Ur as
traditions with an authentic historical core, the consciousness of
history embraces about the same time span as in Hellas. Again, in
exilic and post-exilic times, this consciousness crystallized in the
specifically Israelite conception of a unilinear history that from its
divine origin, through the present, will go on until it has reached its
divinely ordained end. In China, finally, the Three Royal Dynasties
preceding the period of empire go back, by the counting of traditional history, to the early second millennium B.C., a tradition that
the modern critics are more and more inclined to confirm. The specifically Chinese form in which this consciousness of history crystallized is neither the Hellenic cycle now coming to its close, nor
the Israelite history moving toward its divinely ordained end, but a
conception of dynasties that rule by divine decree and lose their
power, never to be regained, when the dynasty has exhausted its
original endowment of divine ruling virtue. Hellas, Israel, and
China thus have in common a millennial consciousness of history
preceding the historiographic form proper. Moreover, we must note
the intriguing fact that, as far as the chronology is reliable, the consciousness seems to range over the same time span, back to a date
in the early second millennium B.C.

The intriguing fact must be noted for later use. It would be hasty
to conclude, however, that we have now found the key to historiographic responsiveness, for there were societies with an even
longer historical memory that did not respond with the writing of
history when they were involved in the same whirlpool of imperial
expansion as Hellas, Israel, and China. Of particular interest are the
cases of Babylon and Egypt. When the Persian rule had been over-
thrown by the conquest of Alexander and replaced by the Diadochic
empires of the Seleucids and Lagids, something like a reassertion of
national consciousness occurred in Babylon and Egypt. About the
same time, *ca.* 280 B.C., both the Babylonian priest Berossus and
the Egyptian priest Manetho conceived the idea of presenting the

king-lists of their respective societies to a public dominated by the conquerors, apparently with the propagandistic intention of contrasting the venerable age of their own societies with the short civilizational history of the new masters. Neither the *Babyloniaka* of Berossus nor the *Aigyptiaka* of Manetho, however, are works of historiography; rather, they cling to an older symbolism, to the historiogenetic form that will occupy us later in the present volume. In both the Babylonian and Egyptian cases, the range of memory over almost three thousand years, even more or less well supported by records, is indeed superior to anything the new imperialists can boast of. And yet, not the representatives of the older societies but the newcomers are the historians. The issue will become even clearer if the responses of Berossus and Manetho are compared with the one of Josephus Flavius. Toward the end of the first century A.D., Josephus wrote his *Jewish Antiquities* with the same propagandistic intent of demonstrating to the Roman conquerors of his time the superior age of the society to which he belonged. In the process he even made himself the advocate of the Babylonians and Egyptians as well, so that in his person the "older" Orient asserted itself against the Greek and Roman upstart. But Josephus was a Jew. He could indeed write history, from the creation of the world to A.D. 66, because he could express himself in the historiographic form he had inherited from his forebears. A long memory alone, it seems, will not make for historiography any more than will a disturbance of order alone.

I have used the inductive method of falsifying tentative generalizations by pointing to an *instantia contraria* in order to eliminate suggestive factors as impertinent to the issue. Neither the destructiveness of an imperial expansion nor the time span of historical memory are decisive for the discovery of history. The quality of history neither adheres to certain spectacular phenomena, nor is it discovered as adhering to them when enough of them have happened over a long time. The inductive method narrowed the issue sufficiently to make it clear that the recognition of events as historical depends on the man involved—though the reader should be warned that this formulation will require substantial revision. If an encounter is to result in the expression of concern with history, and particularly in historiography, the man involved with events must already know what history is; he must already have a conception of order that will enable him to understand the vicissitudes of that order as historical. History seems to be an index that events may receive when certain discoveries concerning order have previously been made.

The question of indices has become thematic in the preliminary inquiry. I shall now elaborate it further by the following propositions:

1. When the primary experience of the cosmos has been disrupted by an experience of transcendence, the constitution of being that hitherto had been interpreted by cosmological symbols must now be reinterpreted by symbols that take into account the newly discovered structure of reality.

2. The experience of transcendence is a movement of the soul, culminating in an act of transcendence in which God and man are constituted as persons facing each other. The movement of the soul is the site of the meeting that in its mutuality is active and passive on both sides, so that the seeker and the sought, the finder and the found can be predicated of both God and man.

3. This movement, with its contraction of divine being into the Within and Beyond of the soul, entails something like a de-divinization of the cosmos that had hitherto been full of gods. The cosmos is metamorphosed into a world with the index *immanent* in relation to divine being with the index *transcendent.*

4. We then must distinguish between a) the separation of divine being from the world including man and b) its specific concentration into a Beyond of the experiencing soul. The general separation makes it necessary to find symbols that will express the presence of divine being as the creative, sustaining, and forming force within the world. For this purpose, Plato created the symbol *methexis,* which in medieval philosophy became the *participatio* of the world, including man, in transcendent being. From the specific concentration into a Beyond of the soul there follow the problems of ordering human existence through attunement to the divine being discovered in the experience of transcendence.

5. Man, existentially ordered by the experience of transcendence, becomes the model of order for man and society. In Plato's *Republic* this model function has grown into the anthropological principle of politics that the order of society is the order of "man

written large." Since, however, man can be the model of society only if his existence is ordered by an experience of transcendence, the anthropological principle must be supplemented by a model conception of the divine being that is experienced in the movement of the soul. In order to solve this problem, Plato coined the term *theology* and distinguished between the true type of theology and the false types. In the context of these distinctions, there appears in the *Republic* as one of the false types the sophistic triad of propositions concerning the gods. Man thus can be the model of paradigmatic order in society only when he himself has been ordered by divine being, when as a consequence he partakes of divine substance, when he has become theomorphic. The theomorphism of the soul, we may say, is the supreme principle of the conception of order that originates in the experience of transcendence and leads to the discovery of history.

6. We must furthermore distinguish between transcendent being a) as a beyond in relation to the hierarchy of the immanent realms of being and b) as eternal being in relation to being in time. This latter distinction has a close affinity, but is not identical, with the distinction made under Point 4 between divine being a) as separate from a world that has become immanent and b) as the counterpart of the soul in the experience of transcendence. The affinity of the first members of the distinctions becomes manifest in the previously mentioned tendency toward a style of Classic philosophy. The affinity of the second members of the distinctions becomes manifest in a tendency to let the realization of eternal being in time as a general problem recede into the background and to focus attention on its realization in the existential order of man and society.

7. Wherever an experience of transcendence has occurred with sufficient intenseness and clarity to disintegrate the primary experience of the cosmos, events can be discovered as having a bearing on the order of man and society in its relation to eternal being. The index that events receive under this aspect is the historical index. In the nature of things, the experience of transcendence itself has the decisive place among historical events inasmuch as it raises the realization of eternal being in time to the level of historical consciousness.

8. I shall refer to the aggregate of symbols developed for the pur-

pose of reinterpreting the constitution of being in the light of an experience of transcendence as symbols of transcendence or the transcendental symbolism, distinguishing them from the cosmological symbolism that interprets the constitution of being in the light of the primary experience of the cosmos. The index *history* is one of the symbols of transcendence.

The preceding propositions have attempted to clarify the essence of the problems created by an experience of transcendence. For this purpose, the experience was treated as if it were an isolated event without social context, as if it were an encounter between God and man that abruptly occurs, without preparation, in an undisturbed cosmological society. It was furthermore treated as if it were always fully actualized to the point where God and man face each other in the act of transcendence, so that a new existential order of man in his presence under God is clearly constituted. In fact, however, the experiences always occur (as far as we know) in social contexts of considerable complexity, and they rarely achieve full actualization. These are the two variables responsible a) for a wide variety of types among encounters and responses, b) for the varying degrees of comprehension and articulation with regard to the problem of order, and c) for the actual appearance or non-appearance of historiography. This manifold of types needs a brief review, with special regard to the discovery of history.

If an experience of transcendence, fully actualized, were to occur in an undisturbed cosmological society, it would probably be incommunicable and meet with no social response, so that there would be no historical record of it. Still, the possibility of such occurrences cannot be roundly dismissed, because there exists the puzzling case of Zoroaster. The curious history of Zoroastrianism, as well as the difficulties we still have today in understanding what happened, will hardly bear any other explanation than the appearance of a prophet in a society insufficiently prepared to receive the truth he has to communicate. The comparatively primitive tribal society in the Iranian hinterland of Mesopotamia's old imperial civilization apparently had not yet developed the sensorium for a spiritual irruption of the rank represented by Zoroaster. Although no certain judgment in this complicated matter is possible, the early deformation of the experience inspiring the Gathas may be respon-

sible for the fact that the new conception of order was never sufficiently clarified to lead to historiographic responses. The Iranian
genius in this respect began to flower only late, in the environment
fertilized by Islam.

Of the successful cases, the Israelite has first claim to attention
because it is closest to the type of a highly actualized experience of
transcendence in opposition to a highly developed cosmological society. Even in this case, however, the spectacularly abrupt exodus
from the cosmological Egypt and the constitution of a new society
under God were amply prepared, as far as the sources permit us to
discern, by unsettling disturbances of the previous order that made
the Mosaic experience of transcendence both intelligible and com-
municable. By the time of Moses, in the thirteenth century B.C.,
Egypt had undergone the troubles of the intermediate periods between the Old and the Middle, between the Middle and the New
Kingdoms. These times of troubles had given rise, especially in the
first Intermediate Period, to literary expressions of suicidal despair
and scepticism with regard to the cosmological order that were of
such intenseness and perspicacity that the non-occurrence of the
spiritual breakthrough is rather less intelligible than its occurrence
would have been; and in the person of Akh-en-Aton a breakthrough
of a sort had actually occurred, though its appropriation as a privi-
lege to the Pharaoh, not to be shared by everyman, prevented its
becoming socially and historically effective. Akh-en-Aton was not
constituted, by his experience, as a man but as a Pharaoh under God;
he remained the mediator of divine presence within the framework
of a cosmological society. From the Hebrew side, though the antecedents are less clear, there is no doubt that the Yahweh of Moses
could be recognized by Moses himself, as well as by the people, as a
God of the Fathers of long standing. Finally, Moses was by birth and
breeding a man between the Egyptian and Hebrew societies, an experience that is always unsettling, as anybody to whom it has happened knows. In spite of all the unsettling disturbances preparatory
to the epiphany of Moses, however, the break with the old order
was much too abrupt for the new order to be carried at once to the
full actualization of its radical potentialities. Moses, it is true,
went one step further than Akh-en-Aton when he let his new
people be constituted in immediacy under God, but it was the
people collectively that was so constituted. Hence, even if the un-

mediated presence had expanded from the Pharaoh to the people, the radical implication of the experience of transcendence—that every man achieves, and can achieve, full human status through his personal existence under God—did not yet fully unfold. Both the expansion and its limitation become manifest in the striking symbolism by which Moses opposed the new order to the old one: In the Pyramid Texts (1a–b) the god greets the Pharaoh with the formula

This is my son, my first-born;

in Exod. 4:22 Yahweh decrees

My son, my first-born, is Israel.

Only under the blows of history, after the fall of Jerusalem, did the universalist implications, always a live undercurrent, make themselves felt in Ezekiel's recognition of everyman as a moral subject solely responsible for his own deeds and misdeeds, as well as in the Deutero-Isaianic conception of Israel's exodus from itself into mankind.

In Hellas and China, the reordering of existence through experiences of transcendence occurs in a setting differing from the Israelite with regard to space, time, and substance of order. With regard to space, the respective areas of Hellas and China lie geopolitically beyond the immediate influence of the older Mesopotamian and Egyptian societies. Hence, the new conception of order does not arise, and does not become effective, in opposition to an empire in cosmological form. With regard to time, the spiritual outbursts occur more than seven centuries after the events reported in the Book of Exodus. With regard to substance, finally, the existence in cosmological form, in the respective areas, was seriously shaken by endogenous disintegration—a process most probably facilitated by the fact that the cosmological order was never institutionalised in a social form of such coherence as the Near Eastern empires.

The Chinese case should be considered first; though beyond the political range of the Near Eastern empires, it is closer in type to them than to the Hellenic. In fact, in China there are to be found symbolisms expressing governmental order that closely resemble those of imperial order in Mesopotamia. Nevertheless, these symbols were not developed in the context of an imperial structure of the same type, for, as far back as the institutional structure can be discerned at all, Chinese kingship had the marks of a ritual rule over the ecumene, with the accents on maintenance and expansion of ritual order rather than of imperial power. By the time of Confucius (551–479 B.C.), this type of ritual rule by one of the Chinese princes over the whole area of federated principalities had declined so far that one can speak of an internal disintegration of the Chinese ecumene. The central kingship had become virtually powerless, and the process had begun in which the rulers of the component principalities were to emancipate themselves from the ecumenic order to the point of appropriating the ecumenic title of *wang* to their local rulership, of entering into rivalry for the overthrow of the ruling dynasty, as well as of developing the conception of a new type of rulership, designated as *ti* in opposition to the earlier *wang*, with overtones of power only uncertainly limited by the declining ritual order. A compact cosmological order, though institutionally not of the imperial type, was dissociating into power and spirit through an emancipation of action from traditional order—an emancipation that led in due course to fratricidal wars among the component principalities until one of them administered the knock-out blow, to use Toynbee's language, and established an empire over the area of what once had been a ritual ecumene. The antagonist to the type of order envisaged by Confucius thus was not a cosmological empire but a rationale of power that was dissociating, through an endogenous process, from the previously compact order. Under these circumstances, the ethos of the ritual kingship acquired for Confucius an aura of the good old times, so that his own conception of order had a strongly traditionalist coloration.

The Hellenic situation was even farther removed from the type of cosmological empire than was the Chinese. In Hellas we find no traces of an imperial symbolism at all, because there was not so much as even a ritual kingship to be clothed by it. The type of ritual order embracing the whole Hellenic society, which would have corresponded to the Chinese kingship, did not go beyond organizations of such precarious cohesiveness as the Amphictyonic Leagues, the late development of the consciousness and name of Hellenes (not yet in Homer), the organization of pan-Hellenic games, or the tenuous organization for common defense in the Persian Wars. The instability of this order, setting aside the major upheavals, is attested by the frequency of minor warfare, conducted in cruel form, over local issues among the poleis, as well as by the tension and civic disorders within them. The internal order in particular, wherever we get an early glimpse of it, leaves much to be desired. The criticisms of Hesiod (*ca.* 700 B.C.), as well as the grievances that compelled the Solonic reform in Athens (596 B.C.), betray the conflict between an order of justice and the unrestrained power drives of personal interest. The actual dissociation of power and spirit can be gauged by the development of a vocabulary for this polarization of order—I mention only, on the one side, the term *pleonexia*, which designates the drive for personal aggrandizement, and, on the other side, the Solonic reflections on the "unseen measure" that is supposed to provide the rule of just conduct. Under these circumstances, the new conception of order found its opposition in a cosmological empire here no more than it did in China.

Nevertheless, the situation did not allow the comparatively simple alignment against a power drive cutting loose from traditional order as in China, because Hellas was burdened—if a burden it may be called—with the magnificent unfolding of its polytheistic myth. The primary experience of the cosmos had not dissolved under the blows of the Doric invasion or the hardships of migration and new settlement on the Anatolian coast but remained the background of the society of gods and men created by Homer. The gods of the epic had become the gods of Hellenic society; therefore, its history of order is pervaded by the ambivalence peculiar to Homeric polytheism. On the one hand, polytheism is possible only when being is interpreted in the light of the primary experience of the cosmos; on the other hand, the Homeric conception of the movements of the psyche resulting in action as movements inspired by the gods is the seed that was to grow into the Aeschylean theomorphism of the soul and, further, into the Platonic conception of the divinely ordered man who realizes in his person the *homoiosis theo.* As a consequence, the experience of transcendence, inchoately present even in Homer, requires the permanent attack on the polytheistic myth, in which it is embedded, in order to arrive at clarity about itself. The attack on the myth—whether in its Homeric form, in local or minor popular forms, or in the cult of the polis—as an "untruth" opposed to the "truth" revealed by the experience of transcendence is the constant theme of Hellenic spiritual history from the first stirrings in Hesiod's *Theogony* through Parmenides and Heraclitus down to the Platonic attack on "dear Homer" that is still liberally misunderstood as an issue in aesthetics. In China this constant theme is missing because Chinese society had never developed a polytheism of the Homeric type; on the contrary, the divine force ordering the ritual ecumene, which seems to have had a personal past, had at an early date assumed the impersonal form expressed by the symbol *t'ien*. The order envisaged by the sages could therefore draw, with a deceptively traditionalist claim, on the ethos of a past unencumbered by polytheism. At the same time, however, the lack of "untrue" polytheism as an antagonist may have been one of the reasons why the "truth" of a transcendent personal divinity—and, correspondingly, the existence of a theomorphic man under God—has never sprung forth from the Chinese experiences of transcendence. The Chinese experience, as far as we know, never culminated in an act of transcendence; and to the incomplete experience corresponded a conception of man that fell short of the full theomorphic status. This less-than-full conception of man I shall call *anthropomorphic*. To this day, the faith in an impersonal source of order has remained a determinant in the resistance of cultivated Chinese to religions with personal gods because of their inferior rationality, while the same faith seems to have affinities, if not with the ethos of communism, at least with its impersonal law of dialectics. Only the second antagonist, *i.e.,* the unrestrained power drive of the individuals, is common to Hellas and China, though even in this common feature the inversion of the time schedule is worth noting. In Hellas the rationalization of the power drive by the sophistic conception of man and society precedes the Platonic attack by a full generation and later parallels Plato's work, while in China the conception of a social order dissociating, or already dissociated from, the older ritual order is systematically elaborated only after Confucius in the work of Shang Yang (338 B.C.) and Han Fei (233 B.C.). In Hellas, Plato attacks the Sophists; in China, the advocates of power politics and benevolent materialism attack Confucianism. With regard to the time schedule of the two antagonists within Hellas, then, one might say that in the first spiritual outburst, represented by Parmenides, Heraclitus, and Xenophanes about 500 B.C., the truth of divine being as transcendent had to be established in opposition to the polis, the people, and its myth, while in the second outburst, represented by Socrates and Plato, the sophistic emancipation had become the primary target.

The phenomena just surveyed have proved to be not self-contained entities to be listed in a catalog of types but display a tendency to enter into various relationships. We could observe the antagonisms, for instance, between the cosmological and transcendental conceptions of order, between myth and philosophy, between philosophers and sophists. The attacks on the myth, then, from Hesiod through the mystic-philosophers to Plato became members of a series of such length in time that we had to speak of a constant in the intellectual history of Hellas. The experience of transcendence, furthermore, did not confine itself to a unique appearance in a definite setting, but the experiences repeated themselves, again forming a series of increasing clarity, so that we had to note a scale of actualization in time and speak of an inchoate mode that could be sensed in the Homeric epic. These relationships are a new class of phenomena, superimposed on the component phenomena, and they present a new problem to be explored. Before this question of the super-phenomena can be pursued further, however, the emancipated power drive requires some attention: It seems to belong neither to the cosmological nor to the transcendental conception of order. Its appearance accounts for the characteristic triangular antagonisms—for the opposition of philosophers in Hellas to both the myth and the sophists, of the power advocates in China to both the ritual kingship and Confucianism.

The antagonism between the philosophers and the advocates of the power drive is serious to the point of deadliness: With the rise of empire in China, the Confucians were persecuted and large quantities of classical writings were destroyed; in the Platonic dialogues, the sophist appears as the philosopher's enemy, threatening him with death by legal proceedings, and in real life the killing is performed with success. This deadliness should be fully realized because there enters into it the fact that the antagonism arises from a conflict, not between the old cosmological and the new transcendental order, but between two conceptions of order, both of which are post-cosmological. The warfare between philosophers and sophists is conducted among parties that have emancipated themselves from the primary experience of the cosmos. The philosopher and the sophist are in fact brothers under the skin inasmuch as they accept the disintegration of the primary experience as their common ground. The bitterness of conflict may make the thesis of a common ground sound odd at first hearing, but we must consider the possibility that from a breakdown of order will arise not necessarily the more desirable order the critics of the old one have envisaged but rather a prolonged period of disorder. Plato was aware of this problem when in the *Epinomis* he counseled respect for the people's myth because uncautious criticism might indeed dissolve it, leaving in the wake of destruction not men on the new level of philosophical existence but people disorganized by their loss of faith. The experience of transcendence, to be sure, exacts a new interpretation of being, but it is by no means certain what form this interpretation will assume once the primary experience of the cosmos has been discredited. It may assume the philosophic form, which interprets the totality of being compactly comprehended in the primary experience, but it also may assume various defective forms according to the willful preferences of the interpreters for this or that segment of reality.

The multiplicity of interpretations subsequent to the rejection of the cosmological type is symptomatic of a new level of consciousness, for the reinterpretation of being, once it has become necessary, brings to acute consciousness the function of man as the interpreter of being—a consciousness that previously had been present only in the less dangerous form of mythopoeic freedom. And once man has become conscious that he is the source, if not of order, of at least the conceptions of order, an autonomy has been gained that can be used in the service of truth as well as of untruth. With the dimension of philosophy there opens the dimension of *philodoxy* (to use Plato's term)—the possibility of opining. Hence, in the new state of emancipation, there are as many conceptions of order possible as there are drives and desires in the psyche apt to harden into centers for organizing them. Only the fact that extravagant conceptions are self-defeating, because they are inadequate for the purpose of ordering human and social existence, puts a practical limit on a range of possibilities that on principle is indefinitely wide. Highly specialized desires, when made the organizational center, will cause severe disturbances in the economy of the psyche; moreover, they will cause a man and his followers to be maladjusted to the exigencies of existence in the world. Cases in point are certain apocalyptic and gnostic sects that indulge their desire for redemption from the evils of this world to the point of expecting the end of the world to be near, and accordingly neglect to provide for the permanent order of man in society. The autonomy, therefore, if misused to indulge special desires, may result in sectarianism; or, if the desire is too special even to attract followers in sufficient numbers to be called a sect, it may reduce the man to the rank of a crackpot or pervert. In order to make an imbalanced conception socially effective, the organizing center must at least be comprehensive enough to provide for the self-sustaining, defensive, and lasting order of society.

Among the imbalanced conceptions there is one that—in spite of the disorder, destruction, and misery wrought in the process of its realization—is better suited than others to the task of providing a lasting order for society. It is the conception motivated, to the exclusion of all other considerations, by the desire to achieve unrestrained ordering power for existence in the world, by the desire to make oneself the ruler of a society and, once this position is achieved, to make the society the ruler over all other societies within reach. I am speaking of the desire to establish an ecumenic empire.

A critic will perhaps wonder why a power drive of ecumenic proportions should be singled out as different from other power drives intending a rule of some duration. The pragmatism of ecumenic expansion, the critic might argue, is no more than ordinary pragmatism pushed to the extreme where dominion is running out of further objects to be dominated. It was no accident, however, that the term *pragmatic history* gained its specific meaning in connection with the imperial expansion of Rome, a meaning that illuminates pragmatisms of less than ecumenic ambitions, also. The extreme of pragmatism, culminating in the conception of world dominion, is related, as its immanentist counterpart, to the conception of a society whose order is informed by orientation toward transcendent being. The "world" that can be conquered is an aggregate of world-immanent objects endowed with a universality for which the conception of ecumenic rule had to draw on the other pole of the Within-Beyond tension—that is, transcendent being. The Alexandrian or Caesarian desire holds its peculiar fascination, not only for the actors but even for the victims, because it heightens the splendor of strength and power by endowing it with the illusionary aura of universality. Ecumenic desire is the ontologically perfect response to the appeal for order going forth from a world that experientially has become immanent. Hence, an ecumenic empire can go far by way of expansion and duration before the illusion of universality is shattered and the tedium of senselessness compels a restoration of balance by accepting transcendental orientation nevertheless. This status of ecumenic order as the ontological counterpart to universal order was admirably discerned by Saint Augustine when he saw in the Assyrian and Roman empires the manifestation of the *civitas terrena* as the antagonist to the *civitas Dei.*

Not all men driven by their lust for power are Alexanders or Caesars any more than all men whose souls move in confusion and seeking are Platos or Isaiahs. The drive for power has its deficient modes, its incomplete actualizations, and its series of preparatory manifestations just as much as does the experience of transcendence. Nevertheless, as early as the consciousness of autonomy becomes tangible at all there is also to be found the awareness of a crucial split in the psyche between spirit and power. As witnesses to this awareness I mention the Homeric conflict of *themis* and *ate,* the later conflict between Solon's unseen measure and the Sophists' *pleonexia* (to which one might add, as Plato did, their *polypragmosyne*), the classic climax in the *eironeia* of Socrates opposed to the *alazoneia* of Alcibiades, and finally the Christian climax in the Augustinian concepts of *amor Dei* and *amor sui.* However multifarious the desires may be, and however many of them may be distinguished by psychological description, they are overshadowed by the sense of a basic dualism in the psyche: Autonomous man can order himself and society either by orienting himself toward transcendence or by emancipating himself as a world-immanent existence. In Augustinian language: Man can live either *secundum Deum* or *secundum hominem.* The differentiation and recognition of the two centers, as well as their antagonism and their struggle for the order of the soul and society, are essentially a part of the historical process once the experience of transcendence has broken the cosmological order. The intimate connection and enmity of the two partners in the process was excellently captured by Saint Augustine when he let his two cities run their course "mingling one with the other through all this time, from the beginning to the end of the world, when they are destined to be separated by the Last Judgment" (*De Civitate Dei*, I, 35; XIV, 1; XV, 1).

The survey of the phenomena was based on certain premises: The context in which an experience of transcendence occurs as well as the degree of actualization achieved by the experience were considered the two variables responsible for a diversified field of encounters and responses. The program of exploring the field, at least with regard to the principal types, was indeed carried out, but in addition to the expected phenomena, the survey revealed relationships among them that constituted something like a class of superphenomena. While the survey thus has produced results beyond expectation, the unexpected part of the result will let the initial premises appear of questionable validity. The context in which the experience of transcendence was supposed to appear turned out to be not a rigid set of institutions, customs, and beliefs but a medium that could be softened by unsettling disturbances to the point of receptivity, while the experience occurred not just once and fully actualized but repeatedly and in various deficient modes. The setting furthermore affected the expression of the experience, and the expressive symbolism became, through communication, part of the setting, thereby increasing its receptivity for future and more articulate experiences. Setting and experience thus lost their identity as they dissolved into a medium in a state of fermentation. The movement manifesting itself in the experiences of definite persons—of a Moses, a Plato, a Confucius—would be present as a ferment in the setting previous to the outburst, while the outburst, though well set off as a phenomenon against the medium in a state of relative quiescence, would not cease to be part of the medium. If the Apocalypse of Abraham recognized a movement in a man's soul, passing through phases of confusion and of seeking preliminary to the act of transcendence, we are now compelled to recognize a movement in society, passing through similar phases preliminary to the actual outburst in a concrete human being. If this, however, is the case, the outburst—even though it can be identified as a distinct phenomenon, sometimes a spectacular phenomenon with consequences of world-historic importance—ceases to be one man's personal affair; it becomes a phase in the movement whose subject is society. Moreover, this transcendental gestation is peculiar not only to the concrete society in which the prophet or sage appears but rather seems to inhere in the whole manifold of concrete societies into which mankind is articulated—as is demonstrated by the parallel occurrence of experiences of transcendence, as well as of other phenomena such as the historiographic responses, in several societies. Mankind as a whole tends to become the subject of the movement that breaks forth in the spiritual outbursts. These tendencies—of the setting and experience to dissolve into a medium of gestation, or of several concrete societies to dissolve into mankind—indicate that the objectifying language of setting and experience will cover the phenomena not in their totality but only with regard to some of their aspects. The phenomena, it is true, are identifiable; they can be ascertained as historical facts by objectifying science. They even can be subjected to the category of causality, as we did when we introduced setting and experience as the variables responsible for the variety of phenomena or when we reflected on the receptivity of the setting as the condition for an experience to be effectively communicated. Hence, the objectifying language has a large field of legitimate application. Nevertheless, the phenomena do not altogether have the character of immanent objects, nor can the relations among them be completely absorbed by the calculus of causality. On the contrary, the survey has again demonstrated the double constitution of history analyzed in the preliminary inquiry: The character of the phenomenon as an immanent object is a secondary stratum within the comprehensive phenomenon that also carries the index of transcendence.

The description of the transcendental stratum in the phenomena obviously has to contend with difficulties of terminology. We started from the experience of transcendence as the movement of the soul in a concrete human being and had to expand the movement metaphorically into social processes in which an indefinite number of persons, and even societies, participated. Such metaphors, by which the experience is made to include the process of which it is a part, are useful to bring the difficulties to attention, but they obviously are no theoretical solution. Since there is no general terminology in existence to describe this class of phenomena, we must create one. For this purpose it will not be necessary to indulge in neologisms; it will be sufficient to assign precise meanings to terms in general use. I shall start with the meaning of *historical* previously developed:

1. The Within-Beyond tension of divine being, compactly present even prior to its differentiation and articulation, is the driving force in the movement that culminates in epochal outbursts. Once an experience of transcendence has actually occurred that is sufficiently intense and articulate to disintegrate the primary experience of the cosmos and its symbolism, events can be discovered as affecting the order of man and society in its relation to eternal being. The index that events receive because they concern the realization of eternal being in time is the *historical index*. The events that receive this index shall be called *historical phenomena*.

2. Historical phenomena have a double constitution. They can be objectified, since they are occurrences in time and space. The character of the phenomenon as an immanent object, however, is a secondary stratum in the phenomenon that as a whole is the expressive response to an encounter. The primary stratum, since it is the carrier of the index of transcendence, shall be called the *transcendental stratum*.

3. The realization of eternal being in time does not occur in a single phenomenon in a single society but in a manifold of phenomena extending through the whole breadth of mankind at any given time. This manifold, furthermore, does not have the character of a crosscut through mankind at one time only but moves through time indefinitely into the future. This process of phenomena in breadth and time we shall call *history*. Since the process has its character of history by virtue of the transcendental stratum in the phenomena, we shall speak of the *transcendental texture* of history.

4. Historical phenomena do not all belong to the same class. The first rank among them is occupied by the experiences of transcendence because a) they raise the realization of eternal being in time to the level of consciousness and because b) they discover in these vicissitudes of consciousness the substance of history and thereby establish the criteria of historical relevance. Beyond the experiences of transcendence there must be considered the unsettling disturbances preceding the experience as well as the disorder fol-

lowing its communication. Of special importance among the consequences of an experience of transcendence are the defective conceptions of order that may arise when the consciousness of human autonomy has awakened with regard to their formation. In general, one may say that an indefinite range of events belonging to the economic, social, governmental, intellectual, and spiritual order of society can acquire historical relevance because closely or distantly—as causes or effects, as social settings, as conditions or consequences—they are related to the central phenomenon, that is, to the experience of transcendence. Moreover, since all these events, as well as their personal and collective carriers, are rooted in the external world, their space and time data will enter the sphere of historical relevance. A wide field of "facts" opens in which almost every event in the life of a man, every datum concerning a society, every act or artifact, may become worth investigating because of its potential claim to be, however humble, a historical phenomenon. At the same time, however, there is the danger of the range being drawn so wide that masses of "facts" with a rather tenuous relation, or none at all, to the center of relevance will be assembled in ponderous pseudo-histories. Still, even such pseudo-histories are themselves historical phenomena, since they represent a type of escape literature characteristic of an age that has lost its sense of relevance.

5. The transcendental texture of history is not an independent entity but arises as a pattern in the constellation of single phenomena. These single phenomena, as we have noted, are not isolated, self-contained occurrences but enter into various relations. An experience of transcendence, for instance, will not occur only once in a society, but several such experiences, in various modes of actualization, will form an intelligible series, sometimes extending over centuries, as did the Hellenic series from Homer to Plato. The same proved true for the antagonisms, with the Hellenic attacks on the myth again forming a series that runs through centuries. Furthermore, the spiritual outbursts and antagonisms, the power drives and empires form patterns extending not only in time through one society but in breadth over several societies. We shall speak of such serial phenomena, whether running through only one society or extending over several, as the *constants* of history. Because these constants, however, do not run through the whole course of his-

tory, but rather are characteristic of limited time-spans, we shall call them *periodic constants.* Correlatively, we shall call a time-span that is characterized by a constant, or by a complex of constants, a *period* of history.

6. Since periods are recognizable only by constants, the periodization of history depends on the constants chosen for the purpose. Since the constants, furthermore, are not confined to processes within a single society but may have their run through several societies, a wide variety of periodizations is possible. To give an example: The conquest of Alexander marks an epoch, since it opens a period that, ever since Droysen, has been called the age of Hellenism—an age well characterized by a complex of constants. If the Alexander conquest, however, be considered as an attempt to establish an ecumenic empire in emulation of the Persian, then the Achaemenid expansion from Cyrus to Darius I will become the epoch that opens the period of ecumenic empires in the Near Eastern and Mediterranean area. In this larger period, the Alexandrian and Caesarean establishments would become sub-epochs. If, on the contrary, we restrict our horizon to Rome, the actions of Caesar and Augustus will become an epoch in Roman history, since they mark the beginning of the Roman imperial period. The attempts at periodization thus will arrive at widely differing results according to whether we select the constant of ecumenic empire as the relevant phenomenon and consequently arrive at a period for a Near Eastern-Mediterranean society or whether we insist that the subjects of periods must be the ethnic carriers of the various imperial drives. Since each of these choices has its validity, the various possibilities of periodization must not be treated as mutually exclusive. If history were to be reduced to the histories of ethnic carriers (in the present case to the histories of Persia, Hellas, and Rome)—because without their internal development leading up to imperial expansion no empires would be established—the phenomenon of the imperial period in breadth, into which each of the three societies reaches with one of its own periods, would disappear from history. If, on the contrary, the constant of ecumenic empire alone were to determine the field of phenomena to be explored, the processes within the single societies preparatory to the imperial outburst would disappear from history. Again, if only the Near Eastern and Mediterranean empires were to be considered,

the broader ecumenic period that also embraces India and China would be excluded from history. Obviously a good deal of historiographic misconstruction is inevitable if the historian is wanting in empirical catholicity—if, for instance, the conventions of national historiography cause him to believe the problems of history to be exhausted by processes internal to ethnic units; or if his conception of Ancient History is limited by a Hellenic-Roman classicism; or if he conceives of the history of the Ancient Orient as confined to the Near Eastern–Mediterranean area, to the exclusion of India and China; and so forth.

7. The transcendental texture of history thus is richly structured by various patterns into which the single phenomena combine to form phenomena of a higher order. Furthermore, the patterns, as we have just seen, do not remain isolated from one another. Periods can form chains of periods; periods of several societies can interlock; and so forth. The aggregate of these patterns I shall call the *configuration of history*. In order to avoid misunderstandings, it should be stressed that this configuration, though it is intelligibly the process of eternal being realizing itself in time, is not the gnostic meaning of history constructed by speculative systems of the eighteenth century and after. The intelligible configuration is strictly a subject matter for empirical exploration. Our knowledge of it, at any given time, will depend on the state of science, which in its turn is determined by a) our knowledge of materials and b) the penetration of theoretical issues. This warning, incidentally, disposes of the much debated question whether history is "subjective" or "objective," for all propositions concerning the configuration can be verified and falsified by the ordinary methods of science. Empirically, the propositions must take into account all the materials available; theoretically, they must reflect the optimal state of analysis achieved at the time with regard to the experiences of transcendence. If the range of subjectivity is nevertheless assumed to be quite large, the apparent largeness can be traced to certain conventions regarding the treatment of history that have come to be accepted as legitimate: From the empirical side it is considered legitimate, under the pretext of specialization, to ignore large bodies of well-known materials, though they would pertain to the configurative problem under discussion; from the theoretical side, it is considered legitimate to replace philosophical analysis by

ideological speculation, by *Weltanschauungen*, by political opinions, or even by what just goes through somebody's head, as the principles for selecting historical phenomena and constructing a meaning of history.

Definitions mark the end of an analysis. With the definitions of history, its transcendental texture, and its structure, the substantive inquiry concerning the question "What is history?" has reached its goal. The complex of structures itself that has come into view with the definitions is a subject matter to be further explored by empirical science. Nevertheless, while the details of the complex do not belong in a study of principles, the general character of the configuration presents an issue that remains to be treated in the present context: It is the issue that arises from the connection between the experiences of transcendence and the actual structure of history. This structure, in spite of the factor of contingency, is not at all a haphazard aggregate of periods; rather, it displays a hierarchical order of long-range and short-range, of dominant and secondary constants; and this order is due to the fact that the experiences are not unrelated phenomena within history but, by their interrelations in time and breadth, weave the very network of the configuration. I have repeatedly stressed that the order adumbrated must not be mistaken for the order constructed by speculations on the meaning of history. Still, for the purpose of clarification, I shall introduce at this point the concept of *eikon* in the sense in which Plato used it in the *Timaeus* when he spoke of time as the *eikon* of eternity. The order in history that can be empirically explored is the *eikon* of the eternal order that lies beyond the reach of science; in this sense we can speak of the eiconic character of the order that is accessible to science. By introducing this concept it will also be possible to characterize more exactly the speculations on the meaning of history: 1) The speculations attempt to bring eternal order within the range of human knowledge; 2) by making this attempt, impossible of realization, they betray their gnostic intent, rooted in the *libido dominandi*; 3) such speculations can achieve empirical verisimilitude in the measure to which they incorporate salient features of the eiconic order; 4) they may have a function in the advancement of science if the features incorporated have hitherto been overlooked or neglected; 5) in spite of this positive function they may have disastrous effects on the order of society, because the eiconic features are presented with the claim to be eternal features; 6) since the speculations, though misconceptions, are conceptions of eternal being realizing itself in time, they will themselves become features of the eiconic order if they are socially effective enough to become constants in time and breadth.

The general character of the configuration presents a fundamental issue because the substance of the configuration is determined by the experiences of transcendence. The experiences, though phenomena in time, weave the *eikon* of eternal order. That history has such a structure with dominant constants by virtue of the experiences has been recognized very early. The consciousness that spiritual outbursts constitute epochs in history that break the even flow of decline and restoration of order and introduce the new structure of before-and-after arose at first in the single societies in which the outbursts occurred. We refer the reader to what has been said in the earlier volumes of *Order and History* on the consciousness of epoch in Israel and Hellas, as well as to the frequent intimations of the subject in the present chapter. Moreover, even the awareness that such constants do not run their course within single societies only but join several civilizational areas together in a society of mankind belongs to antiquity. A striking example is furnished by certain constructions of prophetic succession, such as the self-interpretation of Mani as the prophet who has come to fulfill the task left uncompleted by the Buddha, the Christ, and Saint Paul. Suddenly there springs into vivid relief an ecumene (the term is used by Mani) comprising the Mediterranean area, the Near East, and India as a unity of mankind engaged in the search of spiritual order. In the modern period, with the enlargement of the historical horizon, it was the remarkable parallelism of spiritual outbursts around 500 B.C. that occupied various thinkers and induced reflections on its import for the configuration of history. The issue thus has not escaped notice. Hence, before examining what we consider the dominant constant in the configuration, it will be suitable to survey the recent debate on the parallel outbursts and to appraise its results.

The parallelism of spiritual outbursts was recognized as an important fact in the history of mankind as soon as the data became known. In *Mémoire sur la vie et les opinions de Lao-Tseu* (1824),

40

Abel-Remusat reflected on the curious contemporaneity of Hellenic philosophers, the Buddha, and Lao-tse. He was inclined to attribute it to cultural diffusion. In our time, this assumption has been abandoned on the whole, though one may still run across it as a means to explain some, if not all, of the parallels. Recent thinkers are rather inclined to accord to the parallel outbursts the rank of the most important epoch in the history of mankind, regardless of the question of diffusion. Bergson, for instance, has built *Deux sources de la morale et de la religion* (1932) around this issue. It is true that he does not enter into the problem of periods that is our present concern, but he has distinguished between closed and open societies. The closed society derives its cohesion from the myth; the transition to the open society, wherever it occurs, is marked by the opening of the soul in the experience of transcendence. The experience thus becomes the epoch that determines the configuration of history with its two phases of the closed and open societies. Jaspers, in his *Vom Ursprung und Ziel der Geschichte* (1949), developed the concept of an axial time (*Achsenzeit*) of mankind. This axial time embraces the spiritual processes between 800 and 200 B.C., with a concentration around 500 B.C. when the striking contemporaneity of Confucius and Lao-tse with the Buddha, Deutero-Isaiah, Pythagoras, and Heraclitus is to be observed. In Volume VII of *Study of History* (1954), Toynbee in his turn considers Jaspers' delimitation of the axial time as too narrow. He rather would extend it to comprise the full period from the disintegration of the Syriac, Indic, Sinic, and Hellenic civilizations to the complete unfolding of the four universal religions—that is, of Mahayana Buddhism, Hinduism, Christianity, and Islam. This period would extend from the tenth century B.C. to the thirteenth century A.D.

The account, brief as it was, illuminates the present state of the issue. There is consensus concerning the connection between experiences of transcendence and the configuration of history. Beyond this point, however, the spectrum of opinion betrays a lack of theoretical sureness in treating problems of this class. Abel-Remusat observes a striking contemporaneity of outbursts and takes refuge in the assumption of cultural diffusion. His escape is symptomatic of the variant of positivism that regards symbolisms as cultural curiosities which, if they occur in several instances, must have spread from a center of diffusion. At the time when he wrote, it was not yet clear that symbols express experiences and that, as a consequence, the appearance of similar symbols in widely distant regions indicates the occurrence of similar experiences. If experiences of transcendence occur, they require certain symbolisms for their adequate expression; hence, wherever they occur they will result in the creation of similar symbolisms. The similarity, therefore, is not in need of explanation by cultural diffusion. We do not look for cultural diffusion if people, independent of one another, discover that two times two is four; the feeling that only cultural diffusion will explain the similarity of symbols, if the symbols concern the constitution of being, is due to the positivistic prejudice that only "subjective opinions" are possible with regard to this area. Moreover, the structure of this problem is not materially affected if, in a specific instance, diffusion through social contact should have occurred. The decisive point would still be the readiness to receive a symbolism, because such readiness presupposes confirmation of the symbolism as true by the recipient's own experience. The question of diffusion is therefore only of secondary importance compared with the question of experiences, as well as of the adequacy of symbolisms.

These observations will bring into focus the distribution of outbursts, regardless of diffusion, as the true problem of configuration. There is an obvious temptation to fix on the spectacular outbursts as an epoch in the history of mankind, especially as enough of them occur in the centuries immediately preceding and following 500 B.C. to speak of a distinct clustering. Still, Jaspers' assumption of an axial time is not felicitous. Even if we disregard the aesthetic defect of an epoch that spans five or six centuries and therefore is rather a period, there is something unsatisfactory about an axial time that excludes Moses and Christ. Toynbee's criticisms are well taken. If, however, we follow Toynbee, the axial time will extend over more than two millennia; and if we generously include Moses, and perhaps even Akh-en-Aton, it will extend over more than two-and-a-half millennia—that is, over about half of the known history of high civilizations. The epoch definitely gets out of hand. In the face of this situation, it seems advisable to abandon the idea of an epoch or axial time, at least for the moment, and to assemble first a few historical data as a basis for further theorizing.

Because the difficulties do not arise from an immensity and complexity of materials that would defy theoretical mastering but from the entanglement with preconceived ideas and inadequate constructions, it will not be necessary to build a formidable apparatus. We need no more than selected data on the handbook level to show the distribution of spiritual outbursts in time and space. Their arrangement, proceeding from west to east (see Table I), will at the same time suggest the answer to the puzzling questions. The dates given in the table are in many instances controversial, but within limits so narrow that the picture as a whole will not be affected. Exceptions are the dates for Zoroaster and Lao-tse. In the case of Zoroaster, I have given the traditional date, accepted by Zaehner, but the reader should be aware that good authorities place it higher by as much as two hundred or four hundred years. In the case of Lao-tse, I have followed more recent interpretations of the *Tao Te Ching*, which let its content appear most compatible with the political situation of the fourth century B.C., though tradition makes Lao-tse a contemporary of Confucius.

The table is self-interpretive. The breaking away from the primary experience of the cosmos begins at different times in the various culture areas. In the area designated as Egypt-Israel it begins early in the second millennium B.C., if we accord historical reality to the Patriarchs, and especially to Abraham's exodus from Ur; from the thirteenth century down, Israel's existence in transcendental form is continuous. In the four other areas, the process assumes tangible form roughly after 800 B.C. Concentrations occur both horizontally and vertically. There is a notable parallelism around 600 B.C. between Ionian philosophy, Jeremiah, and Zoroaster. There is another such parallelism around 500 B.C. between the Mystic Philosophers in Hellas, Deutero-Isaiah, the Buddha and Mahavira, and Confucius. But the horizontal must not let us overlook the vertical concentrations in Israel and Hellas, as well as their relative time positions. The concentration in Israel extends from the thirteenth to the sixth century B.C., overlapping with the Hellenic concentration from the eighth to the fourth century B.C. Yet, in spite of their overlapping from the eighth to the sixth centuries, one can hardly extract from the two vertical concentrations a crosscut in time that would justify the language of epoch. Moreover, one should note that the famous center of the axial time around 500 B.C. occurs at a time when the vertical concentration of classic Israel,

43

	HELLAS	EGYPT-ISRAEL
2000		The Patriarchs — ca. 1950–1700
1700		Hebrews in Egypt — ca. 1700–1300
1300		Akh-en-Aton — ca. 1370–1353
1200		Exodus—Moses — ca. 1280 Conquest of Palestine — ca. 1250–1200
1100		Judges—Deborah — 12th century
1000		Samuel — 11th century
900		Nathan — 10th century
800	Epic & Theogony—Creation of the Hellenic Pantheon— Homer, Hesiod — 8th century	Elijah—Elishah — 9th century Hosea—Amos—Isaiah— Micah — 8th century
700	Lyrics — ca. 700–550	
600	Ionian philosophy — ca. 650–550	Jeremiah fl. — 626–585
500	Mystic Philosophers — ca. 550–450 Pythagoras — ca. 582–507 Xenophanes — ca. 570–480	Fall of Jerusalem — 587 Ezekiel fl. — 593–571 Deutero-Isaiah fl. — ca. 538 Rebuilding of Temple — 520–515
400	Heraclitus — ca. 535–475 Parmenides fl. — ca. 475 Tragedy — ca. 500–400 Aeschylus—Sophocles— Euripides Sophistic — ca. 450–350 Historiography — ca. 450–350 Herodotus—Thucydides—Xenophon Socrates — 469–399 Plato — 429–347	
300	Alexander reg. — 336–323	The Jews under the Ptolemies — 323–200
200		Seleucid conquest of Palestine — 200–198

IRAN	INDIA	CHINA
	Eastern expansion of Aryans—Brahamanes & early Upanishads ca. 800—550	
Unification of Medes under Deiokes ca. 715		Eastern Chou Dynasty 770—256
Zoroaster 628—551		
Achaemenian Empire 550—331	Buddha ca. 563—483	Period of the "hundred philosophers" 551—ca. 233
	Mahavira ca. 540—468	Confucius 551—479
Persia under the Seleucids from 312	Invasion by Alexander 327—325	Lao-tse 4th century
	Chandragupta ca. 322—298 Ashoka ca. 273—237	Ch'in Dynasty 221

from Moses to the fall of Jerusalem, already belongs to the past. Considering these facts, therefore, the construction of an axial time for the history of mankind, with a special epoch of concentration around 500 B.C., will appear not only untenable but even apt to obscure the real configuration of history. For the information in the table suggests a process, long in duration and increasing in breadth, by which mankind disengages itself from the primary experience of the cosmos. It begins in the Near Eastern area early in the second millennium; it spreads to Hellas, Iran, India, and China around 800 B.C.; and with the expansion of Christianity and Islam, of Buddhism, Hinduism, and Confucianism it draws ever wider sectors of mankind into its movement. This process is still going on, and its end is not yet in sight. Once this process, with its dimensions of time and breadth, is recognized, it will even be possible to acknowledge the core of truth contained in the debate about an axial time; for if the parallelisms around 600 and 500 B.C. are not the axial time of mankind, they nevertheless are real. This concentration of spectacular outbursts in breadth is symptomatic of the period in which the process expands from the narrow Near Eastern channel to engulf the culture areas from Hellas to China. Although this is neither the first nor the last period, it certainly is a very important phase in the process. Under this particular aspect, Jaspers' construction must even be defended against the criticism by Toynbee, which, while it pleads the comprehensive process against the accent on one of its periods, is liable to obscure the sub-division into periods; and Toynbee's own periodizations, because they are too narrowly tied to his dominant conception of civilizational societies, leave much to be desired. Finally, one must not forget the insight that, in the debate about an axial time of mankind, appears as a premise to be taken for granted rather than as a well-reasoned proposition—the insight that the spectacular outbursts, whether their periodization is satisfactory or defective, are indeed representative for mankind. It would be easy game to expose the arbitrariness of thinkers who award representative function to this or that group of outbursts according to their philosophical or religious predilections, having in common only a hearty aversion to Moses. Whatever their conceits and constructions, I prefer to stress their understanding that in the outbursts *res humanitatis agitur*. Inasmuch as by the outbursts a truth about human existence is discovered, the human vessels of the spirit discover it representatively for mankind; and inasmuch as they realize the truth in their existence, they become the carriers of representative humanity.

On the representative character of the experiences hinges the structure of history. The theory of an axial time would make no sense unless the outbursts were, by their nature, of concern to all mankind. The representative character, however, did not become thematic. The participants, it is true, recognized its importance by the mere fact of their engaging in the debate, but the representative character was presupposed; its implications were not unfolded to the point where its consequences for a theory of the configuration would have become fully visible. A more thorough analysis would not necessarily have brought a better result; on the contrary, it would have shown that the debate about an axial time had to remain inconclusive, because it cannot be brought to a satisfactory conclusion at all. The fixation on the spectacular outbursts, without sufficient regard to their structure, has caused the problem to be stated wrongly. The parallelisms in question, though they undoubtedly occur, must not be construed as ultimate facts in the configuration; rather, they must find their setting in a more comprehensive theoretical context. Hence, the following analysis will first unfold the implications of the representative character; it will then clarify the ontological and epistemological problem presented by the phenomenon; and it will, finally, show that the theory of an axial time must be replaced by a theory of dominant constants.

The experience of transcendence, as previously defined, is a movement of the soul that may culminate in an act of transcendence. In the optimal case, as it brings to acute consciousness the relation between God and man, it will reveal the presence under God as the truth of human existence. An experience of this type would in any case be of importance to the person suffering it; but if the description were exhaustive, if the experience did not contain an additional factor, it would not be a constituent of history. A historian would have no occasion, for instance, to attach relevance to such an experience unless he were writing the biography of a person to whom it occurred—and quite probably he would never write the biography because persons plagued by such oddities would be devoid of historical interest. (This supposition must, of course, be taken *cum grano salis,* for there would be neither history nor historians if the experience did not contain the factor that makes it constituent of history.) This additional factor that makes the experience historically relevant is the truth of order that it reveals with obligatory force for every man. The obligatory force of the experience establishes, in addition to the new relation between God and the man who discovers the truth, a new relationship between the discoverer and his fellow men: The nature of the truth revealed obliges the discoverer to communicate it to the men among whom he lives, while it obliges those within hearing to listen and to receive the truth, as an ordering force, into their own existence. By virtue of its obligatory force, the truth of the experience becomes a center from which radiates a new order for the existence of man in society. Since the new center, however, arises not in a vacuum but within a society with an already established order, and since an old order has the weight of ancestral authority, the consequence of the experience will be disturbances of various types. We remember the earlier discussed antagonisms between philosophers and sophists, sophists and traditionalists, traditionalists and philosophers. The experience thus will not remain enclosed in one man's private life; its occurrence rather will cause a crisis of public order inasmuch as it engenders a conflict between two orders with rival claims to loyalty. Moreover, the parties to the struggle are aware that they are fighting for recognition as representatives of public order, and sometimes the consciousness becomes so acute that philosophers, prophets, and sages develop a special symbolism for expressing the issue. We shall call this symbolism the *transfer of authority.* It is to be found in the three societies that also have developed historiography. In Hellas, it was Plato who transferred the authority of the statesman from the politicians of Athens to Socrates and ultimately to himself. In Israel, Jeremiah arrogated to his person the symbols of royal authority, probably taken from Assyrian kingship, when he spoke the word of Yahweh. In China, the Confucians considered the heavenly mandate of the Chou dynasty to have devolved on their Master. The enumerated cases are the most important ones, but they are not unique in their respective societies; they have pre- and post-histories, so that the transfer of authority is in fact one of the constants that characterize periods of intense struggle for the order of man in society. The larger implications of the symbolism, beyond the range of particular societies, will be suggested if we remember the formula "It was said to the men of old . . . But I say unto you . . ."—the formula by which Christ transferred authority from the old dispensation to Himself as the dispenser of the new law.

The representative character is not a matter of opinion. The experience of transcendence is representative by its essence. Although the essential character was brought out with sufficient clarity in the description, it will not be superfluous to stress the point, because in the psychologizing climate of the age the term *experience* is an almost irresistible invitation to misunderstandings. At worst, the experience might be dismissed as "subjective" in the vulgar sense; at best, it might be misunderstood as the "subject's" experience of something that would then have to be considered its "object." Be it restated, therefore, that the term *experience* signifies an ontic event. It is a disturbance in being, an involvement of man with God by which the divine Within is revealed as the divine Beyond. What is achieved by it is immediacy of existence under God; what is discovered by it is the existence under God as the first principle of order for man. Moreover, the principle is discovered as valid not only for the man who has the experience but for every man, because the very idea of man arises from its realization in the presence under God. Both the reality and the idea of man are produced by the movement; the humanity represented is the humanity produced. In such terms can the representative character of the event be circumscribed. Its various dimensions are perfectly expressed in Israel, for instance, by the identification of the word of the prophet with the word of Yahweh, together with consequences that flow from the identification. When Jeremiah is ordained as prophet, Yahweh touches his mouth and speaks (1:9–10):

> Behold! I put my words in your mouth.
> See! I have put you in charge, of this day,
>   over the nations and over the kingdoms,
> to root up and to pull down,
> to destroy and to overthrow,
> to build and to plant.

Not only the prophet's word is the word of God, but the word also carries with it the authority to destroy and to build—and not only the order of Israel but the order of the nations. The prophet is no more than the mediator through whom the truth of existence is promulgated to all mankind. The spiritual outburst, we may say, has representative character because it is part of the movement by which eternal being realizes itself in time.

The philosopher is not a prophet. The truth as pronounced by the prophet is as valid for him as for any other man; but when the philosopher himself pronounces on the truth of existence, he is not permitted to use the symbols of Revelation or, for that matter, of Myth. His is the realm of Reason; and in the noetic domain the drama of history is not enacted by the *dramatis personae* of a Jeremiah. The interpretation has reverted, therefore, to the language of "eternal-being-realizing-itself-in-time." This expression must be understood as a unit of meaning, as we have tried to suggest by hyphenating its parts. If we were to attribute independent meanings to its grammatical parts, we would easily fall prey to the various fallacies of objectivation. Sooner or later we might land in, for instance, the sophistic triads of propositions analysed at the beginning of the present inquiry. Even worse than the sophistic impasse, however, would be certain derailments that come under the general heading of gnosticism. In order to characterize them, as well as to ward them off, it is appropriate to stress the following series of propositions: There is no entity called "being" that once would exist in the medium of eternity and, after its realization, in the medium of time; nor is there an "eternal being" that suddenly would appear as an object in time; nor a "temporal being" that would be transfigured by the realization and acquire the attribute of eternity; nor are there media of time and eternity with objects flitting from the one to the other. To advance these negative propositions is eminently necessary, considering that in the wake of spiritual outbursts there arise movements of world-historic impact that operate precisely with fallacies of the adumbrated type. Not only will the terms of the ontic event, as well as the tension between the terms, be objectified but even the objects will be personified to become the *dramatis personae* of a new type of myth. Moreover, the fallacious constructions are more than a matter of theoretical error; they are undertaken for the purpose of transposing the disturbance in being into the sphere of human action. The terms and tensions of the ontic event are converted into objects in order to make the movement by which eternal being realizes itself in time an object of human manipulation. A being that suffers from existence in time supposedly can be freed from its prison of temporality and transposed into the perfect state of eternity; and conversely, a perfect being beyond time supposedly can be made to enter time. The imaginary operation thus can perfect being either by freeing temporal being from its worldly prison or by bringing eternal perfection to temporal being within the world. The first method was used by the gnostics of antiquity; the second method, by their modern *confrères.* In either case, the movement of being in the tension of time and eternity is converted into a pneumatic drama designed by the gnostic thinker and hurried by his operations toward its *dénouement* in the final liberation of being and its transition into the state of perfection. Since liberation is the order of the day, and the gnostic mass movements play their great role in the politics of our time, one cannot be careful enough in the analysis of the ontic event, not rigorous enough in determining the meaning of terms.

2

✿

Anxiety and Reason

In the societies of the Ancient Orient the student will encounter a peculiar type of speculation on the course of their order in time. The symbolists who create it let the governance of society spring into existence at an absolute point of origin, and then they tell its history from that point down to the present in which they live. On closer inspection, however, what pretends to be a story of events proves to consist of two parts of widely differing character. Only the later part of the story, the part that issues into the author's present, can claim to relate facts of pragmatic history, while the earlier part, covering an immense time-span of thousands and sometimes hundreds of thousands of years, is filled with legendary and mythical events. The symbolists, it appears, wanted to express what made the historical materials worthy of transmission to posterity by linking them, through an act of mythopoesis, with the unfolding of order in the cosmos. By this method they achieved, within the range of symbolization determined by the primary experience of the cosmos, a speculation on the origin of a specific realm of being, not differing on principle from the speculation on the *arche*, the beginning of all being, in which the Ionian philosophers engaged. Historiography, mythopoesis, and rational speculation thus were combined to produce a rather complex symbolism.

The type is well known as far as the sources are concerned; and the close resemblance among the several instances of its occurrence in Mesopotamia, Egypt, and Israel has not escaped attention. Moreover, it has been well explored, since the symbolism irresisti-

---

"Anxiety and Reason," completed in its present form by about 1968, is found in Box 74, Folder 7, Voegelin Papers, Hoover Institution Archives. See the Editorial Note for more information concerning the title of this piece.

bly invites cracking operations on the part of historians who want to extract from it the rich admixture of empirical facts for the purpose of reconstructing the history of ancient societies. Nevertheless, not only has no attempt been made to identify the type as a symbolic form *sui generis* or to inquire into the reason for its development, but it has remained so far below the horizon of theoretical interest that as yet it has not even received a name. In view of the Israelite instance of the symbolism, in which history is extrapolated back to Genesis in the biblical sense, I propose therefore the name *historiogenesis*.

Once the type is recognized, it will compel questions that concern a philosophy of order. The principal issues are the following:

1. In the first place, if historiogenesis is a speculation on the origin of society, it must be considered a member of a class to which also belong theogony, anthropogony, and cosmogony. The varieties of the class all have in common the quest of origin instituted on occasion of experiences in the several realms of being. As from experiences in the divine, human, and cosmic realm there arises the question concerning the origin of the gods, man, and the cosmos, so from experiences in the social realms there arises the question concerning the origin of society and its order; by the side of symbolisms that express the mystery of existence that puzzles the explorer of divine, human, and cosmic reality there develops a symbolism that expresses the same mystery with regard to the existence of society. However, while the discovery of the class offers the opportunity of defining historiogenesis by the rule of genus and specific difference, it implies much more if we remember that gods and men, society and the cosmos at large are the principal complexes of reality distinguished by cosmological societies as partners in the community of being. The four complexes in their aggregate comprehend the whole field of being, and the four symbolisms enumerated—theogonic, anthropogonic, cosmogonic, and historiogenetic—form a corresponding aggregate covering this field. The addition of historiogenesis to the other three varieties lets the aggregate appear as the phenomenon that is, in the medium of the myth, the equivalent of a speculation on the ground of being in the medium of philosophy. A whole series of questions arises: First, with regard to the function of historiogenesis within the aggregate of the four varieties; second, with regard to the equivalence

of symbolic forms in the various media of symbolization; and finally, with regard to the nature of the constant problems that are
running through a sequence of symbolisms so widely differing in
surface appearance as myth and rational speculation. Especially
from an exploration of equivalence we may expect new light to fall
on fundamental problems of philosophy.

2. Historiogenesis must be considered as an independent phenomenon resulting from the combined efforts of historiography,
mythopoesis, and rational speculation.

With regard to the historical content, I have intimated that modern scholars use the symbolism as a quarry from which they break
the materials for reconstructing ancient history—a quite legitimate procedure, to be sure, since the facts have to be fitted into a
symbolism of a radically different kind. And yet one may feel un-
easy if one sees the remainder of the dilapidated structure discarded, as frequently happens, as dross not worth any further attention. In a recent *Roemische Geschichte*, for instance, the learned
author examines the traditional history of Rome that has historiogenetic character, dismisses its mythical part as "unhistorical
fabulation," and displays no interest at all in the obvious questions
why anybody should have gone to the trouble of fabulating the
fabulation, whether his invention was arbitrary or followed certain
rules, and why the product was officially accepted as the history
of Rome. In the face of such neglect one may ask whether the creation of the myth as well as its acceptance were not also facts of
history? and perhaps facts of considerable importance for the self-
interpretation and cohesion of Roman society? If, however, we recognize the mythical part of the symbolism not as a piece of unhistorical fabulation but as an attempt to provide the reasons that
raise the *res gestae* of the empirical part to the rank of history, the
symbolism as a whole will gain the stature of an historiographic
work conscious of its principles of relevance. The glaring differences of phenotypical appearance notwithstanding, historiogenesis
must therefore be understood to represent, on the level of the
myth, the equivalent to critical historiography—perhaps with the
distinction that the early symbolists were more conscious of their
purpose than some of their later *confrères*. In the case of history we
thus encounter the same issues of equivalence, of identity and con-
tinuity of problems that, under the preceding point, arose for the

case of philosophy; and again we may expect the exploration of equivalence to illuminate the problem of historical relevance.

In the production of historiogenesis, myth and speculation cooperate with the historiographic intention. Since the same pair—myth-speculation—is operative in the other varieties of the class as well, it should be considered a formative unit that may or may not be applied to historical materials. As a matter of fact, wherever it can be dated, historiogenesis proves to develop later than the speculations on the other realms of being; and in some cosmological societies it does not develop at all. But only when the pair is applied to the order of society will the motive of the formative effort become fully manifest as the concern with irreversible time. A society in cosmological form possesses, prior to historiogenesis, symbolisms that adjust its order to the rhythm of the cosmos—*i.e.*, the New Year festivals and other rituals that restore social order to its pristine perfection. Historiogenesis, however, places events relentlessly on the line of irreversible time where opportunities are lost forever and defeat is final. Some implications of irreversibility become plain when the symbolists of an imperial society treat the histories of the conquered societies as part of their own history: The formerly contemporaneous societies are pretended to succeed one another on a temporal line that issues into the empire. One world, it appears, can have only one order, and the sin of coexistence must be redeemed by posthumous integration into the one history whose goal has now become certain. If it furthermore be remembered that the fictitious line is extrapolated to an absolute point of origin so that no extraneous events have a chance of disturbing the one and only course admissible, historiogenesis will appear as a most ruthless construction of unilinear history: It lets the relevant course of events ineluctably run from a cosmic origin to its predestined end in the present of the author's society, whose order alone matters. One may speak of an obsessive concern with the relation of order as it exists, to irreversible time in which it has grown. We may furthermore assume that the same concern with time had previously inspired the purely annalistic records of reigns and events that enter as raw material into historiogenetic speculation, for even annals would be devoid of interest had they no more to record than a rhythmical recurrence of the same. This obsessive preoccupation with unilinear history is clearly incompatible with the assumption, frequently encountered, that early societies are dominated by the idea of cyclical time to the exclusion of all understanding of history in irreversible time.

3. Historiogenesis, once it is recognized in the Near Eastern cases, proves of unsuspected importance for the interpretation of history because of its virtual omnipresence. The earliest instances of the symbolism occur in the Mesopotamian and Egyptian empires. Since they do not break the form of the myth but are conducted well within the range set by the primary experience of the cosmos, one might expect historiogenesis to be peculiar to societies in unbroken cosmological form. The expectation will not be fulfilled, however, since the symbolism also occurs in the Israel, which by its very constitution as a society in freedom under God has broken not only with the cosmological order of Egypt but with the myth of the cosmos itself. It then appears in the context of ecumenic empires in China, India, and Rome as the means for coping with the history of social order. It adapts itself, furthermore, to the ambience of polis and philosophy; assumes a curious form in the "utopia" of Euhemerus, in connection with the imperial expansion of Alexander; gains a new Near Eastern life, through the speculations of Berossus and Manetho, in the time of the Diadochic empires; and even informs the little-known speculation of Clement of Alexandria, where it becomes an odd weapon in the fight against polytheism. Moreover, it has been transmitted by Judaism and Christianity, as well as by pagan revivals, to the medieval and modern West, where it has proliferated into the bewildering manifold of progressivist, romantic, idealist, materialist, and positivist speculations on the origin of history. The symbolism, thus, displays a curious tenacity of survival, from cosmological societies proper to contemporary Western societies whose understanding of the world can hardly be described as inspired by the primary experience of the cosmos. Historiogenesis is one of the great constants in the search of order from antiquity to the present.

The nature of a constant in the search of order, if added to the characteristics of historiogenesis previously set forth, makes possible an odd series of reflections: Both reason and the concern with irreversible time strive for expression in cosmological societies; a speculation of the cosmological type occurs also in societies that have broken with the myth of the cosmos; a speculation on the *arche* of being that we associate with the Ionian beginnings of Hellenic philosophy appears in cosmological empires; a conception of unilinear history that by conventional assumption belongs in the orbit of Israelite-Christian Revelation is to be found not only in cosmological and ecumenic empires but also in modern progressivist societies; and so forth. From this chain of observations emerge two classes of problems that we shall briefly call 1) the styles of truth and 2) the dynamics of change from one style to the other. Because they will occupy us further in this study, their nature need only be adumbrated at this point.

With regard to the first class: Although the nature of man is always the same and his knowledge of reality is always on principle complete, there exist modes of super- and subordination of experiences and their symbolization. In a cosmological society, for instance, the primary experience of the cosmos will dominate all experiences of particular sectors of reality, with the effect that the subordinate sectors can emerge into no more than a state of compact understanding within the limits set by the dominant experience and its symbolism. Moreover, if the myth of the cosmos is broken, for instance by a growth of anthropocentric consciousness or an experience of transcendence, the differentiated insight gained has a tendency to become dominant in its turn and to impose on other experiences the status of only compact expression. Such complexes of super- and subordination of experience we shall call styles of truth. In spite of their imperfection, societies will accept the styles as authentic expressions of truth concerning the order of being and cherish them over long periods of time. The desire for existence in truth is apparently so strong that a society will represent the One Truth by the particular style possible of achievement at the time; the craving for certainty is so intense that the particular type will be endowed with a monopoly of truth to be ardently defended against rival styles. Hence, the opening of new vistas in the search of truth will be followed, as Bergson has observed, by a new closure and monopolization on the level of differentiated insight achieved. With regard to the second class of problems we can be even briefer: None of the styles of truth achieved by a society, even if it lasts thousands of years, is absolutely stable but will give way, under the pressure of a variety of factors, to new types of dominance and subordination.

The two classes of problems just adumbrated determine the organization of the present chapter. Although historiogenesis is a constant throughout history, the presentation of the phenomena will be delimited by the cosmological style of truth. Hence, we shall follow the course of historiogenetic speculation from its first appearance in cosmological societies, not right down to the present but only to the point where the dominance of experience of transcendence makes itself seriously felt. Where to make the incision in a process that has no unequivocal incisions is, to a certain measure, a matter of discretion; for our purpose, we shall break off where historiogenesis merges into historiography, because historiographic problems proper are set by conflicts between the truth of empire and insights gained by an experience of transcendence. The presentation of materials will begin, therefore, with the Near Eastern nucleus of speculation in Mesopotamia, Egypt, and Israel; it will then branch out into the chronologically later, and geographically peripheral, speculations in India and Rome; and it will conclude with the Hellenic and Hellenistic transformations that issue into the idea of world history. The Chinese case, since it lies beyond the first ecumene that extended from India to Rome, will be treated separately in the chapter on Chinese ecumenism. Since the cosmological style, however, is exposed to disintegration, we have also to deal with the dynamics of change. The analysis of materials will be preceded, therefore, by a section on the forces that tend to break the primary experience of the cosmos; and it will be followed by a section on the transformation of historiogenesis in the work of Plato.

Anxiety and Reason [1]

Historiogenesis originates in societies called cosmological because their understanding of order is dominated by the primary experience of the cosmos. This cosmos of the primary experience is nei-

1. See the Editorial Note for a discussion of this work's title, which is taken from this section title (numbered 1 by Voegelin)—the only section title Voegelin used in this piece, originally entitled "Chapter 1: Historiogenesis."

ther the external world of objects encountered by man when he has become a subject of cognition, nor is it the world that has been created by a world-transcendent God. It rather is the cosmos of an earth below and a heaven above; of celestial bodies and their movements, of seasonal changes, of fertility rhythms in plant and animal life; of human life, birth, and death; and above all, as Thales still knew, it is a cosmos full of gods. In the Memphite Theology, imperial order is established by a drama of the gods that, by virtue of the consubstantiality of all being, is performed on the human plane as the drama of Egypt's conquest and unification. In the Sumerian King List, kingship is created in heaven and then lowered on earth; and two thousand years later, in Jewish apocalypse, there is still a Jerusalem in heaven, to be lowered to earth when the time for God's kingdom has come. Yahweh speaks from Mount Sinai, out of a fiery cloud; the Homeric Olympians dwell on this earth, on a mountain reaching into the clouds, and they have quarrels and agreements affecting the historical destinies of peoples in Asia and Europe. The Hesiodian gods Uranus and Gaea are indistinguishably heaven and earth themselves; they enter into a union and generate the gods, and the generations of gods in their turn generate the races of man. This togetherness and one-in-anotherness is the primary experience that must be called cosmic in the pregnant sense.

In cosmological empires, the understanding of history is dominated by this primary experience of the cosmos. History is more than a stream of brute events, which as mere facts would not be worth remembrance because, and insofar as, man engaged in action is conscious of his existence under God. The ruler of a cosmological empire acts by a divine mandate; the existence of the society, its victories and defeats, its prosperity and decline, are due to divine dispensation. When the Hittite king Suppiluliumas (ca. 1380–1346) tells the story of his campaign against Tusratta, the king of the Mitanni, he speaks as the executor of a divine decree and renders account to the Stormgod, whose favorite he is, so that posterity may know of the victory willed by the god. When, in the Behistun Inscription, Darius I (521–486) reports the victory over his domestic enemies, the war assumes the form of a struggle between the Lord of Wisdom and his opponents, between Truth and Lie, so that posterity may know the truth about the Truth that has prevailed. An especially forceful document of this class is the report of Queen Hatshepsut (*ca.* 1501–1480) on the restoration of order after the expulsion of the Hyksos:

Hear all ye people and folk as many as they may be,
I have done these things through the counsel of my heart:

I have not forgetfully slept, but have restored what had been ruined.
I have raised up what had gone to pieces,
> when the Asiatics were in the midst of Avaris in the Northland,
> and among them were nomads, overthrowing what had been made.
They ruled without Re; and he (Re) did not act through divine command
down to my majesty.

I am established on the thrones of Re.
I was foretold for the limits of the years as the one born to conquer.
I am come as the uraeus-serpent of Horus, flaming against my enemies.
I have made distant those whom the gods abominate,
> and earth has carried off their footprints.

This is the command of the father of (my) fathers
> who comes at (his) appointed times, of Re,
and there shall not occur damage to what Amon has commanded.

My (own) command endures like the mountains—
the sun-disk shines forth and spreads rays over the titles of my majesty,
and my falcon is high above (my) name-standard for the duration of
eternity.

When the god commands, by virtue of the divine substance flowing through him the king will command; when the command of the god remains in abeyance, the king is not able to act as a ruler. The will of the god thus becomes manifest, through action or inaction of the ruler, in the order or disorder of society. The king is the mediator of cosmic order that through him flows from God to man; and the historical report bears witness to the dispensation of the gods who govern the existence and order of society in time.

One man's victory is another man's defeat. The proud reports glowing with righteousness were rendered by the victors; the defeated, who have left no monuments, were probably less inclined to praise the splendor of divine-cosmic order. Moreover, the pharaohs who defeated the Hyksos knew that the Hyksos had defeated their predecessors. There is a hint of theodicy in the text when it speaks of the god "who comes at (his) appointed times" and sometimes, for reasons of his own, will not come as desired by man; however glorious and durable the order may be in other realms of being, in history there sways the god who is "the setter up and plucker down of kings." On such occasions, the cosmological style becomes transparent for a truth about God and history beyond the truth of the cosmos. In spite of its embracingness, the shelter of the cosmos is not safe—and perhaps it is no shelter at all. The pride inspiring the reports of victory can barely veil an undercurrent of anxiety, a vivid sense of existence triumphant over the abyss of possible annihilation.

On the strength of these reflections, it would be tempting to indulge in assumptions concerning the causality of changes in the style of truth. The vicissitudes of social order in history, with their undercurrent of anxiety, might ultimately destroy the faith in cosmic order. Since cosmological societies conceive their order as an integral part of cosmic order, the argument would run, the realm of history is the area from which the sense of precarious existence, once aroused, will expand to the cosmos as a whole. If doom is the fate of empire, why should it not be that of the cosmos? A severe crisis of empire might arouse apprehensions of a twilight of the gods who are part of the cosmos just as much as man and society, as well as of the cosmos itself; it might give birth to a spiritual crisis in which confidence in cosmic order will founder and a search for a more reliable source of order be instituted.

Such assumptions concerning the dynamics of change, however, would be disappointed by the actual course of events. Although there is some truth in them inasmuch as the causes adumbrated contribute indeed to a spiritual crisis, it is not the whole truth, for the cosmological order does not in fact break up, however much anxiety the documents betray. Even during the worst political disasters of the Intermediate Periods in Egypt there arose no prophet to proclaim a new order; nor do we hear of revolutionary movements that proposed an alternative to the traditional type of empire. If we survey the endless drama of wars and foreign conquests, of prolonged periods of decline and social disorder, it almost seems as if the undercurrent of anxiety, however much nourished by breakdowns and defeats, would never swell to a stream and sweep away the cosmological style of truth. Moreover, we know already something about the devices that contribute to the durability of the style inasmuch as the very symbolisms that betray the underlying anxiety are also the sedatives that keep it down: In the reports of victory, the sense of precarious existence is quieted by the triumph of the moment; in historiogenesis, anxiety is assuaged by the construction of a one-way line of order in time. Both symbolisms fortify resistance against insights in conflict with the prevailing style of truth. And yet, such protective devices against the upsurge of anxiety will not contain it forever—the style, as we know, has disintegrated after all. Hence, the dynamics of change is puzzling: Why should the myth of the cosmos prove resistant when, under the impact of disturbance in the social sphere, its disintegration might be expected? And where does the critical point lie at which it breaks down nevertheless?

For an answer to these questions one must look to the stratification of experiences in the style of truth. If the primary experience of the cosmos is dominant, it forcefully permeates all experiences of particular, subordinate sectors of reality; and no amount of disorder in the subordinate sectors will shake the faith in cosmic order as long as there is no alternative experience of order to challenge the primary experience on its own ground. Where this "own ground" lies becomes clear from an examination of the symbols by which early societies express their integration into the cosmos. If previously we have roughly spoken of the empire as a cosmic analogue, we now must introduce distinctions in order to discern what is cosmological about the analogies. For this purpose, let us consider one or two symbolisms of kingship.

If a king uses the style of a ruler over the four quarters of the world, he wants to characterize his rule over a territory and its people as an analogue of divine rule over the cosmos. In fact, however, the analogy is not supplied by the cosmos itself but rather by the structure of the universe, more specifically of the earth and the celestial bodies whose revolutions determine the "four quarters." The analogy makes cosmological sense only because the world (in the external sense) and with it the gods, kings, and societies are conceived as consubstantial parts of the cosmos that embraces them all without being identical with any one of them—though we must note a tendency, yet to be explored, to let the embracing cosmos blend into the external universe. Another instance: If the king is symbolized as the mediator of divine-cosmic order, perhaps even himself as a god, again the analogy does not stem from the cosmos itself but rather from the gods. And again it makes cosmological sense only because gods and kings are consubstantial partners in the cosmos—though this time we must note a tendency to let the embracing cosmos merge rather with the gods. The intracosmic sectors of reality, we may generalize, provide one another with analogies of being whose cosmological validity derives from an underlying, intangible embracingness, from a something that can supply existence, consubstantiality, and order to all sectors of reality even though it does not itself belong to the class of existent things. This play with mutual analogies is loaded with suspense because it cannot come to rest on a firm basis outside itself; it cannot give lasting assurance but can do no more than make the particular sectors of reality—in this case, society and its order in history—transparent for the dread mystery of existence. We must therefore conclude: The "cosmos" to which this mystery ultimately attaches is itself non-existent; the own ground of the primary experience turns out to be no-ground; and anxiety is not the fear of a definite threat or event but the response to existence out of nothing.

Existence out of nothing as the dominant experience of early societies might be suspect because it reminds one of modern existentialism. The parallel is well observed, but the suspicion of a modernistic interpretation of ancient materials is unfounded. Rather, the resemblance is caused by the experience of a groundless cosmos, together with the response of anxiety, reawakening among postphilosophic and post-Christian thinkers. Existence out of nothing is indeed the dominant experience in cosmological societies, as evidenced by the special set of symbols developed for its expression. At the center of the myth of order there opens the rich field of symbolisms, which Mircea Eliade has explored in *Mythe de l'éternel retour*—the field of rituals that has, as he astutely observes, the function of abolishing time, of undoing its waste and corruption, and of returning to the pristine order of the cosmos through a repetition of the cosmogonic act. Eliade speaks of the purpose of the New Year rituals as the *'statisation' du devenir*, as the attempt to bring becoming to a standstill and to restore being to the ordered splendor that was lethally flowing away. The people living in the myth sensed the cosmos threatened by destruction through time; and the ritual repetitions of cosmogony purported to "annul the irreversibility of time." The sense of a cosmos existing in precarious balance on the edge of emergence from nothing and return to nothing must be acknowledged, therefore, as lying at the center of the primary experience.

The sense of existence informing the rituals implies a specific sense of time. This implication, if one wants to go beyond conventional generalities, requires more careful analysis than it usually receives. Above all, one must avoid the great source of confusion— *i.e.*, the indiscriminate pooling of early and late phases of cosmological thought—for the cosmological style of truth is exposed to the perversion by which symbols originally expressing experiences are transformed into terms designating objects, just as philosophy and theology are exposed to the corresponding perversions of metaphysical and theological fundamentalism. Only in its early phase can the sense of existence and time under consideration be touched in its purity; it becomes clouded by a variety of factors once the myth has begun to dissolve and the "cosmos" that formerly expressed the mystery of existence is transformed into an object of speculation that can exist in the plural—either as a succession of worlds in time beyond time or as a plurality of worlds in space beyond space. The fundamentalist transformation reaches its full development in Hellenic, Indic, and Hellenistic speculation, though its beginnings can be discerned much earlier. In the environment of this speculation there originates the idea of cyclical time that usually is considered the quintessence of cosmological thought in general, though in fact it does not belong to the cosmological myth proper. Its most articulate expression is to be found in the Aristotelian *Problemata* (XVII, 3): Should we really say the generation of the Trojan War lived prior to us and those who lived earlier were prior to Troy, and so on *ad infinitum*? Aristotle rejects this idea of an infinite regression. The cosmos has a finite time of existence; the later one is in this course the closer one is to the beginning of the next period. Hence, we may be prior to Troy, if Troy should happen to lie at the beginning of a cosmic cycle while we are situated near its end. The Aristotelian argument reveals the reason for assuming a cosmos that runs in circles: Time has become infinite, and since all things must have a beginning and an end, the cosmos must repeat itself in infinite time. The intracosmic problem of an *arche* of things has been transferred to the cosmos as an entity in time. The idea of cyclical time, one concludes, is connected with the idea of infinite time; this idea in its turn is connected with the idea of a world that has become immanent through an experience of transcendence. This whole complex of problems, however, will occupy us in later chapters. For the present, it is sufficient to understand that the infinite time in which things exist is not the time that flies or that will not come, that can be lost or put to use, nor the time that possibly could threaten the order of the cosmos. It is not the time on which Richard II reflects:

> Music do I hear?
> Ha, Ha! keep time: how sour sweet music is,
> When time is broke and no proportion kept!
> So it is in the music of men's lives.
> And here have I the daintiness of ear
> To check time broke in a disorder's string;
> But for the concord of my state and time
> Had not an ear to hear my true time broke.
> I wasted time and now does time waste me;
> For now has time made me his numbering clock:
> My thoughts are minutes; and with sighs they jar
> Their watches on unto mine eyes, the outward watch,
> Whereto my finger, like a dial's point,
> Is pointing still, in cleansing them from tears.

Music is both an order of existence in time and time well ordered by existence. The lines on the royal disaster—on the "concord of my state and time" that was ill kept by action so that the "true time broke"—practically furnish a definition of the cosmological complex existence-time-rhythm-order.

The time of the cosmological style of truth is not a neutral dimension in which things happen but the mystery of possible non-existence inherent to existence; order is not the property of an entity but existence maintained against the danger of its falling into the nothing from which it has emerged. The representation of this concern by two different symbolisms reflects the constant tension between existent things and the ground of existence: Historiogenesis expresses the concern with regard to society as an intracosmic sector of reality, while the rituals express it with regard to the non-existent, embracing "whole" of the cosmos. The two symbolisms do not necessarily refer to different "things," for New Year festivals and coronation rituals pertain just as much to the order of society as do historiogenetic speculations; it is the tension in being itself that requires representation of both its poles.

The tension in being is one of the constant problems in need of equivalent symbolization in the several styles of truth. A glance at one or two instances will confirm the thesis. Eliade's diagnosis of the ritual as an attempt to "annul the irreversibility of time" recalls the *'statisation' du devenir* attempted by apocalyptic speculations. The apocalypses of Jewish antiquity metamorphose the correlative but separate symbolisms of historiogenesis and rhythmical renewal into the one process of history that will issue into the perfect realm. To the believer in a creator-god, the cosmos has dissociated into "this world" of imperfection and the perfect divine ground of being; hence, he does not believe either in the concord of his society with cosmic order nor in the possibility of repairing actual disorder by repetitions of the cosmogonic act. Nevertheless, even if the embracing cosmos is gone, the tension is still experienced, and if the waste of order can no longer be overcome by rituals, the tension can now be dissolved by a metastasis that will put an end to the imperfection of existence forever. Even more remarkable is the occurrence of modern equivalents closely related to Jewish apocalypse. Among the modern apocalypses there should especially be reckoned certain "philosophies" of history that achieve a transfiguration of society, not by divine intervention, but by revolutionary action of man. The tension of cosmic existence thus will not disappear when the primary experience gives way to the challenge of an alternative experience—or there would be no equivalents in the later styles of truth. The proposition, though trivial, must be stressed in view of the assumptions, popular in our climate of positivism, that a change in the hierarchy of experiences proves the truth of the earlier style to have been an illusion and even the reality expressed by earlier symbolisms to have been no reality at all. One should, on the contrary, speak of the illusion of disappearance, for under the dominance of modern gnosticism and scientism the cosmos has been relegated to a position so subordinate that its presence has become almost unbelievable. An ardent Communist, for instance, would be greatly surprised if he learned that by his activities he participates in a cosmological rite of renewal in order to assuage his anxiety of existence.

The fact of equivalents in the various styles of truth can be established easily enough as a matter of empirical observation. More intricate is the question why the tension at the heart of the primary experience does not disappear when the myth of the cosmos is successfully challenged by experiences of transcendence, be they philosophical or revelatory. In order to answer this question at least tentatively, we must examine the nature of the "challenge."

The myth of the cosmos, as previously observed, will not be shaken as long as no alternative is offered to challenge the primary experience on its own ground. Since this "own ground" turns out to be the no-ground of cosmic existence, a challenge can be effective only if it somehow supplies the missing ground. And in fact, this is the quarter from which the challenge comes when the world-transcendent God is revealed as the creator of the world as well as of all things existent in it. Revelation is a spiritual and intellectual revolution inasmuch as the ground beyond no-ground is found at last. Assuming the nature of the challenge to be correctly described in this manner, one would expect anxiety to be immediately blotted out and the cosmological style to be abruptly replaced by the new style of transcendent truth. Contrary to reasonable expectation, however, nothing of the sort happens. Far from causing an abrupt change in the style of truth, Hellenic philosophy and Israelite Revelation rather induce a subtle shading and blending of old and new styles. Even more, in the wake of the great spiritual outbursts people seem to have second thoughts about the truth of the cosmos they abandoned. In Hellas, cosmological awareness increases from the early to the late Plato, from Plato to Aristotle, and from Aristotle to Alexander's cosmic religion. In Israel, the prophets had to permanently struggle against the defections of king and people; the rhythm of defection and return is the symbolism dominating the Book of Judges; we have mentioned the structure of apocalypses; and the hybrid character of a number of Psalms has caused the great debate among modern scholars whether the Psalms in question are indeed the hymns tradition pretends them to be or rather New Year and coronation rituals of the royal period. A closer look at some of the hybrid Psalms will help to clarify the issue.

A good example is Psalm 93. It has a remarkably cosmological tinge, since it symbolizes Yahweh's creation triumphant over a rebellious chaos that may again swallow up creation. First the Psalm praises the established order:

> Yes, the world is established; it shall not be moved.
> Your throne is established from old.
> You are from everlasting.

A Pharaoh could have written the lines for a ritual in praise of Re in one of his moods of ascendancy or even in praise of himself. Actually, Yahweh is meant. The lines immediately following voice anxious concern about the stability of creation:

> The floods have lifted up, O Yahweh,
> The floods have lifted up their voice,
> The floods lift up their roaring.

The praise concludes with the relieved assurance:

> Above the voices of many waters,
> The mighty waves of the sea,
> Yahweh on high is mighty.

The majestic appearance of the cosmos remains victorious, it is true, like the kings of cosmological societies in their reports of victory, and yet there can be felt the characteristic anxiety of the embracing presence in danger of being embraced by time. If in Psalm 93 the accents lie on the rite of renewal, in Psalm 96 they shift to the eternal God:

> For great is Yahweh, and greatly to be praised;
>> He is to be feared above all the gods;
>>> For all the gods of the peoples are nonentities.
> But Yahweh made the heavens;
>> Honor and Majesty are before him;
>> Strength and Beauty are in his sanctuary.

Nevertheless, this praise of the creator-god is introduced by the admonition:

> Sing to Yahweh a new song;
> Sing to Yahweh, all the earth;
> Sing to Yahweh, bless his name.

The admonition betrays the joy that a new song can be sung indeed because the cosmos has been renewed. But then again Yahweh appears as the Lord from eternity:

> Tell among the nations that Yahweh is king;
> The world also is established that it cannot be moved.

The lines sound like a gospel proclaimed by those to whom it has been revealed, to the others who have not yet heard the good news. Revealed knowledge seems to stand against the older experience of the cosmos; one should note that 96:11 invites even the sea to roar its fulness because the sea is no longer the symbol of chaos threatening creation but one of its wonders that gratefully praise the creator.

The hybrid character of the form is obvious: Although Yahweh has been recognized as the lord of creation, the cosmic sense of existence and time is not dead; the other gods are nonentities, but Yahweh is the highest among them as if he were the chief god of a summodeistic empire; Yahweh is the god of his people, as Amon-Re is the god of Egypt, but his revelation as the creator of a stable creation must be communicated to all nations over the earth. No purpose would be served by lengthening the list of contradictions or by further unraveling the tangle of symbols. The hybrid Psalms are units of expression; they demonstrate an intimate togetherness, not felt to be reprehensible, of experiences that apparently exclude one another. Let us look more closely at the structure of experience that makes this odd phenomenon possible.

An experience of transcendence, though it renders an insight convincing enough to determine a new style, does not render a proposition to be verified or falsified like a proposition concerning objects of sense perception. The insight is implied in the experience itself; there is neither a subject nor an object of cognition. As a consequence, no proof is possible through reference to an object accessible to everybody for examination. "Faith is the substance of things hoped for, and the proof of things unseen"—this passage in Heb. 11:1 describes, in a formula never surpassed, the experience as an adventure of the spirit in the realm of existential uncertainty. Faith, though it orders existence through love of its divine ground, does not transmit tangible information. Revelation and philosophy, though they grant a differentiated understanding of the tension between existent things and their ground, do not increase the certainty of insight. Even when faith has supervened, the one and only thing certain about existence remains the uncertainty about its ground. In the experiences both of the cosmos and of transcendence one must distinguish, therefore, between the tension of existence and the degree to which the Logos of the tension becomes differentiated; the differentiation of insight pertains to the Logos, not to the tension itself. If the distinction be made, a number of phenomena in the dynamics of experience will become more intelligible. There are the men who defect from newly acquired faith because it disappointingly offers no higher certainty and return to their former rituals and beliefs, which at least radiate the warmth of the accustomed; or there are the men who lose their faith and fall back on the agnostic certainty of their existence in suspense between anxiety and successful self-assertion; or, finally, the men who find, as in the Psalms, the new faith quite compatible with the firm ground of groundless existence above which their faith has risen. The case of the Psalms especially deserves attention because it shows, better than the others, that the dynamic relations between the experiences of the cosmos and of transcendence are due not to their accidental sequence in time but to their structural relations: Only when faith is in fresh contrast with groundless existence, when the two experiences are still copresent, will faith, brimming with the joy of discovery and relief, erupt into the word and impart its force to the news that must be told to all men of good will. The hybrid Psalms are inspired by precisely this freshness of relief, as at other stages of Revelation are the Songs of Deutero-Isaiah or the Epistles of Saint Paul. Hybridity of experience seems to be the explosive that releases the forces of obligatory communication; and quite probably, on this occasion, we touch one of the roots of language as well as its function in the constitution of society. The experience of the cosmos thus is primary indeed, inasmuch as its core of anxiety in response to groundless existence does not disappear when its understanding of the tension is superseded by differentiating experiences; for the experience of transcendence can do no more than develop the very insight compactly grasped even by the sense of cosmic existence.

In conclusion it will be appropriate, therefore, to cast a glance at the expression of the insight in the cosmological ambiance. We select a Babylonian Prayer addressed, by a penitent, "to whom it may concern" among the gods:

> May the fury of my lord's heart be quieted toward me.
> May the god who is not known be quieted toward me;
> May the goddess who is not known be quieted toward me.

> May the god whom I know or do not know be quieted toward me;
> May the goddess whom I know or do not know be quieted toward me.

With admirable circumspection, the Prayer is directed to all the gods, of both sexes, whether known or unknown. Moreover, the first line appeals to "my lord" as if he were the transcendent God. We are very close to the hybrid Yahweh, who is the highest god among the nonentities. The address as a whole must therefore be considered the cosmological equivalent of an appeal to the divine ground of existence. This function of an equivalent is further confirmed by the following characterization of human existence:

> Man is dumb; he knows nothing;
> Mankind—everyone that exists—what does he know?
> Whether he is committing sin or doing good, he does not even know.
>
> O my lord, do not cast thy servant down;
> He is plunged into the waters of the swamp; take him by the hand.
> The sin which I have done, turn into goodness;
> The transgression which I have committed, let the wind carry away;
>
> My many misdeeds strip off like a garment.

Who would not recall, when reading these lines, the Pauline admonition "Cast off the old man of your former habits, as he is going to ruin through lusts of delusion. Renew yourself through the spirit of your mind, and put on the new man who is created in likeness to God, in justice and holiness of truth" (Eph. 4:22–24) or the parallel passage in Col. 3:9? In both cases, it is the same situation: Man wants to shed the old man like a sullied garment and, by the grace of God, to rise in new existence—with the difference, however, of before and after the Word. The penitent of the Prayer in search of relief has to carry the burden of his "dumbness," while the man of the Apostle's admonition has heard the Word and knows he can find what he hopes for through faith in Christ. The Prayer, though firmly within the range of cosmic experience, leaves no doubt that the shell of the cosmos will be broken through revelatory illumination of human existence.

Anxiety is the response to the mystery of existence out of nothing. The search of order is the response to anxiety. The endeavor to emerge from the "dumbness" of the Babylonian Prayer would be in vain, however, unless a differentiated insight into the Logos of the

71

tension between man as an existent thing and the ground of his existence could be recognized as such; the language of differentiating experiences, of degrees of insight, and even of a Logos of the tension would be empty unless there were criteria by which advances or recessions of understanding could be measured. Frantic and perverse as it sometimes appears, there is reason in the search of order. As Hegel stated the issue: There is reason to be found in history, because reason has been put into it. We must explore, therefore, the role of reason in the search; for this purpose, we shall turn to the factor of rationality in historiogenesis and the related speculations on the origin of intracosmic sectors of reality.

Historiogenesis, theogony, anthropogony, and cosmogony form an aggregate of speculation on the origin of being. This speculative aggregate, to be sure, is still compactly bound by the myth; it has not attained the differentiated symbolism of Hellenic philosophy. Moreover, the speculative varieties composing it are still firmly attached to particular experiences within the several sectors of reality, so that the aggregate is pluralistic in character, it does not ascend to the One Being that is the ground of all being things, as does the vision of Parmenides. Nevertheless, the aggregate covers all of the sectors and must be considered, as previously said, to represent equivalently, in the medium of the myth, the philosophical intention toward the One that is the ground in truth. Even more: This character of equivalence not only pertains to the aggregate but seeps into the component symbolisms severally; for the respective speculations do not confine themselves to their immediate sector of reality but draw into their orbit materials from other sectors. Hesiod's theogony, for instance, with its climax in the Titanomachia, informs us not only about the generations of the gods but also about the civilizational victory of Jovian Dike over more primitive phases of human and social order; his *logos* of the Ages of the World is predominantly an anthropogony, but it also reflects on phases of political and civilizational history, on the ages of the Homeric heroes and their deplorable successors in Hesiod's own time, on the Mycenaean bronze and the Doric iron ages. The cosmogony of the Mesopotamian *Enuma elish* is as much a theogony and an anthropogony and quite probably also contains allusions to such civilizational achievements as the regulation of rivers and the gaining of arable land; and the historiogenetic speculations that are our principal concern extend to theogonic, cosmogonic, and anthropogonic subject matters as well. By virtue of the consubstantiality of all being, a speculation originating in one particular sector of reality can absorb into its range materials from other sectors. Hence the ground of all being becomes visible as ultimately intended, not only through the aggregate of the four speculations but even within the single forms through their mutual penetration.

In order to make the complicated network of experience and symbolization comprehensible at a glance, we shall introduce abstract signs for the elements and construct a formula representing the relations between them:

1. The speculation is motivated by an experience in one of the sectors of reality. The speculative forms corresponding to the sectors are called theogony, anthropogony, cosmogony, and historiogenesis. We shall use the initials of these four nouns for designating the four sectors of reality as t, a, c, and h.

2. The four varieties of speculation corresponding to the four sectors we shall designate as S_t, S_a, S_c, and S_h.

3. As far as subject matter is concerned, the four varieties of speculation do not confine themselves to their respective sectors of reality but absorb into their symbolism materials from the other sectors, divesting them, in the process, of their autonomous meaning and sometimes thoroughly transforming them. Hence, we must distinguish between primary and secondary materials organized by the several symbolisms. This relation we shall express by enumerating the various materials, classified by their sector of origin, placing first the primary materials. The resulting sign will be: $S_t(t-a,c,h)$, $S_a(a-t,c,h)$, $S_c(c-t,a,h)$, and $S_h(h-t,a,c)$.

4. The four varieties of speculation correspond to the four sectors of reality. In their pluralistic manner they exhaust the possibilities of speculation on the origin of being. This character of the aggregate, which makes it equivalent to a philosophy of being, shall be expressed by placing the varieties in order, held together by vertical lines:

$$\begin{vmatrix} S_t & (t-a,c,h) \\ S_a & (a-t,c,h) \\ S_c & (c-t,a,h) \\ S_h & (h-t,a,c) \end{vmatrix}$$

5. The aggregate, though equivalent to a philosophy of being, is not itself a philosophical symbolism but remains within the sphere of the cosmological myth. Neither the single speculations nor their aggregate break with the myth of the cosmos. This subordination to the myth shall be expressed by prefixing a C to the sign for the aggregate:

$$C \begin{vmatrix} S_t & (t-a,c,h) \\ S_a & (a-t,c,h) \\ S_c & (c-t,a,h) \\ S_h & (h-t,a,c) \end{vmatrix}$$

The formula conveys, better than discourse can do, what is meant by a cosmological equivalent to philosophical speculation on the *arche* of things.

Although the formula can also be put to other uses, the present inquiry will concentrate on the questions it raises regarding the equivalence of Myth and Philosophy. This complex can be delimited in the following manner:

In response to his anxiety of existence, man embarks on a search of the ground through acts of mythopoesis and philosophizing. Philosophy is concerned with the two fundamental questions formulated by Leibniz in his *Principes de la nature et de la grâce:* 1) Why is there something, why not nothing? and 2) Why are the existent things as they are, and not different? The same questions are the concern of myth—though for their expression myth is bound to the compact form imposed by the cosmological style of truth. Hence, myth and philosophy can cooperate in producing the mytho-speculative varieties of the aggregate because they have in common the endeavor to relate existent things to a ground that will endow their existence with meaning. Seeking, finding, and giving the ground of things, however, is reasoning; and the act of relating things to a ground is reasoning, whatever symbolic form it may assume. Reason must be acknowledged, therefore, as having a part not only in philosophy but also in mythopoesis, strange as this may sound to the many who still believe myth to be some kind of imaginative play beyond the pale of reason. Nevertheless, though both myth and philosophy have reason at their core, their styles of reasoning differ. In the form given them by Leibniz, the questions concerning the ground of things, regarding their existence and essence, can be asked only after philosophy has differentiated. As long as they are asked within the cosmological style of truth, there prevails the rule of relating things to their ground by relating them to intracosmic things, such as the external universe or the gods. Hence, with regard to the adequacy of styles as a means of expression, philosophy is better suited than myth to formulate the question of the ground.

The complex thus subdivides into a series of interlocking problems. There is, first, the question of myth as an instrument of reasoning. Second, there must be asked the question concerning the core that is common to equivalent symbolizations in the media of myth and philosophy—*i.e.*, the question: What is Reason? And there must, finally, be established the criteria by which the superiority or inferiority of one style can be judged against the other. I shall take them up in order.

Myth as a means of reasoning operates by the rule just mentioned of relating things to their ground by relating them to other intracosmic things. Although there is no exception to this rule within the cosmological style of truth, there exist two fundamental varieties of myth, the one characterized by acquiescence in the rule, the other by a tendency to break it. The first variety may be called the strictly intracosmic, or ordinary, type of myth. The royal symbolisms previously discussed furnish a good example inasmuch as their analogies of being are indeed intracosmic, so that for their cosmological sense they have to rely on the consubstantiality of things supplied by the embracing but non-existent cosmos. To this ordinary type of myth there belongs the overwhelming manifold of instances: Tales concerning the origin of useful inventions or social institutions, of features of the landscape or celestial constellations, of the powers of a shrine or a deity; genealogies of families who trace their descent from a god; genealogies and family affairs of the gods; divine interventions that explain individual actions of man; Homeric prologues in heaven that explain outbreaks, and the course, of great wars; and so forth. To the second type there belong the mytho-speculative varieties of our formula, which tend to break the rule as they attempt to extrapolate the genesis of things to an absolute ground. Supposing the existence of the two types not to be the result of playfulness, it looks as if there were two classes of things requiring the one or other type of myth for their appropriate relation to a ground, and consequently as if there were two types of reasoning.

One cannot expect much help from contemporary sources for an explanation of this odd phenomenon, because all questions of reason have been badly warped by the course that modern philosophy has taken since Descartes. To be sure, it is not impossible to gain access to the problem via Comte's Law of the Three Phases or Schelling's Philosophy of Myth, but the procedure would be laborious; it will be much simpler to go back to a passage by Macrobius, a contemporary of Saint Augustine, since it envisages the very distinction we have in mind. In his Commentaries on Cicero's *Somnium Scipionis*, Macrobius classified the uses to which *fabulae* can be put. Since by his time the term *fabula* had already acquired the meaning of a "false story"—quite similar to the popular meaning of the word *myth* in the English language as "a purely fictitious narrative usually involving supernatural persons, actions or events"—he was especially worried about the use made of *fabulae* by philosophers who supposedly tell the truth. To his satisfaction he found the philosophers using them only for the honorable purpose of veiling the *res sacrae* by a pious garment. And even for this purpose they used them only when they had to speak of the soul, the powers of air and ether, and the other gods. They hardly ever used *fabulae*, however, when the philosopher's discourse dared to rise to "the highest and first among the gods whom the Greeks call the Good (*tagathon*) or the First Cause (*proton aition*), or to the Mind, by the Greeks called *nous*, who contains the original Forms of all things, by the Greeks called *ideai*, and who was born and has gone forth from the highest God."

Macrobius classifies the types of myth not directly but obliquely by distinguishing between their equivalents in the philosophic style of truth. This approach from the hither side of the epoch marked by philosophy has various advantages. In the first place, the whole complex of things potentially covered by myth can be discerned as the *res sacrae*. Moreover, we become aware that even philosophers use *fabulae*, if not for the whole area of *res sacrae* at least for a part of it. By distinguishing between the two sectors of the area, furthermore, Macrobius names the philosophic equivalents of the two types of myth; and by identifying the equivalents, finally, he points to the things requiring either an ordinary myth or mytho-speculation for their treatment. What these things are is clear at least for the second type, for the symbols enumerated on the philosophical side—Platonic Idea, Aristotelian Nous and First Cause, and Plotinic Emanation—are indeed the equivalents of mytho-speculation, no doubt developed to express experiences of transcendence. Less clear is the case for the first type, for this is the sector of *res sacrae* to which even philosophers apply *fabulae* and, in Macrobius' opinion, do it legitimately. Hence, he refers to it only briefly in terms of the myth as "the soul, the powers of air and ether, and the other gods." If the brief reference, however, be supplemented by the longer, though still quite fragmentary, list given for the ordinary type of myth in the preceding paragraph, we obtain a sufficiently distinct impression of the sector. It certainly is distinct enough to answer the question: What happens to the things covered by ordinary intracosmic myth once they have moved into the realm of immanence that differentiates together with transcendence? As to one part, we know, they will grow into the sciences of the external world or enlarge the range of pragmatic action free from "superstition." As to another part, where man is concerned, they will grow into immanent history, psychology, politics, art, and literature. From its vantage point of a philosophical position still close to the myth, the Macrobius passage makes it clear, therefore, that the two types of ordinary myth and mytho-speculation are complementary and form a pattern equivalent to the philosophic distinction of immanence and transcendence. Moreover, since the distinction is present even within the cosmological style of truth, the equivalence of mytho-speculation and philosophy must be admitted to be part of a more comprehensive pattern of equivalences.

The discovery of the more comprehensive equivalence raises a major issue, since both the Macrobius passage and our own examples of intracosmic myth show the gods to belong on the side of immanence. The immanent world, then, would be not profane or secular, as we are accustomed to think under the pressure of Western society in its modern period, but indeed a world full of gods. In the language of Macrobius, it is a sector of *res sacrae*. This verity, though badly neglected today and hardly intelligible to modern man, is of the first importance for understanding the dynamics, as well as the equivalences, in the styles of truth. A few examples will argue the case:

1. Under the cosmological style of truth, man is still fully conscious of the gods being present in the cosmos. When, however, an experience of transcendence concentrates divinity in a Beyond of the world, this primary consciousness may suffer damage. By a non sequitur, immanence may become perverted from a world empty of the gods of polytheism to a world empty of divinity. If the intracosmic gods are an obstacle to understanding the transcendent God, their disappearance may become no less an obstacle to understanding divine presence within the world. The primary experience of the cosmos thus has hold of a truth that may become obscured or even obliterated under the impact of a spiritual outburst.

2. The complemental character of the two types of myth, as well as their equivalence to immanence-transcendence, has been put to something like an experimental test by history. On the one hand, a true conception of immanence will allow the use of the myth even within the transcendent style of truth, as attested not only by Hellenic philosophy but also by the spiritual outbursts of the Buddha in India and of Confucius in China. On the other hand, a perversion of immanence, when it occurs under the philosophic or revelatory style of truth, will not only dispose of the gods of polytheism but also affect the transcendent God. The belief that there could be a secular or profane world under God is erroneous—as Voltaire, who personally favored the compromise of deism, discovered to his grief when under his influence the younger generation, represented by Holbach and La Mettrie, quite consistently turned atheist.

3. An attack on the myth, because it inevitably is an attack on divine presence in the world at large and may involve the transcendent God in its success, is not a harmless pastime. Plato, who attacked the myth in the name of his new truth, became aware of this danger; in the *Epinomis* he cautioned strongly against depriving the people of its myth, because the danger of the people becoming godless was too great. The Church, furthermore, with psychological tact, provided Christian versions of holy places, miracle-working images, and rituals, and developed a host of saints to substitute for the gods. The intracosmic gods, it appears, are not expendable.

4. If a perversion of immanence goes to the extreme of losing the transcendent God, this means the radical loss of any ground to which existence could be related. And if reasoning means relating existence to its ground, the loss of God entails the loss of reason. This latter consequence would make necessary a reassessment of the function of reason in the modern centuries.

Obviously, problems of this magnitude demand careful attention. The two types of myth, as well as their philosophical equivalent of immanence-transcendence, function as a unit in the order of existence; the one cannot be treated without the other. Hence, it is appropriate to clarify the questions of immanence and the immanent gods by a digression, first on the capacity of the myth to survive and second on the disturbance of order through the modern immanentist perversion.

Intracosmic myth need not of necessity become obsolete when a spiritual outburst occurs but can continue in use as a symbolism in which processes in the psyche are related to their divine ground. Inevitably, however, it will suffer a change of meaning when it moves into the sphere of differentiated immanence; for the gods, who in the cosmological style of truth were ultimate reasons for movements of the soul, must now become relay stations, as it were, on the way to the newly differentiated absolute ground. The mediatized gods can no longer be objects of an independent cult, though even the cults die a slow death. Nevertheless, the difference should not be exaggerated, important as it is. As a matter of fact, the relay function is preformed within the cosmological style of truth inasmuch as all intracosmic reasoning has to rely for its cosmological validity, as we have repeatedly stressed, on the consubstantiality of all existent things provided by the embracing but non-existent cosmos. Relating one intracosmic thing to another would not make much sense if the assumed ground were not irradiated with ultimacy from the embracing but as-yet-unknown ground. With the transition from one style to the other, one might say, the relay function no more than reverses direction: In the cosmological style of truth, the ultimacy of the myth relays the ultimacy of the cosmos to the thing to be related to a ground, while in the styles of transcendence, the myth is consciously a play of divine presence, always presupposing, and leading toward, the divine ground ultimately intended. Between the extreme types, moreover, a whole series of transitional types has room for unfolding. In the Homeric epic, for instance, the freedom of mythopoesis is so great and the imputation of human actions to divine interventions so liberal that the actions of the gods who direct the human play sometimes impress one as a divine play directed by a more remote divinity—and that, in fact, it is, through the divine presence in Homer's soul. The road is not over-long from the Homeric use of the myth to the Platonic creation of the God who, without benefit of intermediate gods, pulls the human puppet by the various-metaled cords. In spite of a closeness to the style of transcendence that makes the epic transparent for man's existence under God, however, man himself, to say nothing of God, is so little differentiated that Homer's language does not even have a word signifying *soul.* Only centuries later, by the time of Heraclitus and Aeschylus, can one speak of an immanent soul, now designated as psyche; and this soul has become theomorphic to such a degree that its processes can be represented by a play of the myth in which the gods have recognizably become the cords of the Platonic Player of the Puppets. The play of the gods has so knowingly become a play of the soul that it can even dispense with man as the actor—the Aeschylean *Prometheus,* the great drama of the immanent soul, is enacted exclusively by divine and semidivine *dramatis personae.* In view of the transitional phenomena, one may consider the relay function inherent in intracosmic myth to be the basis of mythopoetic freedom on which depends the immanent unfolding of epic, lyric, and dramatic art.

Myth thus never need atrophy. It can survive on principle because, in relation to the absolute ground, it acquires the relay function in reverse; and it does survive as a convenience, because it has developed into a sophisticated instrument for expressing nuances in the life of the soul that cannot be easily replaced, and in fact never has been effectively replaced, by the development of an immanent rival language. This, however, is not to say that myth has not been supplemented by later symbolizations of divine presence in the world. To philosophy we owe the stark symbol of Reason (*nous*) that erects the having of a ground, the participation in it, and the ordering of existence by such participation, into the nature of man, while to Christianity we owe the *imago Dei,* the spiritual movements of the soul through Grace, and above all the presence of God in history through Incarnation. The noetic and pneumatic experiences of transcendence thus bring forth an insight into existence and its relation to the divine ground, surpassing by far cosmological understanding and relegating myth to the second rank. Still, myth not only survives but, in our time, even revives in response to the perversion of immanence in the period of enlightenment and ideology.

The acute perversion of immanence that begins with Enlightenment is a revolt against the socially dominant perversion of transcendence through the fundamentalism of ecclesiastic Christianity. This context, though it is not our present concern, must be mentioned because it affects the structure of the revolt; for the perversion is not a return to the pre-transcendent, cosmic sense of existence from an unknown ground but an advance beyond the style of transcendence to a wilful groundlessness, *i.e.*, to a rejection of the transcendent ground already known and a refusal to engage in search of it through faith. If the revolt were to be isolated from its context, there would remain nothing but a stupor of existence, personally not to be sustained for any length of time and useless as a truth of order in society. The revolt, however, has become a force in the order of Western society—and could become one because it was not a stupor but a disorder of existence, on principle of the same structure as the disorder it opposed. If the tension of existence toward the divine ground can be transformed into an objectified truth whose possession numbs the tension, the same can happen to the revolt if it accepts the perversion of transcendence, throws the ground out together with its fundamentalist incrustations, and dogmatizes itself as an existence carrying its ground within itself. Fundamentalism is the denominator common to the correlative perversions of transcendence and immanence. Hence, when the opposing ranks close in battle the result is a tragic, and sometimes comic, entanglement in intellectual positions only half intended but held with the full intolerance and fanaticism peculiar to possessors of objectified truth. The revolt is plagued by an essential incongruity between experience and symbolization; for the strand of authentic revolt against the ground, by itself no more than a stupor of existence, lies beyond means of expression, while the strand of desire to recover a ground that has become invisible through the fundamentalist perversion of transcendence must express itself in symbols of senseless militancy against the ground. The difficulties of the balancing act can be discerned in Hegel's case. In his rejection of the fundamentalist God he is as sure as any enlightened *philosophe*; in his *Phaenomenologie* he informs us that "God has died." Nevertheless, a thinker of his spiritual sensitivity cannot fall into such obvious traps as atheism, materialism, or a psychology of religion. The experience of transcendence is a reality after all. But what can one do if, on the one hand, God must be understood as the objectified existent thing of the fundamentalists, while, on the other hand, under the pressure of fundamentalism He cannot be understood as the non-existent reality of the ground? Hegel's solution of the aporia, a masterpiece of constructive genius, is his ontology of a consciousness that maintains itself in an Archimedic suspension before and beyond the tension of immanence-transcendence but that is nevertheless linked 1) to immanence, inasmuch as the truth of Revelation can be penetrated by the dialectics of human reason, and 2) to transcendence, inasmuch as the dialectic penetration is an *opus* of the third and final person of the Trinity (the Spirit, *Geist*) coming to its self-consciousness. The construction is a monument to the powers of speculation—but unfortunately, somewhere in the procedure the mystery of existence gets lost and the uncertainty of the ground gives way to the certainty of Hegel's system.

With the construction of a system we touch the ambiguity of a search of order conducted in revolt against the ground; for when man assumes the posture of revolt, he will be flooded with anxiety, and when he is prevented from responding to anxiety by a true search of the ground, he will find relief in the creation of fictitious grounds. As early as the seventeenth century, Pascal diagnosed this problem of modern man and spoke of the *divertissements* that intend to dissolve the ennui—*i.e.*, the threatening stupor of existence. I shall use his term *divertissement*, or diversion, to designate the fictitious grounds developed in response to anxiety. These diversions of the eighteenth and nineteenth centuries do not have the comparatively simple structure of assuaging devices in the cosmological style of truth but reflect the ambiguity of wilful groundlessness. The immanentist apocalypses, for instance, which characterize the period, betray the underlying anxiety just as much

82

as does an Egyptian report of victory; but since they are prevented from relating precarious existence to its true ground, their assuaging appeal must go to a self-made ground—that is, to the "system." The system is the assuaging device, developed as a response to anxiety, when man in revolt has sunk not into stupor but into spiritual impotence. As far as the search of order is concerned, a system is a futile enterprise; for the shell of certain knowledge, stifling a true search of the ground, perpetuates the state of groundlessness it intends to relieve. Socially, however, it can become a successful, and therefore dangerous, game, for a system is fundamentalist truth with a vengeance. From a perversion of transcendence there always lies an appeal to the reality perverted; but from a system there is no appeal. With the true ground, the openness of existence toward the ground is lost; from the fictitious ground, there can be derived no more than a fictitious existence insulated against reality. When man functions as God, therefore, the cords pulled by the Player of the Puppets become the bars of a prison; and the believer in a system wants to draw everybody into the prison he has built around himself.

The context in which the perversion of immanence is to be placed must be mentioned once more. The diversionist, it is true, responds to anxiety with the creation of a fictitious ground; he furthermore displays no particular zeal to rediscover the ground. All too frequently, he even enjoys his self-made existence, under the labels of freedom and reason; but he is not the one who has caused the groundlessness of existence in the first place. The ground of existence, not easily to be rediscovered, was lost by the perversion of transcendence—and that misfortune must be charged to the fundamentalism of ecclesiastic Christianity. The ecclesiastic perversion of transcendence must be acknowledged as the socially more comprehensive phenomenon if one wants to understand the phenomenon of positive responses to anxiety that do not go in the direction of the Churches. There were a great number of people for whom the Churches lost their faith, but not all of them would become diversionists; and between the embattled fundamentalisms there runs a stream of positive response, sometimes meandering through the positions left and right. One of the most important among them, distinguished by its massiveness, is the revival of the myth and its function. It wends its circuitous way through the channels of immanent science and literature and is quite as characteristic of the period as are the ideological diversions. The revival begins with the prelude of Romantic orientation in the field and then branches out in the establishment of a solid science of the myth through psychology, archaeology, Oriental studies, philosophy, philology, and the comparative science of religions. The movement is not always as conscious a search of the ground as are the systems an attempt to prevent it. Not rarely one encounters in the field of comparative religion admirable studies written by authors who apparently are not touched by the spiritual content of the materials they explore, so that the reader is baffled by the question why the author should have devoted the time of his life to a study of phenomena that he considers senseless. But the fact of the study remains; and if its motives are opaque on the surface, one still may surmise the disquiet that urges a man to let his work flow over this field. The pressure of the socially dominant diversions, it is true, casts a shadow of bad conscience, sometimes quite noticeable, on this oblique seeking of the ground by means of historical and philological methods applied to extant documents of seeking. Nevertheless, the general character of the revival as a movement of revolt against the revolt and, as an attempt to restore order through reestablishing the relation to the ground, cannot be denied. Nor can its effects. Brilliant breakthroughs like Frazer's *Golden Bough* or the work of Freud and Jung have influenced their generations and enlarged the horizon of men in search of order against the waste by time; a whole stratum of reality lost has been regained by adding the dimension of myth and dream again to an understanding of the psyche that had degenerated in the nineteenth century to the antics of a radically immanentist psychology. Moreover, the myth has not remained a mere object of inquiry but has become an active force in the creation of new symbols expressing the human condition. The new situation will be suggested if there be named representatively the work of James Joyce, William Butler Yeats, and Thomas Mann. In relation to the perversions both of transcendence and immanence, the revival must be acknowledged as a ritual restoration of order. The truth of a cosmos full of gods reasserts itself.

In the course of the revival, as we emerge *au bout de la nuit* and our eyes regain a measure of their sight, there also emerge symbols hearkening back to pre-ecclesiastic and even pre-Christian voicings of spiritual need. In fact, they recall cosmological symbolisms. I am thinking of T. S. Eliot's symbol of the Waste Land, which expresses the cumulative effect of a long period of Waste Time:

> Here is no water but only rock
> Rock and no water and the sandy road.

And in this Waste Land

> What are the roots that clutch, what branches grow
> Out of this stony rubbish? Son of man,
> You cannot say or guess, for you know only
> A heap of broken images, where the sun beats,
> And the dead tree gives no shelter, the cricket no relief,
> And the dry stones no sound of water.

But in this utter desolation of the time, through which the Son of man drags himself forsaken by the Son of man, there still is alive at least an apprehension of divine presence:

> Who is the third who walks always beside you?
> When I count, there are only you and I together
> But when I look ahead up the white road
> There is always another one walking beside you
> Gliding wrapt in a brown mantle, hooded
> I do not know whether man or woman
> —But who is that on the other side of you?

The third man on the way to Emmaus, at one time revealed, is now wrapped and hooded. This is not the unknown god, not yet revealed, to whom the Babylonian Prayer is addressed but the revealed God who has become unrecognizable. The symbolism resembles the Babylonian penitent's language of the god whom I know or don't know, who may be a god or a goddess. But a perversion of transcendence does not turn into a pristine faith in the gods. The presence, though divine, is enigmatic. The penitent of the Waste Land who has lost God cannot cry out to the enigma as to a god not yet fully known. He can only say of himself, in retrospect: "I was neither Living nor dead, and I knew nothing." And that state is less than the Babylonian's aliveness; it is the state of the shadow. Eliot's lines describe, more truly than Hegel's "God has died" or Nietzsche's "God has been killed," existence when it has become shadowy through the loss of its ground.

The Waste Land does not lie behind us, but we are emerging from

85

it, though sometimes unwittingly and unwillingly. The difficulties will become apparent from a case of the pilgrim's progress in revolt against the way he walks, offered by Benjamin Rowland's *Art and Architecture of India* (1953). The author, about to deal with a world of art in the medium of the myth, addresses his readers as follows: "This is a book written primarily for Westerners in a period when no approximation to the ancient Indian and Medieval Christian concepts of art as a form of devotion any longer exists. . . . This book is not written for those unhappy few who, unable to adjust themselves to the materialistic present, seek refuge in the traditional past." No sterner a stance in the Waste Land could be expected from a modern man doing his duty. And yet, Rowland's book is a perceptive study of a "traditional past." The ways of devotion are devious.

Eminent scholars consider the Babylonian New Year festival something like a prototype of myth and its function. In the festival, the king performs a ritual combat that symbolizes the victory of the god over the forces of chaos; and the priests recite the *Enuma elish*, the story of Marduk's victory over Tiamat. The festival is an integral symbolism that defies classification as either an ordinary myth or a mytho-speculation. Nevertheless, it is not a third type of myth, for the *Enuma elish* no doubt belongs to the cosmogonic variety of our formula and changes neither content nor structure when used in the ceremony of the festival. Rather, one would have to say it acquires an additional dimension when it is recited in explanation of the *dromenon*—i.e., of the action performed by the king; inversely, the king's action, which otherwise would be an irrelevant exercise, is drawn into the myth and becomes a ritual of cosmic renewal when it is performed, under certain conditions of time and space, to the accompaniment of the recital. Only if joined in the festival will cosmogonic story and ritual together have the function of restoring the order of existence in society; and only the joint phenomenon, together with its restorative function, is "myth" in the full sense. In a comment on the festival, Samuel S. Hooke remarks about truth and function of the myth: "Here we have the original meaning and function of myth. The truth of the myth lay in the fact that it described, in symbolic language, a real situation. The function of the myth lay in its power, in conjunction with the ritual, to maintain that situation in being." The myth in the sense of a tale is not the whole of myth; it is a dead truth unless it becomes incarnate in the order of existence through ritual enactment. Without such enactment, the symbols will become Eliot's "heap of broken images" and existence will fall into disorder. To myth in this full sense apply the following reflections on its relationship with reason.

If the act of relating things to their ground is indeed an act of reasoning, regardless of the symbolic form it assumes—be it that of myth, philosophy, revelation, apocalypse, or gnostic speculation, ancient or modern—then to the act of reasoning will pertain what Hooke considers the true property of the myth—*i.e.*, "its power, in conjunction with the ritual, to maintain that situation in being." Supposing this transfer of function from myth to reason to be justified, the functions of symbolization in all of these cases can be linked with reason by a number of generalizing propositions. We may say for instance:

1. Not only myth but every symbolism expressing the tension of existence has its component of truth as it conveys an insight into the Logos of the tension;

and:

2. Not only mythopoesis but every act of symbolization belonging to this class has the purpose and effect of bringing forth, maintaining, or restoring the order of existence, personal or social.

Moreover, if previously there had to be noted the function of historiogenesis and reports of victory as anodynes of anxiety, the restricted observation can now be generalized:

3. All acts of symbolization expressing the tension of existence have the functions both of assuaging anxiety and preserving order.

And finally, since all of these functions have something to do with the endeavor to relate existent things to their ground, we may say:

4. The cosmic sense of existence out of nothing, the waste through time, decline and restoration of order, responsive anxiety, and the search of order have as their common center that clearing in existence to which such terms as *nous*, or *intellectus*, or reason have become associated.

Whether the transfer of functions from the act of symbolization to the act of reasoning, as well as the subsequent generalizations, is tenable or not will depend on the meaning of reason now to be explored.

What is Reason? Since the clearing in existence is not an existent thing but existence illuminated so as to make visible the tension toward its ground, it will not be surprising if so thingless a something has caused numerous meanings to cluster around the term. That is not to say that the meanings agglomerate haphazardly about a something that escapes precise description; on the contrary, they articulate the dimensions of the clearing with great precision. Still, a clearing in existence is not a tangible object of the external world to which one can refer, with sufficient power of identification, by a name; it can be identified only by measuring out and articulating its dimensions. Hence, I shall enumerate ten meanings of reason, arranged in such a sequence that the principle of their accumulation becomes intelligible. The list, however, will not be exhaustive; all meanings induced, for instance, by a revolt against the ground or by identification of the ground with man, have been excluded.

> Reason as the consciousness of existence from a ground;
> reason as the transcendence of existence toward its ground;
> reason as the creative ground of existence, in the sense of the Aristotelian Nous as the First Cause;
> reason as man's faculty to understand himself as existing from a ground;
> reason as man's faculty to articulate his understanding through formation of ideas;
> reason as perseverance in concern about the relation to the ground (the Platonic *zetesis*; seeking; state of Grace);
> reason as the effort to order existence by the insight gained;
> reason as the persuasive effort, the Platonic *peitho,* to induce other men's participation in reason;
> reason as a constituent of man through his participation in the reason of the ground (Platonic *methexis*; Thomasic *participatio*);
> reason as a constituent of society through everyman's participation in the common ground, in the sense of the Aristotelian *homonoia.*

Since the perversion of immanence through positivism is a social force in the discourse of our time, the interpretation of the list will appropriately be prefaced by a few cautions: The meanings enumerated do not refer, in the manner of concepts, to objects of the external world but are terms articulating the field of non-existence inherent to existence. By "field of non-existence," furthermore, there is to be understood an area of reality with a definite and recognizable structure but empty of existent things. The phrase "empty of existent things," finally, must not be taken to mean "populated with imagined or illusionary things," since the area is devoid of all thingness. With these safeguards we can proceed to analyze the list by groups of meanings:

1. The enumeration begins with the meaning of reason as a clearing in existence: Existence is illuminate with consciousness. Consciousness, in the sense of the clearing, has neither a subject nor an object. Man, it is true, is its carrier, but he cannot be its subject, since this consciousness is not an act intending an object but an awareness of existence out of nothing. It is this non-cognitive awareness that imparts to existence its tension and provokes the response of anxiety.

2. The enumeration, then, expands to the poles of the tension. From the side of man, existence is discovered to have a dimension beyond his thingness toward a ground. The "beyond," however, is not a thing existent outside man but a direction in the non-existent reality illuminate with consciousness. This directional character of consciousness is what is called transcendence. As far as the opposite pole of the tension is concerned, it again imparts a direction to the reality illuminate with consciousness, variously called the ground, origin, *arche, aition, idea,* cause, and pleonastically, creative ground or cause.

3. Consciousness, as an illuminated tension in the field of non-existence, is ontologically founded in man as its carrier. Man can be said, therefore, to have the faculty of reason in the sense that he can form an idea of himself as an existent thing with a consciousness by which he is aware of his existence from a ground. By articulating his consciousness he discovers himself as the thing having it—*i.e.,* as man having reason. The terms used in the process of articulation we shall call *ideas.* To this class of ideas, hitherto used without further characterization, belong such terms as *existence, field of non-existence, existent things, consciousness, tension, poles of tension, ground, no-ground, nothing, origin, cause, idea* (in the Platonic sense), *clearing, illumination, articulation, ideation,* and so forth. One of the most important terms in the series is the *idea of man,* for the formation of metaphysical concepts with

regard to the nature of man is a secondary phenomenon, founded on the discovery of man as the carrier of a consciousness in tension toward the divine ground. The confusion of idea and concept of man, as later parts of the present study will show, is the source of serious disorders of human existence in society.

4. The next group of meanings is concerned with reason as the ordering force of existence. For the ground of which man is conscious is not a thing that once upon a time has caused other things, including man, to exist but a power of origin, continuously radiating through consciousness the obligation to order existence toward the ground. The fulfillment of this obligation requires the efforts that are called virtues when they have become habits of order. The existential virtues in the eminent sense are the efforts to keep existence open toward its ground and to persevere, in seeking the ground, the Platonic *zetesis*, in resistance to the disorder of existence through opinion. These efforts are at the root of the phenomenon called conscience. The formation of the dianoetic and ethical virtues in the Aristotelian sense depends on the development of the existential virtues. These habits of action provide the backbone of order—as virtues to personal existence, as institutions to existence in society.

5. Reason articulating itself, finally, recognizes the field of nonexistence as the area of consubstantiality with the ground. Accordingly it develops the idea of human reason as participating, within the limits allowed by non-cognitive awareness of the ground, in the *ratio eterna*. The ground is constitutive of existence through being present in it. This structure of consciousness is expressed, with regard to personal existence, through the Platonic and Thomasic ideas of *methexis* and *participatio;* with regard to existence of man in society, through the Aristotelian idea of *homonoia*, the participation of all men in the same *nous*.

To reason indeed, as the analysis shows, there pertain the properties attributed by Hooke to myth. They can now be reformulated more precisely: The truth of the myth lies in the fact that it articulates, by its specific means of symbolization, the field of nonexistence inherent to existence; the function of the myth lies in its power to keep existence in order by keeping it open toward its ground. From this reformulation I have omitted any reference to the ritual, because ritual, though a distinct phenomenon, is no more than part of myth in the full sense. Moreover, what this full sense is can now be stated more clearly, because the same issue of a full sense opposed to a deficient mode is peculiar also to the sphere of reason. For the meanings of reason enumerated will not provide, in their aggregate, a sum of information about the clearing in existence as an existent thing. The meanings were developed by acts of articulating the clearing experienced in existence, and they must ineluctably remain a dead truth, "a broken image," unless the acts of articulation are re-enacted by the reader or hearer of their original accounts. No more than the truth of myth can the truth of reason be conveyed by information; it must be acquired by an act of meditative articulation and thereby be made the ordering force in existence. The inherence of action in the truth of reason was concentrated by Aristotle in his conception of the life of reason (nous) as *theoretike energeia*, as contemplative action. Only *theoretike energeia*, not the knowledge of philosophic doctrines, has the power of ordering existence truly to the point of inducing a state of *eudaimonia*. The action of contemplation is the philosophic equivalent of ritual in myth. We conclude, therefore, that the properties of the myth indeed pertain to reason, that reason lies at the core of all symbolizations relating existence to its ground, and that the generalizations are justified.

The inquiry concerns the role of reason in the search of order. It is well to recall the concern at this juncture, when criteria for the superiority of the philosophic over the cosmological style of truth have to be established, in order to avoid the pitfall of premature conclusions. For at first sight, the issue looks deceptively simple. If the question of superiority hinged on nothing but the adequate symbolization of the non-existent ground, one might argue that both myth and philosophy engage in reasoning when they relate things to their ground. Myth, however, reasons by means of relating things to other intracosmic things of a higher rank, while philosophy differentiates the clearing in existence and articulates the non-existent ground. Hence, differentiated reason is the criterion by which philosophy must be judged a more adequate means of reasoning than myth. This argument is valid, and the conclusion will remain true, all further complications notwithstanding. Nevertheless, in the light of the preceding analysis, the argument is unsatisfactory in several respects:

1. In the first place, the argument might be misunderstood as a piece of facile phenomenalism unless its unavoidably objectifying language is accompanied by a bodyguard of cautionary negatives. For neither are the styles of truth objects in the external world; nor is differentiated reason a property attaching to a style like a color; nor is there an observer outside the styles of truth who could recognize reason as a property. As soon as the negatives are introduced, it becomes clear that the judgment of superiority can be rendered only from inside the philosophic style of truth to which the present inquiry belongs. The judgment thus is immanent to the dynamics of change in styles.

2. Reason is not a style of truth. One can advance from myth to philosophy but not "from myth to reason." This fact—that reason is not itself a style of truth though it lies at the core of all the styles—has various consequences that are apt to diminish the luster of philosophy. Order in existence, for instance, corresponds to a man's actualization of his relation to the ground through ritual, meditation, faith, and prayer but does not correspond to the degree of differentiation. Hence, reason may be highly effective in the order of cosmological societies when it has not yet articulated the field of non-existence; it may seriously impair the order of existence when it has differentiated but is not actualized through meditation; and it may become a source of disorder rather than of order when it is bandied about as a topic of the time, as in the Age that derives its name from Reason. If the dimension of actualization be taken into account, as it must, the superiority of philosophy appears less convincing. Moreover, one must not overlook the fact that no society has ever accepted philosophy as its style of truth. There are cosmological, Christian, Islamic, Buddhist, Hinduist, Confucian, and ideological societies, but there never has been a philosophic society in history. Nobody has ever seriously tried to realize Plato's idea of the *kallipolis;* and however carefully Aristotle has demonstrated the higher rank of the philosopher's life, societies prefer to be ruled by politicians. And finally, even when philosophy is cultivated in societies dominated by another style of truth, as in Islamic or Christian societies, there arise such problems as those of a double truth of faith and reason or of a subordination of philosophy to theology as its handmaid. Such oddities point to limitations in the truth of philosophy; there seems to be more to

existence than the Logos of the tension that can be differentiated by a noetic experience.

3. The most serious defect of the argument, however, is its restriction to the question of the ground. The noetic experience, it is true, differentiates the field of non-existence as the site of the tension toward the ground. But the tension has two poles, only one of them being the ground; the other one is the man who experiences the tension. Furthermore, the event of the noetic experience is ontologically founded in man as an existent thing among others in the world. In brief: Non-existence is inherent to existence, so that man cannot differentiate the field of non-existence without differentiating the field of existent things of which he is a part. When the clearing in existence becomes illuminate with consciousness, the community of intracosmic things dissociates into the world of existent things and their non-existent ground. These implications of the noetic experience with regard to the world of existent things proved to be tardy in unfolding, however, because the carriers of noetic and pneumatic outbursts were primarily interested in the discovery of the ground, as well as in the more immediate consequences of their discovery for personal and social order. The discovery of non-existence, to be sure, made immediately visible the existent things as a field to be explored and led to the brief but splendid flowering of Greek science. But this promising development was cut short by the closing in of cosmology on the new level of insight achieved by the Classic philosophers, and it has taken the better part of two thousand years, as well as the additional pressure of Christian transcendentalism, before differentiated non-existence could become fully effective in the rise of modern science. This differentiation of the field of existence, at long last achieved, must be considered the second criterion by which the truth of philosophy can be judged superior to the truth of myth.

The vicissitudes of reason in societies whose prevalent style of truth is non-philosophic are subject matters for later parts of this study. The first and third points just raised, however, concern the tension of existence, its poles, and its Logos; they pertain to the dynamics of change from myth to more adequate means of reasoning. Although the superiority of philosophy over myth can be argued only from the level of differentiated reason, the points of superiority are recognizable as such because the corresponding inadequacies of myth make themselves felt within the cosmological style of truth as gropings toward more perfect expression of a truth imperfectly discerned. The core of reason exerts a pressure of its own that manifests itself in various transitional phenomena on the scale of compactness and differentiation. Through a series of representative texts, I shall document the transition from mytho-speculation to differentiated reason, first with regard to the unknown ground and second with regard to the field of existent things.

We have distinguished between ordinary myth and mytho-speculation. While myth in general relates to other intracosmic things as their ground, the varieties of mytho-speculation construct aetiological chains that elongate the genetic line until a cause is reached that is believed to be the highest one in the cosmos and therefore to be eminently qualified to make the whole chain expressive of the non-existent cosmic ground. This symbolism of the chain allows for a series of varieties by which the intactness or beginning dissolution of the cosmological style of truth can be gauged. The chain can either present itself in its finished form and be accepted as a genesis of things from the highest cause down, or it can be presented in the process of construction from the existent thing up to the highest ground. Moreover, since the chain is motivated by an authentic search of the ground, it is not simply discarded when an experience of transcendence occurs but carefully examined, criticized, and related to the new insight. Hence, I shall give examples for both the finished form and the process of construction, as well as for the relating of the chain both to pneumatic and noetic experiences.

Experientially, a mytho-speculative construction always begins from the thing to be explained and ascends to the ground considered the highest, as witnessed by the mythopoetic freedom in changing the highest ground, or any links in the chain, according to the requirements of the social situation. This process of construction, however, need not be in the foreground of consciousness. On the contrary, if anything is characteristic of stable cosmological societies, it is the insouciance about conflicts between successive extrapolations to the ground within the same society, or between simultaneous extrapolations in well-known neighboring societies. Nobody seems to worry when a Babylonian high-god replaces a Su-

merian in a cosmogony, or when neighboring Egyptian and Mesopotamian empires both claim to represent the order of the cosmos
on earth. This lack of concern about the process of construction
and the experience motivating it, as well as about conflicts that
after all might cast a doubt on the value of the construction, manifests itself in the unquestioned acceptance of finished symbolisms
that tell the story of a genesis from the highest cause down to the
existent thing. An instance of such an unquestioned genesis is furnished by a Babylonian incantation against toothache. The ache
was supposed to be caused by a worm finding his living in the
diseased area. As in the New Year festivals, the priest-physician
would combine his operation (the ritual) with a story of how the
worm came to be:

> After Anu had created heaven,
> Heaven had created earth,
> Earth had created rivers,
> Rivers had created canals,
> Canals had created marsh,
> Marsh had created worm—
> The worm came weeping before Shamash,
> His tears flowing before Ea:
> "What will you give me to eat?
> What will you give me to drink?"

The gods offer him ripe figs and apricots as a habitat. But a worm
of such ancestry is choosy; he insists on a place between the teeth
and the gum, and that he is accorded by Shamash and Ea. In this
Babylonian instance, the cosmological symbol is still intact.

The story of a genesis from the highest cause down, however, can
be reversed, so that the aetiological chain will be transformed into
a series of questions from the existent thing up. This is the procedure of numerous dialogues in the Upanishads. An instance of the
competitive questionings, by which the wisdom of the Brahmana
Yajnavalkya is tested, is the following passage:

> Then Gargi Vachaknavi asked.
> "Yajnavalkya" she said, "everything here is woven,
> like warp and woof, in water. What then is that in
> which water is woven, like warp and woof?"
> "In air, O Gargi," he replied.
> "In what then is air woven, like warp and woof?"
> "In the worlds of the sky, O Gargi," he replied.

The questioning lady then drives the Brahmana through the following causes: The world of the Gandharvas, of Aditya (the sun), of Chandra (the moon), of the Nakshatras (the stars), of the Devas (the gods), of Indra, of Prajapati, and finally the worlds of Brahman. The questioning concludes:

> "In what then are the worlds of Brahman woven, like
> warp and woof?"
> Yajnavalkya said: "O Gargi, do not ask too much, lest thy
> head should fall off. Thou askest too much about a deity
> about which we are not to ask too much. Do not ask too much,
> O Gargi."
> After that Gargi Vachaknavi held her peace.

The Indian dialogue operates with the same apparatus of intracosmic causes as the Babylonian incantation. And yet, the reversal of the aetiological chain is more than the exploitation of a formal possibility. The descent from the highest cause down comes to rest on the thing to be explained, its emphasis lies on the objective order among things in the cosmos, while the ascent from the existent thing up, from the "everything here" (closely related to the Heraclitian "this cosmos here"), moves the tension of existence with its unrest of the quest to the fore. Even though the unknown ground remains unknown, and too much questioning is threatened half-jokingly—but only half, with the sanction that your head will fall off—man and his search of the ground have become the center of concern. A great step forward is taken toward the polarization of existence that will result in the confrontation of man with God. One may speak of a partial illumination of the field of nonexistence by consciousness.

When the breakthrough toward the transcendent ground actually occurs, the symbolism of the chain is not simply discarded; the dynamics of change is continuous and produces specific symbolisms that show the experience of transcendence on the point of its emergence from the primary experience of the cosmos. An example of such continuous change into the pneumatic type is the Apocalypse of Abraham (Chaps. 7–8), an Essene document, to be dated probably in the first century B.C.:

> More venerable indeed than all things is fire
> for many things subject to no one will fall to it. . . .

More venerable even is water,
    for it overcomes fire. . . .
Still I do not call it God,
    for it is subject to earth. . . .
Earth do I call more venerable,
    for it overcomes the nature of water.
Still I do not call it God,
    as it is dried up by the sun. . . .
More venerable than the earth I call the sun;
    the universe he makes light by his rays.
Even him I do not call God,
    as his course is obscured by night and the clouds.
Yet the moon and stars I do not call God,
    because they, in their time, dim their light by night. . . .
Hear this, Terah, my father.,
    that I announce to you the God, the creator of all,
    not those that we deem gods!

But where is He?
And what is He?
—who reddens the sky,
who goldens the sun,
and makes light the moon and the stars?
—who dries up the earth, in the midst of many waters,
who put yourself in the world?
—who sought me out in the confusion of my mind?

May God reveal Himself through Himself!

When thus I spoke to Terah, my father,
    in the court of my house,
The voice of a mighty-one fell from heaven
    in a cloudburst of fire and called:
Abraham! Abraham!

I said: Here am I!
And he said:
    You seek the God of gods,
    the Creator,
    in the mind of your heart.
    I am He!

The Apocalypse is carefully organized. There is a first part, closely resembling the dialogue of the Upanishad with its series of questions. When the aetiological chain is exhausted, however, there follows not an evasive closure of the quest but the flat announcement of the extra-cosmic god as the object of the search. When this point is reached, furthermore, the head does not fall off, but the further search is recognized as useless, because knowledge beyond this point is possible only through the self-revelation of God. And the climax of the experience, finally, comes through the revelatory confrontation of God and man, couched in the symbolism of the Thornbush Episode.

A well-organized text of this kind, with considerable literary ancestry, is not a primitive document. The Apocalypse is a sophisticated analysis of the transition from cosmological truth to pneumatic experience by a great spiritualist. It deserves more attention than, as far as I know, it has hitherto received.

The aetiological chain, it would seem at first sight, is introduced only with the intention of polemics against a strongly cosmological environment. But there is more to it than the explicit denial of a series of divine presences, of "those that we deem gods"; for the chain of the cosmological style is, in fact, transformed into the *via negativa* of the mystic who, roaming through the immanent realms of being, cannot find God until, after their exhaustion, the search comes to its rest in transcendent reality. This transformation, however, is possible only because the chain, especially when it assumed the form of questioning, is already a *via negativa* on which the wanderer presses toward the ultimate ground. We become aware of the equivalence between cosmological chain and post-cosmological *via negativa*. But why should the chain, whatever its form, not be discarded when the ground is reached through a pneumatic experience, as obviously it was by the author before he sat down to write his Apocalypse? The answer is given through the announcement of the creator-god, inasmuch as it restores an otherwise superfluous chain to its dignity by recognizing it as the order of existent things created by the ground. Hence, the discovery of the ground does not condemn the field of existence to irrelevance but, on the contrary, establishes it in its true importance as reality that derives its meaning from the ground; and inversely, the *via negativa*, ascending over the hierarchy of being, leads indeed to the ground, because the ground is the origin of the hierarchy. Through the pneumatic transformations of the chain, the dissociation of the cosmos has again advanced a step. The Babylonian incantation accepted the finished chain as the objective order of intracosmic things; the Indian dialogue moved the process of questioning into the center and made the border of transcendence visible, without, however, doubting the order of the intracosmic chain; the Essene Apocalypse abolishes the intracosmic order and replaces it by an order of creation that leads to the creator god. Nevertheless, the order of creation does not lead by itself toward the creator but does so only when there is a heart in search of God. The "mind of the heart," in the Apocalypse, is the Aramaic equivalent to the Hellenic *psyche* and the Augustinian *anima animi* as the term designating the site of the search—a site that comprises both immanence and transcendence but is itself not to be located either immanently or transcendentally. The text makes admirably clear the non-existent reality of the tension—of God seeking man, and man seeking God—the mutuality of seeking and finding one another—the meeting between man and the beyond of his heart. Since God is present even in the confusion of the heart preceding and motivating the search itself, the divine Beyond is at the same time a divine Within. Subtly the unknown author traces the movement from Within to Beyond as it passes from the confusion of the mind, to the search of the unknown that is present in the search as it was in the confusion, and further on to the call from beyond— until what in the beginning was a vague disturbance in that part of reality called the heart has become a clear confrontation in the "Here I am" and "I am He." This analysis of a pneumatic search culminating in revelation, superbly free from all objectivations, disengages the field of non-existence from the primary experience of the cosmos without losing the field of existence. The Apocalypse of Abraham (Chaps. 7–8) is a masterpiece, comparable in rank to the analysis of erotic tension in the *Symposion.*

The series of transitional phenomena will properly be concluded with Aristotle's noetic quest of the ground in his Theology—*i.e.,* the work traditionally called *Metaphysics.* The term *theology* had been coined by Plato and was used by Aristotle as a name for philosophizing on the ultimate ground (*proton aition*); alternatively, he used First Philosophy (*prote philosophia*) and Wisdom (*sophia*). Nothing in the work, however, indicates that he knew he was dealing with Metaphysics. The principal sources for the issues of present interest are *Metaphysics* [Book] I and [Book] II, to be supplemented by some further passages. Book I, conventionally designated as the "historical survey" of predecessors, serves as introduction to *Metaphysics;* Book II, whatever the controversial details of its origin, looks like a briefer and perhaps earlier introduction to the same work, editorially inserted in the present place because it elaborates some points only touched upon in Book I. The achievements of Aristotle come under two heads: He developed 1) a symbolism for expressing the dimension of history in the search and 2) a terminology for making the search and its history intelligible. The two achievements are interdependent.

First, the new symbolism. I have put the term "historical survey" in quotation marks because it is misleading. The Introduction, it is true, offers a wealth of information on the course of Hellenic philosophy from Thales to Plato and Speusippos, but it is not a history of "ideas" or "doctrines" in the modern sense. If the scattered remarks of Aristotle (II.i; III.i) on his intentions in writing the "survey" be assembled, they can be summarized as follows: Aristotle deemed the complexities of the noetic quest so enormous that one man alone could never reach the goal; many a trial and error were needed to overcome the difficulties, many a tentative approach to achieve a great result in the end; hence, to ignore the earlier attempts would entail not only the risk of repeating mistakes of the past but also the loss of partial solutions already gained; anybody who wants to bring the secular quest to a successful conclusion must, therefore, study the earlier attacks on the problems he wishes to resolve; and finally, Aristotle feels obliged to render an account of the discussion with the predecessors because otherwise he would fail to discharge his debt of gratitude toward thinkers to whom he owes the formation of his own state of mind (*hexis*). The introduction, it will appear from these remarks, moves in the tradition of the Platonic dialogue, even though the emphasis has shifted from the present to the past. Hence, more appropriately than a "survey" it would be called a dialogical critique or an intellectual autobiography—especially since it has decisive points in common with the intellectual autobiography of Socrates in Plato's *Phaedo.* The numerous and astonishing inaccuracies, furthermore, that occur in Aristotle's account of his predecessors' philosophic intentions should be charged to the emotions of a critique that is less interested in historical exactness than in the clarification of problems. After all, there is such a thing as productive misunderstanding. Such reservations notwithstanding, the introductory critique is a new symbolism that intends to establish the continuum of noetic search as a relevant structure in history; for *Metaphysics* I expands the dialogic filiation of Socrates and Plato so as to embrace the Hellenic thinkers from the Ionians, and even Homer and Hesiod, down to Aristotle's own present. By the same token, it expands the present of the search—*i.e.*, the event of the actualized tension of existence toward its ground—so as to embrace past events of the same type. The past of time is discovered to have a present when the present of time dissociates into the two presents of existence and non-existence, for non-existence does not cease to be real when its carriers in the world of existent things have sunk into the past. When the field of non-existence becomes illuminate with consciousness, and philosophy has differentiated reason as the core of all endeavors to relate things to their ground, reason is recognized as one of the constituents of history. This last formulation, however, goes beyond the intentions of the critique, since Aristotle recognizes reason not as one of the constituents but as the one and only. His relevant structure does not embrace more than the noetic search of the Hellenic philosophers, and the course of this search is conceived as coming to its predestined end in Aristotle's own effort. The introduction thus has a strong touch of the ineluctable unilinearity that is peculiar to historiogenesis. Nevertheless, the achievement is real: Aristotle's Theology has disengaged the Logos of the tension from its cosmological compactness, and with the differentiation of reason in personal existence, it has laid the foundation for a philosophy of man in historical existence. In the Theology, the search of the ground catches up with itself, as it were, and becomes thematic as the concern of man. That is not to say that the noetic search has reached its goal; on the contrary, it keeps going on, and no end is in sight. Still, an epoch has been reached, acknowledged as such through the ambiguity attaching to Aristotle's work, for in retrospect from his own present, he conceived his Theology as the culminating effort of philosophic team work in the dimension of history—a conception next to forgotten. In retrospect from his successors' present, the final Theology has become the first Metaphysics—the great arsenal of analysis and terminology on which philosophers are drawing to this day in their defense of Reason in societies dominated by styles of truth other than the philosophic.

Second, the terminology. One cannot disengage the field of non-existence from cosmological compactness through an act of philosophizing without articulating its dimensions. By means of the terminology—all too easily taken for granted once it has been developed—one can trace, therefore, the actual labor of disengagement and gauge the measure to which the effort has been successful. I shall order the terms by groups that will make the Aristotelian quest of the ground intelligible with regard to both its success and limitations:

1. Above all, Aristotle not only engages in the quest of the ground but makes the quest itself thematic as the concern of man through which his manhood is constituted. Man lives in ignorance (*agnoia*) and moves toward knowledge (*episteme*). But he would not know about his ignorance, and consequently not even try to escape from it (*pheugein ten agnoian,* 982b20f.), unless he were made aware of it by an experience of restlessness or disquiet. Since the Greek language has no exact equivalent to what we have called anxiety in response to existence out of nothing—the Greek *agchein* not having proliferated by meanings and terms like the Latin *angere*—Aristotle characterizes the experience more concretely by the verbs *diaporein, aporein,* and *thaumazein. Diaporein* can mean (the same as can *aporein*) the passive state of being at a loss or in doubt, to be in difficulty or in want; but also, more actively, it can mean the raising of a difficulty or question. The two strands of meaning indicate, on the linguistic level, an experience of restlessness that is active and passive at the same time. On Aristotle's theoretical level this structure of the experience splits into the perplexed questioning (*diaporein*) and the difficulty (*aporon*) that is its target (982b12ff.); and the transition from the compactly active-passive experience to the distancing of subject and object enables him to place the difficulties, together with their questioning, on a scale ranging from common objects of curiosity to greater ones, such as the changes of sun, moon and stars, and finally to the origin of the cosmos (*tou pantos genesis,* 982b17). Even though there is no term for anxiety, it becomes clear that *diaporein* ultimately refers to the raising of

the cosmogonic question in the attempt to overcome the state of anxiety. *Thaumazein*, then, means wondering or marveling, sometimes with the connotation of a marveling aroused by admiration for the splendor of a spectacle, as for instance of the cosmos. When, however, Aristotle speaks of *thaumazein* as the origin of all philosophizing (982b12f.), he has in mind a "wondering why things should be as they are" (983a14f.), thus implying in the *thaumazein* the quest of the ground. The terms *diaporein* and *thaumazein*, finally, become practically synonyms when they are linked in the definition: "A man perplexed (*aporon*) and wondering (*thaumazon*) is conscious (*oietai*) of being ignorant (*agnoein*)" (982b18). In the light of this definition, ignorance is not an inferior state of knowledge but the pole of a tension of which man becomes aware through the experience of perplexed wondering.

2. Man wants to emerge from ignorance. *Metaphysics* I, by its opening statement, suggests the other pole of the tension: "All men by nature reach out for knowledge [*tou eidenai oregontai*]." The conventional translation of the phrase as "desire to know" is not wrong, since *oregesthai* (to reach or grasp for a thing) can indeed also mean to yearn or desire. Still, the translation here offered is preferable, because further on in the text (982a32ff.) Aristotle formulates the same thought, this time however substituting *hairein* (take, grasp, seize) for *oregesthai*, and *epistasthai* (to be assured, feel sure, to know a matter) for *eidenai*. As in the case of *diaporein* the passive perplexity was less important to him than the active raising of the question, so in the case of *oregesthai* he is less interested in passive desirousness than in the active reaching out for knowledge. Moreover, the verb *epistasthai* itself acquires in his usage a curious streak of grasping. As perplexed questioning tended to split into questioning (*diaporein*) and perplexing difficulty (*aporon*), so the possessive knowing splits into an active knowing or inquiring (*epistasthai, episteme*) and the knowables (*episteme, episteta*) it tries to reach. This split serves again the purpose of distinguishing objects of knowing and of placing them on a scale. The ascent of *diaporein* from minor matters to the ground of the cosmos is paralleled by an ascent of *episteme* from technical knowledge and inventiveness, to the immediate causes of particular things (*hekasta*), and finally to the first causes (*ta prota kai ta*

aitia) of all things (981a13–982a20). *Epistasthai* and *hairein*, when linked in a phrase to mean "reaching out for knowledge," practically function as a compound designating an ardent search (982a33).

The factor of rank in the types of knowledge is furthermore enforced by adding the adverb *malista* (to the highest degree) to *episteme, episteta,* and *hairein,* so that there is a supreme reaching out for supreme knowledge of the supremely knowables—i.e., for the first causes of things (982b1ff.). (One is tempted to recall *to malista panton,* the supremely real, in Plotinus V, 5, 11). The knowledge (*episteme*) of the eminently knowables Aristotle calls Wisdom (*sophia,* 982a20–982b8); and this Wisdom is the subject matter of the search (*zetesis kai methodos*) in which he is engaged in the present work (983a21ff.). The meaning of *oregesthai,* finally, becomes fully differentiated when Aristotle identifies (1072a26ff.) the object reached for (*orekton*) with the object of intellect or reason (*noeton*). Only the apparent good is an object of desire or appetite (*epithymeton*); the first, or real, good (*proton kalon*) is the object of rational will (*bouleton*). This gamut of terms and meanings suggests a noetic meditation comparable to the pneumatic in the Apocalypse of Abraham: Knowledge moves from minor perplexities, through the hierarchy of being, to confrontation with the divine Nous—who, in retrospect from confrontation, is recognized as the Prime Mover whose moving was present even in the first stirrings of *thaumazein-diaporein* and *oregesthai-hairein.* The unrest of perplexed questioning comes to its self-understanding when the human *nous* discovers as its *noetikon* the divine *Nous.* Hence, the sense would not be tortured if the opening statement were paraphrased: "All men are by nature in quest of the ground."

3. Noetic confrontation with the ground entails historical confrontation of philosophy with myth. Hence, the two styles of truth must be identified by names. They must furthermore be characterized with regard to what they have in common as well as with regard to their difference; and there must be detailed the reasons for preferring philosophy to myth. In all of these respects Aristotle's feat of articulation is remarkable. The terms for the two styles, it is true, he inherited from Plato, who already had the meaning of philosophy (*philosophia*) fully developed in opposition not only to myth (*mythos*) but also to opinion (*doxa*). The full articulation of what myth and philosophy have in common, however, comes with

the opening statement of *Metaphysics*, declaring the quest of the ground to be the constituent of man quâ man. All men are aroused by the same *thaumazein*, but they can express their wondering about the ground of things by either myth or philosophy. Hence, "the *philomythos* is in a sense a *philosophos*, for myth is composed of wonders" (*thaumasion*, 982b18ff.). The term *philomythos* as a name for the philosopher's counterpart in relating things to their ground appears for the first time, as far as I know, in this passage. Regrettably, it has been received by the Western language no more than has Plato's *philodoxos* (lover of opinion), so that we are compelled to use more idiomatic, though more clumsy, circumscriptions. It looks as if success had been denied to these valuable articulations of historical types, because no society has ever adopted philosophy as its style of truth; the terms opposing a new style to an old one that have been successful—such as Israel and the nations, or Christians and pagans—originate in the pneumatic rather than in the noetic sphere. The passage just quoted is noteworthy furthermore because it connects the wonders (*thaumasia*) of the myth with the motivating *thaumazein*. At first reading one might suspect a play of words, perhaps with the intention of ranking myth lower than the new philosophizing that is free of such wonders—in which case the *thaumasia* would mean something like "supernatural explanations" in the modern derogatory sense. This interpretation, however, is precluded by what we know about Aristotle's attitude toward the myth. His late confession "The more solitary and isolated I am, the more of a lover of myth [*philomythoteros*] I am becoming" leaves no doubt about the attraction myth held to him as a philosopher. Hence, the passage should be given the chance to mean what it says: that *thaumasia*, if not as adequate, are at least as effective an answer to *thaumazein* as are the symbols of philosophy. In order to understand this proposition, one must remember that the quest of the ground is an exploration not of causal relations among world-immanent existent things but of the field of non-existence. In this field, the ground of existence remains an impenetrable mystery even if it receives the names of Nous or God; and the same is true for the manner in which existence derives from the ground, even if this manner receives such names as *kinesis* or creation. The Nous of the philosopher is no less a *thaumasion* than the marvels of the myth, even though the term be reserved to the latter. Aristotle, who still lived close to the myth (to say nothing of his Platonic education in such matters), recognized the mystery of existence as the constituent area of the marvelous and the miracle. In spite of such understanding, however, he was adamantly critical on the point that the place of *thaumasia* is not in philosophy. In the closing passage of *Metaphysics* XII, 8, he speaks of the thinkers of old who bequeathed to posterity, in the form of the myth (*en tou mythou schemati*), a tradition that the celestial bodies are gods. This belief of the forefathers (*patrios doxa*) he declares to be divinely inspired and manifestly true (*phanera*), and it should be retained. In fact, he lets it enter into his conception of the Prime Mover of the cosmos. The rest of their tradition, however—that the gods are human or animal in shape—he believes to have been added for the edification of the vulgar, and it must be discarded by the philosopher. What myth and philosophy have in common, thus, is the recognition of the ground as divine; what distinguishes them is, on the one hand, the cosmologist's mythopoetic freedom to fill the area of mystery by *thaumasia* and, on the other hand, the philosopher's discipline not to elaborate on the mystery and thereby to obscure the structure of non-existent reality.

4. Since both myth and philosophy are engaged in the quest of the divine ground, they both can lay claim to the title theology (*theologia*). At this point we touch the limit of Aristotle's effort at articulation, for the intracosmic gods of the myth are not the philosopher's Nous; if theology were to apply to both myth and philosophy, it would have to be qualified as compact and differentiated, or mythical and philosophical theology. Instead of such adjectives, we find in *Metaphysics* a variety of approaches that in their aggregate betray a fundamental uncertainty:

(a) In the just quoted passage from XII.viii (1074b1ff.), for instance, Aristotle wants to separate (*chorizein*) the acceptable from the unacceptable gods of myth as if they were neatly separable entities indeed. Philosophical theology then would become myth minus the *thaumasia,* and as a consequence, the celestial gods of Aristotle would be intracosmic gods.

(b) In I.iii (983bff.), on the contrary, he draws a sharp line between theologizing (*theologesantes*) thinkers who set gods as the first causes of things and philosophers (*philosophesantes*) who replace the gods with matter or elements. He reflects, for instance, on Thales, who declared water to be the *arche* of things, and compares this attempt with a Homeric passage where Oceanus and Tethys are presented as the parents of creation (*genesis*). What he has in mind clearly is the question of equivalence: Both myth and philosophy express the quest of the ground (*arche*), but the theologizer finds it in intracosmic divinities, the philosopher in water.

(c) The uncertainty becomes most tangible in the multiplicity of names for the philosophical effort. The name *theologia*, which had been coined by Plato, appears in the subdivisions of philosophy by subject matter into the three theoretical philosophies or sciences of physics, mathematics, and theology (1026a18ff.; 1064b1ff.). Alternatively, this highest of the theoretical sciences is named the divine science (*theia episteme*, 983a7f.) because it deals with first causes and because all believe that god is "a sort of *arche*." Moreover, God is the sole and chief possessor of this knowledge (983a9ff.), while man becomes his partner in it when he explores as much of it as the ultimate cause lets become visible of things divine (1026a18). First Philosophy (*prote philophia*, 1026a24), Wisdom (*sophia*, 981b26ff.; 996b1ff.), and Science of Being quâ Being (*to on he on*, 1025b3ff.) are used as synonyms for theology. In one of these contexts, finally, there appears the characterization of Wisdom or Theology as the highest and most authoritative science, which the others, as her handmaidens, may not contradict (996b12). Before we can pronounce on the reasons of the uncertainty, a few additional sources that have a bearing on the question must be examined.

5. Aristotle understands his noetic quest of the ground as bringing to fruition what mytho-speculation had intended. With regard to the vocabulary for dealing with the problems of the aetiological chain, it is fully developed. There are terms for things (*ta onta, ousiai*), their causes (*aitia*), the chain or series (*euthuoria*) of causes, the position of causes on the chain as intermediate (*meson*), last (eschaton), and first (*proton*), for infinity (*apeiron*) and limit (*peras*) of a series, and for the first cause in its quality of an origin or beginning (*arche*) of all things (994a1ff.). With regard to the argument, it is directed against the Ionian and Italian philosophers who tried to construct an aetiological chain by means of hyletic causes. Aristotle

considers this procedure plagued with the fallacy of an infinite series, because matter or an element is no true beginning of anything—"for wood does not make a bed, nor bronze a statue, but something else is the cause [*arche*] of change" (984a25). The generation of one thing from another can not go on indefinitely, such as, *e.g.*, flesh from earth, earth from air, air from fire, and so forth without a limit (*peras*); neither can, in an ascending chain, man be moved by air, air by the sun, the sun by strife, and so forth (994a1ff.). This type of chain is inadmissible because an intermediate term is always the cause of the immediately following one without being a first cause; in an infinite series, however, all terms are intermediate, and therefore none is the first. "Thus, if there is no first term there is no cause at all" (994a19). Not just anything, it appears, can serve as *arche;* but if the intracosmic gods are denied to the philosopher, and matter falls under the ban as well, what is it? The question becomes acute on occasion of human action and its final cause: "The what-for of a thing is its fulfillment [*telos*], *i.e.*, it must not be for the sake of another thing but all things must be for its sake; hence, if there is to be a last term [*eschaton*] of this kind, the series must not be infinite [*apeiron*]; for if there is no last term, there is no what-for. Those, however, who insist on an infinite series do not understand that thereby they abolish the nature of the good [*ten tou agathou physin*], for nobody would try to do anything, if he did not reach the end with it. Also there would be no reason [*nous*] in the world; for man, as he has reason [*nous echon*], will always act for an end—fulfillment [*telos*] is an end [*peras*]" (994bff.). This argument of Aristotle's, fundamental in *Nicomachean Ethics* and *Politics*, is conventionally called teleological— but teleology unfortunately is no more than a dignified but unfounded opinion about the order of things once the question of *telos* is taken out of its experiential context. As the passage just quoted shows, this context is the experience of man's reaching out, by means of his *nous*, for the no ʾtikon. The argument for the limited chain would be badly misunderstood if it were taken for an attempt to "prove" the limit or its nature. On the contrary, it shows certain constructions to be untenable because they are in conflict with the noetic experience. That the chain has to have a limit, and the limit a certain nature, is not the result of the argument but is its premise derived from exploring the noetic dimensions of non-existence. This position, however, compels questions concerning Aristotle's criteria in judging a construction true or false. A modern intellectual would gladly jump to the defense of Ionian philosophers and Sophists and truculently demand: What proof do you have for the existence of a First Cause or a Highest Good? Obviously, if Aristotle's position is to make sense, reason and truth must mean more than ratiocination and its result; reason must be a something that implies as its content, as it were, the truth about the area of reality covered by the symbolism of aetiological chains.

6. With regard to this complex of questions, Aristotle's articulation has not fully emerged from cosmological compactness inasmuch as the term *aletheia* has to carry the meanings of both truth and reality. As a consequence, the principal passage on *aletheia* (993b20ff.), though perfectly clear with regard to its intent, is next to untranslatable into a modern language, and the translations offered inevitably must pay their tribute of distortion to the ambiguity of meaning. The interpretation must resort therefore to paraphrase and commentary. Aristotle begins with the general proposition that philosophy is "knowledge [*episteme*] of truth-reality [*aletheia*]." Injecting the active strain of *epistasthai*, he then continues: Theoretical knowledge issues into truth-reality as its fulfillment (*telos*), while practical knowledge issues into action; for practical men, even when they investigate how a thing is, will not study the everlasting but the here and now about it. "But we [the philosophers] do not know what is true-real apart from the cause." The stage is now set for the argument proper: In the aetiological chain, the cause ranks higher than the thing it causes, and *causing* means imparting reality of the same kind to the thing caused. "The thing that imparts to other things reality of the same name [*to synonymon*] is, in relation to these other things, supremely the thing of this kind [*malista auto*], as, e.g., fire is hottest because it is to other things the cause of their heat." The conception of reality and causation exemplified by the instance of heat, then, is generalized to apply to all existent things with regard to their being as things: "Hence, the most true-real [*alethestaton*] thing is that which to other things is their cause of being true-real [*alethes*]." The immediately following sentence, drawing the conclusion for the first causes (*archai*) of things, is so tightly constructed that it can be rendered only by paraphrase: Since this world of our experience has

always the structure of existent things, their causes (*archas*) must of necessity be always the most true-real (*alethestatas*) things. They cannot be only sometimes true-real (*alethes*) and sometimes not, nor is there a further cause imparting being (*einai*) to them, but they are the cause to the other things. Hence all things (existent things as well as non-existent *archai*) have the character of truth (*aletheia*) that corresponds to their being (*einai*). This subject matter is resumed in *Metaphysics* XII by the formal statement "Everything [*ousia*] is generated by what is of the same name [*ek synonymou*]" (1070a4f.). On this generating *arche* hang "the heaven and the physical universe [*physis*]" (1072b13ff.)—especially the *nous* by which we recognize the synonymity of the *arche*. For reason (*nous*) is moved by the intelligible (*noeton*), the first among intelligibles is substance or thing (*ousia*), and the first among substances is the first by actual being (*energeia*) (1072a30ff.). The noetic act (*noesis*), however, makes *nous* participate in the *noeton* (or makes it one with the intelligible in the mode of participation [*metalepsis*]); or inversely, that which is receptive of the *noeton* or *ousia* is *nous* (1072b20ff.). Moreover, while the noetic act is on principle always concerned with what is best in itself, the act of the highest rank (*malista*) is concerned with what is best in the highest rank (*malista*, 1072b19ff.). Hence, the thing (*ousia*) that is the origin of all things, and especially of *nous*, must be a *noesis noeseos*, a noetic act acting on itself—i.e., an *actus purus* (1074b35). The existence as *actus purus*, however, is marvelous (*thaumaston*) (1072b26). The philosopher, if he has to dispense with the *thaumasia* of the myth, has at least a *thaumaston* in the end.

3

The Eclipse of Reality

By an act of imagination man can shrink himself to a self that is "condemned to be free." To this shrunken or contracted self, as we shall call it, God is dead, the past is dead, the present is the flight from the self's non-essential facticity toward being what it is not, the future is the field of possibles among which the self must choose its project of being beyond mere facticity, and freedom is the necessity of making a choice that will determine the self's own being. The freedom of the contracted self is the self's damnation not to be able not to be free.

The contraction of his humanity to a self imprisoned in its self-hood is the characteristic of so-called modern man. It becomes recognizable as a personal and social process in the eighteenth century, when man begins to refer to himself, not as Man, but as a Self, an Ego, an I, an Individual, a Subject, a Transcendental Subject, a Transcendental Consciousness, and so forth; and it reaches an intense clarity of its own structure in the twentieth century, when a Jean-Paul Sartre, whose formula I have used in describing the contracted self, submits this type of deficient existence to the analysis of his *L'être et le néant.*

As neither the man who engages in deforming himself to a self ceases to be a man; nor the surrounding reality of God and man, world and society does change its structure; nor the relations between man and his surrounding reality can be abolished; frictions between the shrunken self and reality are bound to develop. The man who suffers from the disease of contraction, however, is not inclined to leave the prison of his selfhood, in order to remove the

"The Eclipse of Reality," completed by about 1969, is a typescript found in Box 76, Folder 5, Voegelin Papers, Hoover Institution Archives. The first fifteen pages of the typescript were published in 1970 (*cf.* the Editorial Note on this text).

frictions. He rather will put his imagination to further work and surround the imaginary self with an imaginary reality apt to confirm the self in its pretense of reality; he will create a Second Reality, as the phenomenon is called, in order to screen the First Reality of common experience from his view. The frictions consequently, far from being removed, will grow into a general conflict between the world of his imagination and the real world.

This conflict can be traced from the discrepancy of contents between realities imagined and experienced, through the act of projecting an imaginary reality, to the man who indulges in the act. First, on the level of contents, a reality projected by imagination may deform or omit certain areas of reality experienced; reality projected, we may say, obscures or eclipses First Reality. Ascending from contents to the act, then, one can discern a man's intention to eclipse reality. This intention can become manifest in a large variety of forms, ranging from the straight lie concerning a fact to the subtler lie of arranging a context in such a manner that the omission of the fact will not be noticed; or from the construction of a system that, by its form, suggests its partial view as the whole of reality to its author's refusal to discuss the premises of the system in terms of reality experienced. Beyond the act, finally, we reach the actor, that is the man who has committed the act of deforming his humanity to a self and now lets the shrunken self eclipse his own full reality. He will deny his humanity and insist he is nothing but his shrunken self; he will deny ever having experienced the reality of common experience; he will deny that anybody could have a fuller perception of reality than he allows his self; in brief, he will set the contracted self as a model for himself as well as for everybody else. Moreover, his insistence on conformity will be aggressive—and in this aggressiveness there betrays itself the anxiety and alienation of the man who has lost contact with reality.

But what is Reality? Moving with conventional language, we had to use the term in more than one sense, and the several meanings seem to be at cross-purposes: A reality projected by imagination, it is true, is not the reality of common experience. Nevertheless, a man's act of deforming himself is as real as the man who commits it, and his act of projecting a Second Reality is as real as the First Reality it intends to hide from view. The imaginator, his act of imagination, and the effects the act has on himself as well as on

other people, thus, can claim to be real. Some imaginative constructions of history, designed to shield the contracted self, as for
instance those of Comte, or Hegel, or Marx, even have grown into
social forces of such strength that their conflicts with reality form
a substantial part of global politics in our time. The man with a
contracted self is as much of a power in society and history as an
ordinary man, and sometimes a stronger one. The conflict *with* reality turns out to be a disturbance *within* reality.

The multiple meanings of reality are not caused by loose usage of
the term, but reflect the structure of reality itself. To be conscious
of something is an experiential process polarized by the cognitive
tension between the knower and the known. The several meanings
of reality can be made intelligible by going through the successive
acts of reflection on the process of consciousness: If, in a first act of
reflection on the process, we turn toward the pole of the known,
the object of cognition will be the something we acknowledge as
real. If, in a second act, we turn toward the pole of the knower, the
human carrier of cognition as well as his images and language symbols referring to the known, will move into the position of the
something to be acknowledged as real. And if, in a third act, we
turn toward the experiential process and the cognitive tension as a
whole, the process will become the something we acknowledge as
real. Following the acts of reflection, the meaning of reality moves
from the known to the knower and ultimately to the process that is
structured by the participation of, and by the cognitive tension between, the knower and the known in the experience. The consciousness of reality becomes a process within reality.

Only on the level of reflection established by the third act there
will come into view the problem of disturbances in the process. In
the commonsense attitude of everyday life, we take the experiential process as undisturbed for granted: The knower refers to the
known through the images and language symbols engendered by
the event or process that we call experience, and living in this attitude we assume the experiences will be reliable and the symbols
engendered will truly refer to the known. Nor will the philosopher
surrender common sense when he engages in reflective thought,
but will assume reality to be knowable in truth—even to the limit
of knowing in truth that some things are unknowable. In Hellenic
philosophy, where the problem becomes thematic for the first time,

the term *aletheia* is burdened, therefore, with the double meaning of Truth and Reality; and even a speculation that deviates in its course as widely from common sense as Hegel's does, starts from a reality known by sense perception with truth and certainty. This commonsense assumption concerning the truth of images, on which the main line of philosophy is based, will have to be qualified, however, when we encounter persons who produce imagery at variance with the images supposed to be true. Imagination, it appears, can cut loose from reality and produce the sets of images that we call Second Reality because they pretend to refer to reality though in fact they do not; and, setting aside the phenomena of error or of imperfectly articulated experience, imagination will cut loose in this manner, when the imagining man has developed centers of resistance to participating in reality, including his own, so that his imagery will no longer be true but express reality in terms of his resistance to it. We are faced with the phenomenon of a cognitive tension of consciousness that will retain its form of referring to reality even when in substance the contact with reality has been lost for one reason or another. Moreover, since imagination can eclipse but not abolish reality, not only the form of consciousness will be retained, but the whole reality of common experience that apparently has been lost will remain present to consciousness, though its presence will now be marked by various indices of non-reality according to the character and degree of the disturbance. For reality eclipsed but not abolished will exert a pressure to emerge into consciousness, and thereby to achieve full status of reality, that must be countered by acts of suppression—a reality to be eclipsed can be relegated to the limbo of oblivion that we call the unconscious; or it can remain semi-conscious as a disturbing background to reality imagined; or it can be consciously denied the status of reality, as in the dogma of no-God; or it can induce a state of revolt, because it cannot be denied but is sensed to be hostile, as in certain Gnostic speculations. A man deformed, thus, can well be conscious of his deformation, and indeed may experience his existence as a hell in which he is condemned to act as if he had the freedom of a man undeformed.

The major thinkers who suffer from the compulsion to deform their humanity to a self are never quite unaware of what they are doing. From the eighteenth to the twentieth century, the stream of Second Realities is paralleled, therefore, by a stream of self-analysis. There are the surprisingly frank confessions of the intellectual tricks employed in accomplishing the imaginative feat of the moment; there are the conscientious explanations why the present Second Reality had to be produced in opposition to those already encumbering the public scene; and there are the shrewd inquiries into the author's self that compels him to do what, at the same time, he senses to be a misdeed. Self-analysis is so much the accompaniment of imaginative projections that the age of Second Realities has become the great age of Psychology. A peculiar compound of insight and intellectual dishonesty has developed; and this honest dishonesty has become an enduring twilight mode of existence, replacing the clear existential rhythms of degenerative fall and regenerative repentance. A character of compulsive action against better knowledge, very marked for instance in Marx and Nietzsche, pervades the process of deformation and must be considered in part responsible for certain oddities of its historical contour—such as the tiresome elaboration of problems into irrelevant detail, the resumption of problems exploded long ago, epigonal revivals of positions one would have thought abandoned for good, in brief: a compulsive repetitiveness that defies all rational predictions of an end when the problems are exhausted. When, for instance, an imaginative outburst of such grandeur as the Hegelian attempt at salvation through conceptual speculation (*Begriffsspekulation*) had run its course; when it, furthermore, had been followed by Max Stirner's exposure of the contracted self in its naked misery as the motivating core of all current philosophies of history, projective psychologies, and new humanisms; when, thus, the Second Realities protecting the self had been torn to shreds, and nothing was left to be done but to abandon the contracted self and stop the deformation of humanity; one might have expected [Stirner's] *Der Einzige und sein Eigentum* (1844) to have a sobering effect on the intellectuals engaged in the game of deformation. But nothing of the sort happened. On the contrary, at the time when Stirner wrote and published *Der Einzige,* the young Marx prepared a new philosophy of history, improved on Feuerbach's projective psychology, developed one more humanism, and imagined a revolution that would metamorphose man into a Superman and thus redeem man, society, and history from the evil of alienation. That is not to say that we cannot discern an advance of insight through the cycles and epicycles of the process; today we certainly know more about its problems than the thinkers of the eighteenth century possibly could know. Nevertheless, neither the recognition of advancing insight, nor the increased sophistication of analysis or the aesthetic satisfactions it grants, must blind us to the fact that Sartre's *moi* of 1943 is still lost in the same dead-end as Stirner's *Ich* of 1844. The process has run itself to death, both metaphorically and literally, and yet it does not stop. Modern man has become a bore.

I have stressed the compulsive repetitiveness of the process, the atmosphere of slaves treading the mill without hope of escape. Perhaps I have stressed it too strongly. Existence in the twilight zone of projective imagination and self-analytical insight, it is true, pertinaciously preserves its structure during its long course from the middle of the eighteenth century to the present. Nevertheless, the manifestations of the constant mode of existence are more than individuals of a species, and their sequence in time is more than a series of interchangeable events. For deformed existence has its dynamics; and the dynamics intrudes a distinct pattern into the course. Let us list the rules of the dynamics:

1. When imaginators of Second Realities proceed to act on their imaginative assumptions and try to make the world of common experience conform to their respective dreams, the areas of friction with reality will rapidly increase in number and size.

2. As the world of common experience can be eclipsed but not abolished, it will resist its deformation and, in its turn, force the imaginators to revise their Second Realities. Imaginative projecting will not be given up as senseless, but specific projects will be changed in detail or replaced by new ones. During the period under discussion, revisionism is a common phenomenon, caused by the refusal to dissolve the contracted self and to stop projecting.

3. When conflicts with reality compel revisions with some frequency over a period, the activity of projecting can pass from a phase of comparatively naïve indulgence to one of a more critical occupation with the standards of projects. For a Second Reality must, on the one hand, satisfy the requirements of the contracted self and, on the other hand, contain enough uneclipsed reality not to be ignored as a crackpot scheme by the contemporaries. There is a remarkable advance from the comparatively loose anthropologies and philosophies of history of the eighteenth century to the tight interlocking of Hegel's *Phaenomenologie, Logik, Philosophie des Rechts,* and *Philosophie der Geschichte.*

4. When a more or less stable balance between the contracted self and satisfactory Second Realities has been achieved—as it has by the work of Comte, Hegel, and Marx—the interest can shift from the construction of further Second Realities to the problems of deformation. The twilight mode of existence can become an independent field of study.

Under pressure from the dynamics just adumbrated, the process of deformation has developed a recognizable and intelligible pattern in history: There are to be noted two periods, of about equal length, marked by the shift of accent from the projection of new Second Realities to the inquiry into the type of existence that engages in their projection. In the century from Turgot, Kant, and Condorcet to Hegel, Comte, and Marx, the weight lies on the construction of philosophies of history, of the great designs that will justify the deformation of humanity as the meaning and end of history, and assure the contracted self of its righteousness when it imposes itself on society and the world at large. In the century from Kierkegaard and Stirner, through Nietzsche and Freud, to Heidegger and Sartre, the weight shifts toward the inquiry concerning deformed existence. The early philosophers of history and the late existentialist thinkers, thus, are more intimately related than the surface differences of their fields of interest would suggest. For the shift of weight means that the early constructs, purposely designed to eclipse historical reality, have performed their task so well that, to the latecomers in the movement of deformation, history is, if not altogether, at least sufficiently dead not to disturb by memories of a fuller humanity the concern with the contracted self.

To the texture of man's existence in general belong the moods. We must avert to the issue of the moods, because the age of the contracted self has engendered a whole sheaf of neologisms that express fluctuations of mood, such as *optimism, pessimism, egotism, altruism, egomania, monomania,* and *nihilism*—a fact that suggests that existence compulsively deformed has a mood peculiarly its own. Moreover, the dynamics of deformed existence has caused a historical polarization of the fluctuations similar to the shift of accent from the projection of Second Realities to self-analysis. For the shift of accents is accompanied by a change of mood from eighteenth-century exhilaration by the projects of building a new world, and confidence of being equal to the task, to twentieth-century disorientation, frustration, despair, and sense of damnation in face of the accumulated results of projecting.

We can approach the question of the peculiar mood through Hegel's recall, in his *Philosophy of History,* of the general excitement aroused by the events of the French Revolution:

> As long as the sun stands in heaven and the planets revolve around it, has it not happened that man stood on his head, that is on his thought, and built reality in conformity to it. Anaxagoras had been the first to say that Nous governs the world; but only now has man gained the insight that thought should govern spiritual reality. This was a splendid sunrise; all thinking beings shared in celebrating the epoch. The age was ruled by a sublime emotion, the world trembled as the enthusiasm of the spirit [*Geist*] pervaded it, as if only now the divine had been truly reconciled to the world.[1]

The text is of particular value to our purpose because it is couched in one of the several languages of deformation. The question of the new languages will be treated in a later context; let it suffice for the present that coining a new language, either by giving new meanings to familiar terms or by inventing new technical terms, is one of the most effective devices for eclipsing reality. That Hegel's recall is written in one of these newspeaks makes for certain difficulties of understanding, but it also makes us more sharply aware of the unity of texture, of the style that characterizes deformed existence from the compulsive deformation of humanity, through the deformation of language and the projection of Second Realities, to the odd moods that accompany the operation.

At first reading, the text seems to be a piece of nonsense because the sentences will apparently not render a coherent immanent meaning. If we assume both Thought and Spirit to be translations of the Greek Nous, and therefore to be used as synonyms, how can Thought have come to govern the Spiritual World? If we try again and assume Thought and Spirit not to be synonyms, but only Thought to translate Nous, what is meant by the Spirit it has come to govern? But when we read on and learn that the world has been pervaded by the enthusiasm of the Spirit, now that Thought has come to govern the world, it sounds as if Thought and Spirit were the same after all. Well, there are no answers to such questions

---

1. Georg Hegel, *Philosophie der Geschichte,* ed. F. Braunstaedt (Stuttgart, 1961), 593. This is Voegelin's translation.

arising from close reading; the text will remain unintelligible as long as we expect it to be consistent by commonsense logic. The difficulties will dissolve, however, and the text render its meaning, if we accept Hegel's dialectical logic—that is his project of a Second Reality. If we read the passage in the light of Hegelian dialectics of history, the Nous of Anaxagoras and Aristotle will be the divine Spirit that governs a world removed from divinity; Thought will be the name of the divine Spirit when, in the dialectical course of history, it has gained the "objective form" of human thinking that enables it "to reach effectively into external reality" because now it is immanent to the world in which it operates; and the Spiritual World will be the world of man, society, and history in which the divine Spirit, having gained the objective form of human thought, operates effectively. If in this manner we provide a dictionary for translating the language of dialectics into the language of common sense, the text will become intelligible: Hegel, it turns out, is a metastatic thinker who believes that man can transform the world, which exists in tension toward God, into the very Realm of God itself. Ordinary man, of course, cannot accomplish this extraordinary feat—first the divine Spirit must have become incarnate in the Thought of man, and that it has done in the events of the French Revolution. History has found a new epoch, for the divine, which had been only imperfectly reconciled to the world when God became man in Christ, has come to be truly reconciled to the world now that the Thought of man has provided the divine Spirit with its objective form. Hegel conceives history as moving from the Nous that governs the world, to the God who becomes man, and finally to the man who becomes God. To Hegel, God is dead because man-god at last has come to life and will create a new realm in his image. To sum it up: The Hegelian man-god has eclipsed the reality of God and history and thereby gained both the freedom and authority to project Second Realities and impose them on the world. Shorn of the paraphernalia of dialectics, Hegel's Thought is a contracted self that closely resembles Sartre's *moi.*

The mood of deformed existence is subject to remarkable fluctuations. Hegel recalls it as a state of elation—but he has to recall it. The elation of the years in which he worked toward the great outburst of his *Phaenomenologie* of 1807 is no longer quite the mood of the time when he wrote the recall, more than twenty years later—even though in his later years he had not at all abandoned his views of reconciliation or of salvation through projecting a speculative system. The milder fluctuations, it is true, can be explained by the disenchantment following the realization that an imaginative project does indeed not effectively transform reality. But how do we account for the great historical oscillations between the extremes of exuberant confidence and black despair?

The spiritual disease that causes such extremely disparate symptoms was diagnosed by a healthier mind than Hegel's, by Jean Paul, in his *Vorschule der Aesthetik* of 1804. At the time when Hegel was elated Jean Paul wrote:

> When God sets—like the sun sets—on an age, then soon the world will be in darkness: the scorner of the All (*des All*) respects nothing but his own self, and in the ensuing night he is afraid of nothing but his own creatures.[2]

As if he had Hegel's text lying before him and were devising the most suitable counterformula to the recall, Jean Paul describes the sunrise of Thought as the sunset of God. When the contracted self rises, the reality of God will be eclipsed; and since God can be eclipsed but not abolished, the mood of elation cannot be sustained; the presence of God makes itself felt in the fluctuation of the mood from the earlier confidence of self-assertation to the later anxiety and despair.

Moreover, when the phase of despair has been reached in the process, the man who experiences it must express it by means of the very symbols used by Jean Paul in his diagnosis. Jean Paul's symbols of Night and Nothing reappear when Nietzsche describes the mood of the men who murdered God, in *Froehliche Wissenschaft* (Aphorism 125):

> What did we do when we cut the earth loose from the sun? Whither is it moving now? Whither are we moving? Away from all suns? Are we not falling all the time? Backward, sideward, forward, in all directions? Is there still an above and below? Are we not groping as through an infinite nothing? . . . Is there not night falling and evermore night?

Hegel was elated because God at last was dead and the man-god had convincingly revealed himself in the events of the French Revolution; Nietzsche knew despair because by his time insight

---

2. Jean Paul, *Sämtliche Werke* (Weimar, 1935), XI, 22.

into the problems of deformation had advanced far enough to make him aware that God certainly had been murdered but that the man-god, the Superman, had yet to appear.

But let us return once more to Jean Paul; for not only had he diagnosed the darkness underneath Hegel's elation, eighty years before it was experienced and expressed by Nietzsche, he also knew why the Superman, in whom Nietzsche still placed his hope, would never appear and make an end to the falling and groping in the infinite Nothing. In the *Vorschule* he speaks of the spirit of the age (*Zeitgeist*), its "lawless arbitrariness" and its "egomania," and then continues:

> It [the *Zeitgeist*] would egomaniacly annihilate the world [*Welt*] and the All [*All*], in order to empty the field and to gain free play for itself in the Nothing.[3]

The empty field of Nothing results from the eclipse of reality; Jean Paul has recognized its imaginary character. No projection of a man-god can overcome the Nothing, for the Nothing has been projected, by the man who deforms himself, for the very purpose of indulging in the projection of the man-god. Man can eclipse the reality of God by imagining a Nothing, but he cannot overcome the imagined Nothing by filling it with imagined somethings.

To recognize the empty field of the Nothing as resulting from an act of imagination, however, is not to say that there is not a real problem of nothingness; on the contrary, man can project the imaginary field of the Nothing only when he has really fallen into nothingness by contracting his humanity to a self. Thus, on the level of the mood, with regard to Nothing and Anxiety, we encounter a compound of reality and imagination, corresponding to the compound of insight and intellectual dishonesty that characterizes deformed existence. Or inversely, the deformation of existence affects the whole of its texture down to the mood that moves in the amplitude of elation and despair.[4]

Eclipsing reality is a complex operation. It can be made fully intelligible—with regard to its purpose, its structure, its rules of con-

3. *Ibid.*
4. The preceding pages are those previously published in 1970. Voegelin's typescript continued without interruption into the text printed here.

struction, its frictions and revisions, and its ultimate failure—only by the analysis of concrete instances of deformation. We shall now proceed, therefore, from the general description of the process to a case study.

The form that the case study has to assume is determined by the characteristics of the historical process. They are, on the one hand, the constancy of the twilight mode of existence throughout the period from the eighteenth to the twentieth century and, on the other hand, the shift of accent from projection to self-analysis. If only the first characteristic were to be considered, any case chosen at random would be satisfactory; in view of the second characteristic, however, the case, in order to be representative, must be a pair of cases: an early one, representing the exuberance of projecting, and a late one, representing the predominance of self-analysis. The documents best suited to our purpose proved to be, for the eighteenth century, three lectures from Friedrich Schiller's course on Universal History and, for the twentieth century, Jean-Paul Sartre's chapter on "Bad Faith" from his *L'être et le néant*.

The three lectures from Schiller's course are the introductory lecture on the question "What Do We Call, and to What Purpose Do We Study, Universal History?" and the two further lectures, "On the First Community of Men, in the Light of the Mosaic Document" and "The Mission of Moses." In the introductory lecture, Schiller concentrates so exclusively on his imaginative project of Universal History that the contraction of humanity to a self— which must be presupposed, if one wants to make sense of the project—becomes only marginally thematic. The two following lectures, however, give us direct access to the process of contraction. Hence, I shall deal with the Moses lectures first.

The Moses lectures share with the introductory lecture the unshaken confidence that projecting a Second Reality is a meaningful enterprise. Schiller is not reflectively concerned with the existential sense of his operation but simply constructs an image of the self, apparently with the best of conscience, by deforming the meaning of biblical symbols and by replacing them with the imagery of contraction. The resulting catalog of deformations and transformations is of considerable value for our purpose, because the realities to be eclipsed are explicitly enumerated and correlated with the eclipsing images. The transformations I have selected are the ones that have a direct bearing on the issue of contraction:

1. Schiller deforms the meaning of the Fall of man, as related in the Book of Genesis, by interpreting it as the emancipation of reason from nature. The voice of God, prohibiting man to eat from the Tree of Knowledge, he changes into the voice of man's natural instinct. Man's disobedience to his instinct is "the first manifestation of his self-activity, the first venture of his reason, the first beginning of his moral existence [Dasein]."⁵ This reinterpretation of the Fall resumes the ancient gnostic inversion of the Fall of man as a Promethean revolt against God.

2. If the symbolism of God and man in the tension of command and obedience is to be superseded by the tension between nature and reason, the pneumatic experience that engenders revelatory symbols must itself be eclipsed. To this purpose, Schiller transforms the history of Moses into the history of a Freemason who was able to overcome the "polytheistic superstition" by a "Deistic" conception of God. This is the story: In high antiquity, an unknown Egyptian priest had observed the "physical economy of nature" and conceived the idea of "a general connection of all things." Moreover, he had advanced from this "idea" to the conception of a "Highest Being," of "a sole and supreme intellect," as the "Demiurge" of the "general connection" (383–85). The priest communicated his new truth about God to select persons able to share it; the group formed a small temple community and organized a mystery cult in order to hide the truth from the vulgar; and the community perpetuated itself through the initiation of new members who could advance to the full knowledge of truth only by a series of degrees. The precautions were necessary because Egyptian

5. Friedrich Schiller, *Historichen Schriften* (Weimar, 1970), 399, Vol. XVI of Schiller, *Werke*, ed. Lieselotte Blumenthal and Benno von Wiese. All quotations from these lectures are taken from this source. The first lecture, "What Do We Call, and to What Purpose Do We Study, Universal History?" ("Was heißt und zu welchem Ende studiert man Universalgeschichte?"), is found on pp. 359–76; the second, "The Mission of Moses" ("Die Sendung Moses"), on pp. 377–97; and the third, "On the First Community of Men, in the Light of the Mosaic Document" ("Etwas über die erste Menschengesellschaft nach dem Leitfaden der mosaischen Urkunde"), on pp. 398–413. Subsequent citations to these lectures will be given by page number, parenthetically in the text.

society and government were institutionally geared to polytheistic superstition, so that free propagation of the truth might have led to revolutionary upheavals, probably ending in the slaughter of the cult members. The Egyptian mystery of Deism and its cultic organization served as a model to the Freemason lodges of the eighteenth century. Moses himself, thus, had nothing to do with the origins of Deism. However, though he was born a Hebrew, he had been educated as an Egyptian priest and initiated in the Deistic cult. When he became the liberator of his people, his conscience would not allow him to give them a false religion of the polytheistic type, and yet, considering their degraded state, he could not divulge to them a truth about God they were not able to receive. In this dilemma, there occurred to him the idea of equipping the one and true God with the appurtenances of a polytheistic divinity, including such revelation stories as the Thornbush Episode, and of leaving it to reason to disengage, in a millennial history, the truth from the falsehood in which he had to clothe it. When the truth that had been the property of a small community was transformed in this manner into the religion of a people, it could become historically effective, so that "after a slow evolution" the doctrine of the one God, accepted by the people as a matter of "blind belief," did at last mature "in the brighter minds to a concept of reason [Vernunftbegriff]" (376). Disguising the truth of the Demiurge and transferring the disguised truth to a people thus was the great achievement of Moses. In its wake, Israel had its role in universal history, because Christianity and Islam were built on the foundation of Moses. Moreover, "in a certain sense it is incontestably true that we owe to the Mosaic religion a good deal of the Enlightenment we enjoy today" (376). Hence, without "denying the unworthiness and baseness of the people [die Unwürdigkeit und Verworfenheit der Nation]," we must respect Israel as "an impure and mean vessel, used to preserve something very precious" (376).

3. The God who reveals himself is dead, but there still remains the pale god of man's Deistic conception. By a reflection on the meaning of Providence, Schiller lets him pale so far that he becomes practically invisible: In the life of Moses, in his brilliant idea of disguising the Demiurge as Jehovah, and in the role of Israel in history, we must acknowledge "the great hand of Providence [Vorsicht]" (381). By providence, however, must not be understood

124

"the Providence which, by the violent means of miracles, inter-
feres with the economy of nature," but the other providence that
has given "to nature such an economy that even extraordinary
things can be brought about in a quiet manner." Once "providence," which still smacks of an agency beyond nature, has done
the work of incorporating its plans into the economy of nature, it
can be treated as synonymous with a "destiny" immanent to nature. Schiller states that, in view of the people's degradation, no
Hebrew could have become the liberator of Israel. He then asks,
"What device [Ausweg] did destiny choose to achieve its purpose?"
and he answers, it let a Hebrew be educated as an Egyptian, so that
he could "become the instrument for the nation to escape from
bondage" (381). Through a series of transformations—God of Revelation, god of Deism, anonymous providence, immanent destiny—
Schiller arrives at an image of the agency responsible for meaning
in history that is practically Hegel's List der Vernunft.

4. A further act of transformation needs some unraveling. The
pertinent passage introduces the personnel that propagate biblical
and Enlightenment symbols respectively. Schiller calls the two
types the "people's teacher [Volkslehrer]" and the "philosopher"
(400): The "people's teacher" is justified when he speaks of the
event told in the Genesis story as the Fall and draws useful moral
doctrine from it; but not less justified is the "philosopher" when
he considers the same event to be the decisive step of human nature toward perfection. The Fall, it is true, transforms the perfect
child of nature into an "imperfect moral being," and yet it elevates
man from an "automaton" of nature to a moral being which, though
imperfect, is destined to climb the historical ladder at the top of
which it will reach self-rule (Selbstherrschaft). At first sight, the
passage appears to rank the two types of personnel as equal inasmuch as each type has hold of one part of the full truth. The impression is deceptive, however, for Schiller has reduced the truth of
faith to a moral doctrine useful for educating the common people,
with the term people to be read in the derogatory sense of a lower
intellectual rank. As a consequence, the prophets, theologians,
priests, and presumably also Christ are degraded to teachers of a
doctrine for the people, while the Enlightenment philosophes are
promoted to an intellectual elite having converse among themselves. The new "philosophers"—classical philosophers are never

mentioned—represent "self-activity [*Selbsttätigkeit*]" (399) and the advance of man toward "self-rule [*Selbstherrschaft*]" (400); they represent the historical "climbing of the ladder." The "people's teachers," on the other hand, are cast in the role of a reactionary clergy bent on preserving the state of imperfection. The principal transformations hidden in the involved text seem to be the following: Schiller, first, transforms the truth of revelatory experience into a "doctrine," so that he can oppose to it the doctrine of the contracted self; or, more accurately, he finds the transformation in the ecclesiastical environment of his time, accepts or pretends to accept it as the truth of faith, and opposes to it the equally doctrinal truth of self-active reason. He then transforms the degenerative, doctrinal form of Christianity current in his environment— with considerable justification—into a people's truth to which he can oppose the truth of reason as the truth of an intellectual elite. Finally, he transforms the people's truth of his time—and here his good faith would have to be doubted, unless we could plead the general philosophical illiteracy of the age in his favor—into a truth characteristic of an early phase in the history of mankind, now to be superseded by reason that has come of age (*mündig*) (399). By means of these transformations Schiller eclipses the reality of revelatory and philosophical symbols together with the reality they express. The past is dead; we are living in an apocalyptic present in which a backward "people" is to be led toward maturity by the historical vanguard of the "philosophers."

5. Finally, there emerges the terrestrial paradise as the purpose of the deforming operation. Man is destined to be "the creator of his happiness and only that part of it which he owed to himself will determine the degree of his happiness" (399). The state of innocence he has lost through the awakening of reason he will regain through the use of his reason, for "from a paradise of ignorance and servitude" he will advance, "and if it takes many thousands of years, to a paradise of knowledge and freedom" (399). The paradise to be regained by Grace and Faith thus will be eclipsed by the paradise to be regained by self-activity and reason. The deformer of his humanity will enter an imaginary state of paradisical existence by means of an imaginary act of self-salvation.

Human existence has a number of dimensions: Man exists as a consciousness in the tension between time and eternity; his existence as consciousness is founded in his existence as a body in the time of the external world; and his existence both conscious and bodily is not only personal but social and historical as well. A deforming operation, in order to eclipse the reality of existence effectively, would have to extend its imaginative projects in all of the several dimensions. The deformations of the Moses lectures, however, do not eclipse the whole of existential reality but pertain primarily to consciousness in its dimension of person-society-history. God is deformed to an economy of nature and man to a self-activity of reason, so that the tension between time and eternity can be eclipsed by the tension between nature and reason; the Fall is deformed to a Revolt, so that man can become his own creator and savior; the revelation to Moses and Israel is deformed to the rational ideas of an Egyptian Deist and the ingenious devices of Moses; the history of salvation—ranging from the Fall and Moses through Israel, Christianity, and Islam to the Enlightenment—has become the process in which the truth of reason is being disengaged from superstitious dressings, until the terrestrial paradise of rational self-rule is reached, or about to be reached, in Schiller's own present. The Second Reality arising from the deformations thus roughly corresponds to the *historia sacra* symbolism of Christian tradition. At least a part of the Second Realities developed in the process of deforming humanity apparently has the purpose of providing the contracted self with a sacred history that will satisfy its requirements.

The *historia sacra* of the Moses lectures is complemented by the *historia profana* of the introductory lecture on Universal History, in which Schiller is not concerned with sacred history but with the civilizational gap between Western and primitive societies. The discoveries made by the European navigators in distant seas and lands have resulted in "a spectacle both instructive and entertaining" (364): There are the peoples of various degrees of civilization (*Bildung, Kultur*) surrounding the Western world like children of various ages standing around a grown-up, recalling to him by their example what once he had been and from where he began. A wise hand seems to have preserved these primitive (*rohe*) peoples to the time when we, in our civilization, would have advanced far enough to apply the discoveries to ourselves and to reconstruct the lost beginnings of our race from this mirror (364). A look at primitive societies will tell us what we have been; a look at contemporary Western society, what we are now. In the present state of our world we enjoy the advantages of a balanced system of states, of the institutions of property, marriage, and family, and of internal security. Man's abilities are no longer tied down by the necessity of survival; he is free to follow the call of his genius. Religion has been ennobled by philosophy; Leibniz and Locke have done as much for the dogma and morality of Christianity as the brush of Raphael and Correggio for its sacred history. The asocial troglodyte has become a civilized thinker and man of the world; all thinking heads are linked by a cosmopolitan bond (*weltbürgerliches Band*). The beginnings were "barbarian"; the present is the "age of reason" (366–67).

The movement "from one extreme to the other" (367) is the subject-matter of universal history. But how does one write the history of an inexhaustible stream of events, especially as we have only incomplete knowledge of it? Schiller formulates the rules that will enable us to perform the task:

1. "There is a long chain of events reaching from the present moment back to the beginnings of the human race, interlocked like cause and effect" (370). Universal history is rectilinear and must be constructed from the present backward. "The real sequence of events descends from the origin of things to their newest order; the universal historian ascends from the most recent state of the world toward the origin of things" (372). From the inexhaustible "sum of events" the historian will select those that have "an essential, incontestable, and easily traceable influence" on the present state of the world and the state of the presently living generation. "That is the world history that we have" (372).

2. Our knowledge of world history has gaps. "Only now and then light falls on a wave" in the "continuously running stream of events" (372). It is the task of "philosophical intellect" to connect the fragments by artificial links, so that "the aggregate will be raised to the rank of a system, to a rationally coherent whole" (373). The historian has a right to proceed in this manner because of "the unchangeable uniformity of natural laws and of the human mind" (373). Gaps in our knowledge can be reconstructed by analogy with events that lie within our horizon of experience.

3. One of man's properties is his instinct of harmony (*Trieb . . . nach Übereinstimmung*) (373). He wants to assimilate everything

to his own "rational nature" and to raise every phenomenon to its "highest effectiveness" (*i.e.* to "Thought" [*Gedanke*]). He wants to transform cause and effect into means and end; he does not want not to recognize teleological order in reality. Since, however, there is no such order visible in reality, "he takes this harmony out of himself and transplants it into the order of things, i.e. he introduces a rational purpose into the course of the world and a teleological principle into world history" (374). The gaps in such a teleological pattern "will be partly confirmed, partly refuted by the facts" (374). But that is where the gaps in our knowledge come in handy: As long as "important links are missing," the historian will declare the issue to be undecided, and in that pleasant case, the opinion will prevail "which offers a higher satisfaction to the intellect and a greater happiness to the heart" (374). The historian, Schiller recommends, should use the method with caution, but even when he is careful, he will be delighted by the small efforts at construction, because they are steps on the way toward resolving "the problem of world order" (374).

The rules are exhilarating. But we must remember that the lecture was published in November of 1789, the year of the French Revolution, and it has all the freshness and as-yet-unclouded optimism of the revolutionary period. It is frank to the point of naïveté in setting forth the intellectual tricks to be employed in the construction of a Second Reality, and it exhibits, therefore, the mechanism of eclipsing reality much more clearly than the system of Hegel a generation later. With regard to falsifying history, Hegel, Comte, and Marx certainly are not less ruthless than Schiller, but they are less exhibitionist with regard to their methods. Nevertheless, whether the operation is conducted overtly or is veiled by a fog of semiconsciousness, there still remains the question why anybody should spend the time of his life with the game of falsifying history at all. On this question again Schiller's frankness does not fail us; what is buried in the volumes of the later philosophers of history as an incidental remark he states explicitly: The study of universal history will accustom man to participate in the past and to anticipate the future, with the result of overcoming "the limits of birth and death which enclose the life of man narrowly and oppressively"; universal history will create "the optical illusion" of expanding "the shortness of life to an infinite space" (375). Moreover, "the individual will be imperceptibly absorbed [*hinüberge-führt*] into the species"; universal history lets man experience "the last destiny of things" (375)—*i.e.*, to be a perishable link in the chain of events—and will induce him to fasten his own perishable existence (*Dasein*) to "this imperishable chain" (376). We must respect the generations of the past for their contribution to the treasure we have inherited from them and pay to the coming generations the debt we cannot pay to those of the past. In this way, every merit has access to "immortality, to the true immortality I say, where action lives and goes on to be a living force [*weiter eilt*], even though the name of the actor should be left behind" (376). Schiller believes that the reduction of man to an "individual of the species" and the submersion of the mortal individual in the immortal stream of human history will gain for man an immortality of which as a person he has no hope. The barriers of birth and death that are felt to be the walls of a prison cannot be abolished, but they can at least be made invisible by the "optical illusion" of participating in universal history. The occupation with universal history turns out to be the opium for an intellectual who has lost Faith.

Schiller's operation of eclipsing reality is conducted with superb self-analytical consciousness. The lectures are indeed so clear with regard to the purpose, scope, and method of projecting a Second Reality that beyond the remarks I have made incidental to the various points no further explanations are necessary.

And yet this self-analytical lucidity flowers from existential darkness. We are in the garden of the *fleurs du mal.* The clarity remains internal to the operation; it does not extend to the mode of existence that will induce a man to resort to the imagination of Second Realities as an anodyne for his anxiety and alienation. The issue of the mode of existence is touched, to be sure, when Schiller informs us that constructing a Universal History will gain for the imaginator the optical illusion of true immortality. But this lucid consciousness of indulging an illusionary satisfaction deepens rather than dissolves the mystery. With regard to its existential roots, the act of deformation remains as obscure as ever.

Moreover, Schiller does not indulge in some private dreaming but delivers lectures to an audience. Not only does he take his own existence in the twilight zone of honest dishonesty for granted beyond need of explanations, but he is sure that his audience will not ask unpleasant questions with regard to this point either. The social situation of Schiller's lectures thus differs radically from the one presupposed by Aristotle when he delivered the *logoi* of his *Metaphysics*. For the members of Schiller's audience are not meant to be "men who by nature desire to know"—if they were, there would be trouble. They are rather assumed to be men who by nature desire to live in a world of imagination and will be ardently interested, therefore, in the lecturer's feat of constructing such a closed world and furnishing it with tasty items of interior decoration.

The lectures thus raise a series of questions to which, in spite of their clarity, they give no answers. Even more, it is the darkness of this very clarity that forces the questions. What kind of reason is it that will indulge in un-reason under the pretense of reason? Is it reason at all? What is the existential disorder that will cause a man who considers himself a philosopher to indulge in intellectual dishonesty in public? And what kind of audience will give its existential assent to the grotesque performance? Obviously questions of this class, because they question the mode of existence that is taken for granted by both the lecturer and his audience, cannot be answered by further exploring the contents of the lectures. Unless we want to throw our hands up in despair, we must confront the unreasonable performance with reason that does not take un-reason for granted.

In order to find the entrance to the maze of problems suggested by such questions, we shall confront the imaginator with Reason in the person of a philosopher. Let us imagine a "man who desires to know" sitting in Schiller's audience. How will the lecturer and his performance impress him?

There is a man standing up there on the podium who believes in Deism, in the self-activity of reason, and in the "beneficent middle-class, the creator of our whole culture," as the guarantor of "an enduring happiness of mankind." He candidly tells us he is going to construct a Universal History in the light of his bundle of idiosyncratic beliefs. He promises to disregard reality and to deliver a construction that will let his set of idiosyncrasies emerge as the end of history. To that purpose he will, on the one hand, omit what does not fit and, on the other hand, fill gaps in the historical record with stories of his own invention, such as the tall story about Moses. He engages in this construction because he likes to feel surrounded by a harmonious world of which he can understand the order. He knows quite well that no such order is to be found in history but, don't worry, he will put it in, so that we can be pleasantly surprised when he finds it there. He seems to take for granted, on the whole, that the idiosyncratic beliefs that he is going to discover as the meaning of history are something like an order. Still, he wants to make sure. Hence, he puts the label of "reason" on his set of beliefs, so that the resultant construction can rank as "thought" or "rational concept." At last he confesses to the sore spot in his existence: He suffers from a claustrophobic feeling that life is a prison between the walls of birth and death. Because he does not consider such a prison the proper habitat for a man who has come of age, he surrounds himself with an imaginary world tailored to his stature. Apparently the lecturer has never heard of the human condition, for his illusions of grandeur will be satisfied by nothing less than an expansion of his limited existence to infinite space.

The lecturer's performance will strike the man who desires to know as the manifestation of a spiritual disturbance, of madness in the sense in which the Greek tragedians and philosophers have used the term. Moreover, the man sitting in the audience will conclude that precisely under the aspect of spiritual disturbance the performance is of interest to us. If the lectures were no more than dilettantic or obsolete pieces of experience, they would merit no attention. If the grotesque features of the performance were to be considered a syndrome of alienation in the psychopathological sense, Schiller would be a clinical case. The performance deserves close attention because the lectures are not in search of truth within the reality of common experience, though they don the form of a *bona fide* search of truth and are delivered in the social setting of a university, and because the grotesque features of the performance, caused by the lucidly conscious attempt of simultaneously reaching and avoiding truth, are a syndrome not of clinical but of spiritual alienation. Although we cannot yet venture into etiology, the performance presents the appearance of a pneumo-pathological case.

The confrontation has brought into focus the relation between reason and existence as the key problem. I shall deal with the relation first from the side of reason.

Reason, it appears, is not a faculty of man that will autonomously and invariably function by its own laws but rather a *modus operandi* of consciousness that is disturbed when man deforms his humanity to a self. There can be a twilight zone of honest dishonesty, bearing the marks of compulsiveness, because the operations of the mind are affected by the very processes on the existential level to which the clarity of the imaginator's operation does not extend. Right reason, the *recta ratio* of the Stoics, is dependent on the order of existence.

Moreover, the relation between reason and existence is a problem not only in the order of personal existence but in society and history as well. Schiller's performance as a lecturer requires an audience that will give its existential assent. If the existential assent is not forthcoming—if, for instance, as we have imagined, a man who desires to know sits in the audience—the problem of rational order in society becomes acute. When the philosopher encounters the imaginator, two modes of reason encounter one another. The question arises whether rational discussion is possible between men who represent the two different modes of existence and reason and, if not, what form the encounter will assume. In the imagined confrontation we have cast Schiller's auditor in the role of an observer. Extrapolating this role, we may say that the "man who desires to know" will not enter into Schiller's argument with agreement or objection because rational discussion presupposes a community of existence in truth. There is no sense in arguing with a man who compulsively distorts, omits, and invents facts in order to imprison himself in an imaginary world. Rational discussion is impossible. The role of the observer, however, will not satisfy the exigencies of an encounter in every respect and under all circumstances, because the imaginator's operation is not wholly but only partially unreasonable. A project of Second Reality, if it is effectively to eclipse First Reality for any length of time, must have incorporated sufficiently large, important, and emotionally appealing sectors of the reality of common experience to be acceptable by the standards of the audience to whom it is addressed. Since, furthermore, the great imaginators are frequently men of unusual intellectual powers, vast knowledge, and psychological perspicacity, there may indeed be much to be learned from them about such sectors of First Reality as they have incorporated. A philosopher would ignore the works of Hegel only at his peril, even if he shudders at the idea of constructing a speculative system with the purpose of improving on salvation through Christ. Within certain limits, therefore, rational discussion is possible, even though, in order to watch the limits, the imaginator's fundamental deformation of reason must be countered on the philosopher's part by an equally fundamental wariness of the observer.

The limits must be watched carefully indeed, because the discussion can remain rational only as long as it moves within the areas where Second overlaps with First Reality. As soon as the questions concerning the order of existence, which the imaginator's clarity leaves in darkness, are touched, the rationality of the discussion will be deformed by the existential antagonism of the interlocutors. It will assume the form of "war and battle" that Plato described and analyzed in his *Gorgias*. The man who desires to know and is willing to learn from an imaginator must remain aware that even the most important information concerning facts and the most brilliant thought subordinate truth to their function in the imaginative construction. If he is not on his guard, agreement on points that overlap with First Reality may suck him into the vortex of existential deformation. The great projectors of Second Realities are social forces because they are able to transform rational agreement on an unexceptional point into sweeping existential assent to the deformation of humanity. They are surrounded by the social fields of secondarily deformed humanity in their schools, adherents, admirers, vulgarizers, followers, fellow-travelers, and so forth. Inversely, the imaginator must always be on his guard, because he can never be certain when he enters a discussion that Reason will not suddenly raise its ugly head. His interlocutor may be a man who desires to know and will therefore not abide by the imaginator's rule of the game that a discussion must never touch the question of existence, for if this question were touched, not only would the project have to be abandoned, but the imaginator's existence itself would be in danger of being engulfed by its own nothingness.

The depth of anxiety aroused by the pressure of reason can

be measured by the violence of the imaginator's reaction. When Socrates in the Sophistic environment of the *Gorgias* trespasses on the forbidden ground of existence, he is confronted with the threat of murder. The modern deformers of humanity, when they have gained power in the form of a totalitarian government, use the same threat as their *ultima ratio,* while in the so-called free societies they use milder forms of violence, such as social boycott. What happened to Camus after the publication of his *L'homme révolté* and the break with Sartre is a representative example of the treatment meted out in a Western society to a man who dares to think. Still, the social success of violence for the time being is not a sign of existential victory, for parallel with the contemporary use of violence there has emerged the peculiar argument that Karl Mannheim has called the general suspicion of ideology (*der allgemeine Ideologieverdacht*). When the man who desires to know trespasses in a discussion, he will run against the embattled imaginator's last line of defense—that is, against the argument that all pursuit of truth, even the philosopher's, is an operation of imaginative projecting. There is no First Reality; there are only Second Realities. This argument, however, can hardly be considered a defense; its use rather acknowledges the breakdown of the deforming operation in the twentieth century, for if there is no First Reality to be eclipsed, the construction of a Second Reality is no longer the bang that accompanies the rising of a new world from the death of an old one, but the whimper in which all reality dies. *Nous sommes dans le nihilisme*—as Albert Camus has summed up the situation.

In conclusion, the philosopher's and the imaginator's reason are not the same. Discussion that is supposed to be rational degenerates to the existential "war and battle" because two conceptions of reason, manifesting two different modes of existence, are pitched against one another. Since the indiscriminate use of the term *reason* for either of the two conceptions is an inexhaustible source of confusion—and today more than ever before in the history of deformation—it is necessary to introduce terminological distinctions. The original conception of reason is the philosopher's. Reason, *nous,* is the name the classical philosophers have given to man's consciousness of tension toward the divine ground of his existence. Plato's philosopher, or Aristotle's man who desires to know, is the man who wants to exist consciously and actively in the truth or reality of this tension. Reason in the philosophical sense is the undeformed knowledge and reality of human existence. In the so-called Age of Reason, the *philosophes*, Plato's philodoxers, developed an image of reason that served the purpose of eclipsing the reason of man's undeformed existence. This new image of the *philosophes* does not emerge from an analysis of existential tension but is developed in the course of their imaginative projecting. It belongs, in its varieties, to the content of the various projects. In order to distinguish the two conceptions of reason terminologically, I shall speak of the philosopher's noetic and the imaginator's doxic reason.

Second, I shall deal with the relation between reason and existence from the side of existence.

The notion of doxic as distinguished from noetic reason has imposed itself because Schiller's operation, on the one hand, claims to be undertaken as a work of reason while, on the other hand, it defies rational analysis on its own terms. Moreover, the difficulty is caused less by faulty reasoning on Schiller's part than by his outrageous misrepresentation, in the name of reason, of reality in common experience. Reason, it turns out, is not merely an operational algorithm but has existential content. Regarding the content, the philosopher's reason is man's tension toward the divine ground of his existence becoming luminous to itself, while the philodoxer's reason is an image designed to obscure the reality of existential tension. In order to prevent existence from becoming luminous, the imaginator replaces man and his consciousness by an imaginary Self, endows this homunculus with a special consciousness—*i.e.*, with doxic reason that will not question the premises of his construction—and ascribes to the manmade man the status of full humanity. The doxic reason of the Self, finally, will take care that the areas of consciousness to be eclipsed will be properly deformed, or transformed, or omitted, or denied status of reality. The clarity of the operation thus creates the obscurity of existence surrounding it.

The Self just described will not betray the secret of its maker: It will tender no direct information concerning the structure of the existence it is designed to eclipse, and it hides the indirect information it offers in the fact of its being projected by an imaginator behind the pretense of being the imaginator himself. As long as the homunculus is taken at the value of Man he puts on his face, the existence to which he owes his existence remains in the darkness of doxic clarity. The Self is a fortress impenetrable to rational analysis as long as we treat doxic reason as if it were noetic reason. I have devised the course of analysis so as to make this point clear: It is not enough to let the philosopher observe the operation, for he can observe no more than the oddity of the performance and surmise the underlying spiritual disturbance. Nor is it enough to pursue doxic reason into the haunts of its premises, for the pursuer can drive the Self to the border at which its argument becomes a nihilistic futility, but he cannot go beyond this limit. The analysis, to be sure, must pass through these phases in order to establish the pneumopathological character of the case, but if it is not to end in a futility that matches the futility of nihilism, it must raise the understanding achieved in fact to the consciousness of an insight: The thinker who thinks the thought of his Self has lost the luminosity and, with the luminosity, the identity of his existence as man.

As the last proposition shows, the analysis can advance beyond the critical point only by appealing to the existential content of reason. The structure of existence itself must be introduced to cope with the imaginator's attempt to eclipse it, and the philosopher's luminosity of reason and existence provides the standard by which every man's, including the imaginator's, reason and existence are to be critically measured. To be sure, the philosopher's existence as the standard has been implied in the present study from its beginning—or we could never have spoken of First and Second Realities, of an imaginator, a contracted Self, and the deformation of humanity—but we must state its use explicitly now that the analysis has been pressed to the point of questioning the imaginator's identity of existence. Using this standard, the issue of identity can be stated succinctly: A man's identity is constituted through existence in tension toward the ground of his existence. Man, however, can reject his own identity; he can imagine a Self, endow it with doxic reason, and let it engage in projecting Second Realities. He can, furthermore, remain sufficiently unconscious of what he is doing to pretend with a show of good faith that he himself is the Self he has imagined and that the activities of the Self are his own thoughts and actions. Since he cannot abolish the reality he tries to eclipse, finally there will develop in his consciousness a tension between the false and the true selfs, between the false identity claimed and the true identity disclaimed. His existence is structured by two selfs.

Although the loss of identity here described is related to schizoid and schizophrenic states of consciousness, I must warn against jumping to suggestive conclusions. The problem of this relationship, as we shall see, is rather complicated. The specific nature of the spiritual disturbance under discussion will be better realized through a recall of the Hellenic advice, *Gnoti seauton*. The command of the Delphic God to man to know himself as man before the God is the counterpart to Yahweh's command, Thou shalt have no other gods before my face. If the divine command to know yourself (reflexive pronoun) preparatory to achieving the philosopher's luminosity of existential tension is perverted into the human, perhaps a psychologist's, command to know your Self (object), the effect is the same as in the case of disobedience to Yahweh's command: Existence in the truth of the command is broken. The truth of existence can be destroyed through manmade images bearing the face of God just as much as through manmade images bearing the face of Man. The death of God and the death of Man are correlative phenomena; both the making of gods and the making of Selfs manifest man's loss of his identity.

The loss of identity entails a complex structure of existence. There is a true self and an imaginary self, each equipped with a reason, a consciousness, and even a conscience of its own; and there is a comprehensive consciousness that has to accommodate them both, with no identity of its own and therefore in permanent danger of falling into nothingness. Moreover, between the two selfs there extend variegated and fluid relations. The imaginary self can be so predominantly productive that its work gives the public signature to the personality of the thinker, with the true self kept under the hatches of unconsciousness. Or the true self, rarely or more frequently, can stir and cause frictions, such as overt expressions of skepticism regarding the validity of the imaginary self's operations, or the fluctuations of mood on the scales of optimism-pessimism and elation-despair. Or, perhaps the oddest variety, both of the two selfs can be actively productive with no major conflict in the imaginator's personality becoming apparent. The Schiller who delivered the untragically optimistic lectures on Universal History is also the Schiller who wrote the tragedy of *Wallenstein;* the Hegel who constructed a speculative system is also the Hegel who wrote the magnificently realistic study of the English Reform Bill; and the Sartre who finds in existence only the meaning projected by the Self is also the Sartre whose fictional and dramatic characters get involved in tragic situations because their projects of meaning are not attuned to the sense that existence has, independent of their projecting.

It is not advisable, as I have said, to apply psychiatric categories to phenomena of this class, or to stretch the selfs with their subtle fluctuations of conscious–semiconscious–unconscious on the Procrustean couch of the psychoanalytic conscious and unconscious. The phenomena of deformed existence rather belong to the same class as the phenomena of spiritual crisis, of *periagogé* and conversion, of the old man and the new man, of the Pauline two egos, or the remarkable complexities of Saint Augustine's existence. A man's consciousness, it is well to remember, is not a durable object but an intangible process of sustaining its own identity; the nothing is always there to open its abyss when the defenses are weakened. The processes of consciousness and the struggles for identity of existence are a well-circumscribed area of reality, the experiences are intelligible in terms of the language symbols they have engendered, and the phenomena are in no immediate need of being explained through reduction to the psychopathological level—though the extreme forms of existential disintegration will frequently be of help in understanding phenomena of pneumopathological deformation. Even if one of the great imaginators displays clinical symptoms beyond a doubt, one must avoid mixing up psychiatry with the analysis of a spiritual disturbance, or one may get entangled in affairs like the famous "two careers" of August Comte.

I shall use the "madness" of Comte to clarify some points of method. The case will, furthermore, be of value for understanding the problems of an imaginator's social success and its limits, of the existential assent given by the public, of the phenomenon of secondary deformation, and of the transformations that a Second Reality suffers in its transition from an imaginator's doxic consciousness to the semiconsciousness of the public.

There is agreement among historians on the facts of the case. At the time, the case centered in the assumption of an early "intellectual" phase in the work of Comte, represented by his *Cours de philosophie positive* (1830–1842), and a late "religious" phase, represented by his *Système de politique positive* (1851–1854). Because of its scientistic intent as well as its antitheological and antimetaphysical bias, the *Cours* appealed to a number of scholars and philosophers, among them John Stuart Mill and Emile Littré. When the volumes of the *Système* began to be published and the religious system of Comte unfolded with its dogma, cult, catechism, and calendar, the admirers of the "intellectual" Comte were greatly embarrassed. They had to assume a "break" in the life of the thinker, since the "intellectual" Comte could be accepted, but the "religious" Comte had to be rejected. Thus the formula of the "two careers" was coined. For personal reasons, Littré was deeply touched by the developments; he went so far as to stigmatize the religious phase as a manifestation of "madness" and linked it, with the support of Madame Comte, to the clinical periods of Comte's derangement. The assumption of the "break" and the "two careers," as well as the attempt to declare the second Comte a madman, however, ran into the difficulty that Comte could prove, by reprinting his early essays of the 1820s, that his career had never suffered a break. In the two series of the *Cours* and the *Système* he had executed the program conceived in his youth; one could not accept the one without the other, for only if understood as a unit did the *Philosophie* and the *Politique* make sense. The grandiose projective unity of Comte's work could not be doubted. From the projective unity of the work and the charge of madness as the premises, one would have to conclude disjunctively that if the late work was insane, the early work was, too; if the early work was sane, the late work had to be accepted as its consistent elaboration and fulfillment. The charge of madness petered out in a sordid comedy with a lawsuit and was never seriously renewed; the question of the "two careers" that had provoked the charge was left adrift. Thus far the facts of the *cause célèbre*.

In order to disentangle the issue of existential structure from the facts, we must first eliminate the charge of "madness." Whatever Comte's neurotic troubles may have been, his work is an imaginative project of the same type as Schiller's, characterized by internal clarity of the operation and surrounding darkness of existence. There is no more madness in the projecting of Comte than in the projecting of Turgot or Condorcet, Kant or Schiller, Hegel or Marx. We must, furthermore, eliminate the assumption of a "break" in his projecting. The *Cours* is the great meditative process by which Comte transforms himself into the representative man of the new Positive Age; thereafter he consistently presents himself as the inaugurator of the new age, as the Founder of the new Religion of Humanity and its first Pontiff. The difficulties of Comte are not to be found in his work considered as a project of Second Reality; the troubles arise from the frictions with First Reality. There is something in the late work that the admirers of the "intellectual" Comte were not willing to swallow. The assumption of "two careers" thus makes sense if it is understood as an expansion of projecting beyond the limits to which society would give its existential assent.

The symbol of the "two careers" expresses the refusal of existential assent to the late work. It is valid not only for the situation that engendered it but expresses a pattern in the history of deformation that is running on even now, a century after Comte's death, so that the acceptance and rejection of the early and late work respectively is still a live issue.

The ideas of the "intellectual" Comte have entered the consciousness of secondarily deformed existence and become an ingredient in the mishmash of ideological clichés that the "modern man" of the twentieth century considers to be "thought." On this vulgarian level, they are recognizable in the widespread resentment of theology and metaphysics among intellectuals, as well as in the rich crop of successor symbols to Comte's "positive" age, such as the "post-Christian," "pagan," "neo-pagan," "secularist," and "immanentist" ages. The stadial construction of history, though it did not originate with Comte, has become through his work one of the most effective instruments of social terrorism, frightening spiritually and intellectually defenseless people into conformity with some age declared to be theirs by this or that group of activist intellectuals. The replacement of rational debate by existential terror, with its destructive effects on man's free existence in society, was already recognized by John Stuart Mill as a crucial factor in Comte's work, and its potential for oppression was rated by him higher than governmental encroachments on civil liberties. In this sense, the "intellectual" Comte is being accepted and has become a force in the deformation of humanity.

More complicated is the rejection of the "religious" Comte. Regarding this strand in the history of deformation, we must distinguish between the lingering of the Comtean sect as an obscure conventicle and the not-at-all obscure treatment of the late projective work of Comte.

The institution of the Religion of Humanity as a cult was socially rejected inasmuch as it has never found numerous adherents. That will surprise nobody who has visited the Comteist chapel in Paris, in the neighborhood of the Archives Nationales, and has been depressed by the pathetic sentimentalism, tastelessness, and shabbiness of its mural and sculptural decor.

The late work as an imaginative project, on the other hand, does not suffer from neglect. On the contrary, it has become the object of intensive historical research in such special studies as Georges Dumas' *Psychologie de deux messies positivistes: Saint-Simon et Auguste Comte* (1905) and Frank E. Manuel's *The Prophets of Paris* (1962). Yet I wonder whether these excellent and sympathetic studies are not continuing the rejection of the "religious" Comte in the more subtle form of historical enshrinement. Moreover, without prejudice to their quality of historical scholarship, the classification of Comte as a messiah or prophet encounters similar difficulties of method as the earlier charge of madness. If the psychiatric reduction lowers the work of Comte to a level of neurotic derangement to which it has not sunk, the interpretation as messianism or prophetism raises it to a spiritual level it has not attained. The genteel enclosure in categories that miss the structure of spiritually disturbed existence rejects the "religious" Comte just as much as did the cruder attack of Littré.

Phenotypically, to be sure, there is something messianic or prophetic about the late work of Comte, yet in order to ascertain more precisely what this something is, we must first admit unequivocally that Comte was neither a messiah nor a prophet. If we take these terms seriously, as in a philosophical study we must, they do not denote a man who eclipses his true self by a Second Reality and as a consequence has lost his identity of existence—*i.e.*, his tension toward the divine ground—but on the contrary a man who lives in the reality of the tension and proclaims its truth. Messianic and prophetic personalities represent optimal identity of existence. The follower of Christ is a *homo Dei* (2 Tim. 3 : 17), not a Comtean *homo humanitatis*, and the Pauline letter just quoted, as if it were aimed at the voluminous systems of the imaginators, speaks of the *semper discentes, et nunquam ad scientiam veritatis pervenientes*, of the men who teach and teach but never arrive at the knowledge of reality in truth (*aletheia, veritas*, 3 : 7). We must distinguish, therefore, between true prophetism that proclaims the truth of existence and the phenotypical prophetism that appears as part of an imaginative project. The prophetism of Comte belongs to the imaginative projecting of his contracted self, not to the true self that by means of projecting he tries to eclipse. The homunculus, it appears, can be endowed not only with doxic reason but also with an imaginary prophetic spirit that will proclaim a message of imaginary salvation. For reasons that will be set forth in a later part of this study, we shall call this projected spirit of prophecy the gnostic endowment of the homunculus. The addition of gnostic spirit to doxic reason completes the imaginary man who will eclipse both philosophy and faith, or rather their derivative doctrinal forms of theology and metaphysics, which alone were within the range of Comte's understanding. Imagining a prophetic truth of salvation, of course, will make the imaginator no more a prophet than his dream of doxic reason makes him a philosopher. Nevertheless, imagining a positive messiah on top of a positive philosopher in order to relegate the Hellenic and Judaeo-Christian imperfections to the past in one sweep is a splendidly logical fantasy, worthy of a French thinker who, in the wake of the Revolution, is conscious of representing the culture of France, which is the culture of the West, which is the culture of mankind, in the age of perfection it is about to enter.

The very consistency and perfection of the performance make all the more intriguing the question of why the contemporaries were profoundly shocked by its later part, though otherwise they were eager to give their existential assent to Promethean enhancements of the contracted Self. Moreover, the question of why gnostic messianism does not have the same appeal as doxic reason arises not only with regard to Comte. Although his case was the most spectacular one, there was quite a pride of imaginary prophets who suffered disappointment. Whether it is Fourier's modest reflection that not for the first time in history is God using an obscure man to proclaim the most important message to the world, or Fichte's quiet confidence that the philosopher of the *Wissenschaftslehre* is Christ, or Hegel's discreetly proud consciousness of having done better than Christ, or Comte's flamboyance of replacing the Era of Christ by the Era of Comte, the one-upmanship on Christ did not work.

In answer to this question, one could write a volume on the historical causes that keep messianic projecting socially within the confines of conventicles, sects, and schools. Fortunately, however, this is not necessary; the mere reference to a course of history that does not conform to the course projected by the imaginator implies the answer we are looking for: History in First Reality is a dimension of man's full existential structure, whereas the history imagined by the prophet is a project devised to protect the contracted self against the pressure of First Reality. Moreover, the contracted self is itself a product of imagination; not only the stadial construction of history with its ages but also the discoverer, inaugurator, founder, prophet, or messiah of the new age belong to the contents of the project. There are no ages and their prophets in the history of common experience. The gnostically enhanced homunculus is a "prophet" or "messiah" only in Second Reality; in First Reality, he is the phantasy of a pneumopathological case. Hence, the answer to the question of whether a "messiah" will succeed or not must be given by the rule previously formulated that the success of a project depends on the relation between its contents and the exigencies of man's full existence in society and history at a specific time.

In a society of men who live in the truth of reality, an attempt to eclipse this very reality will be no more than a personal oddity and have no social success at all. If, on the other hand, a society consists of a large proportion of men who suffer from the same spiritual disturbance as the imaginator, his projecting will have success, provided his project keeps close enough to the civilizational state of the society, or at least of its politically, economically, and

socially most important sectors. A project of romantic agricul-
turalism will not do too well in an industrial society, because a return to the soil is not to the taste of urbanized masses. Radical
"anti-civilizational" projecting on the lines from Rousseau and the
more rabid Fourier to the surrealist André Bréton—who wrote the
Ode à Charles Fourier (1947) and considered going out in the street
with a revolver and shooting at random as the most suitable expression of his opinion concerning the state of civilization—is condemned to remain a marginal phenomenon. Projecting, in order to
have social appeal, must include a hard core of First Reality, changing with the social and historical situations. In the eighteenth and
nineteenth centuries, examples of hard cores are Schiller's beneficent middle class, Humboldt's and Hegel's bourgeois society in
combination with the Prussian state, Saint-Simon's and Comte's
entrepreneurs and capitalists, and Marx's industrial workers; in the
twentieth century, the hard core must be revised to accommodate
the middle class of the industrial society, the governmental and
economic bureaucracies, the managers and technicians, and the
armies.

Although the hard core is necessary to secure pragmatic appeal,
the essence of an imaginative project is its proclamation of a new
truth about man's existence in society and history. If the imaginator seeks acceptance for his truth, he must equip his project with
symbols of authority in matters of truth. The acceptable symbols
of authority, however, are strictly limited, because the truth of
existence is not a matter of opinion but a process of insight, carried
on in history by the men who, in a critical situation, experience the
tension of existence and express it by means of symbols. There are
no more than two principal types of "prophetism": the Greek and
the Israelite. The term *prophetes* originally denotes the Greek
seers and poets in their capacity as speakers of the gods. Pindar can
say of himself: "Reveal [*manteuo*], O Muse, and prophesy shall I"
(fragm. 150). And the prophetic poet—epic, lyric, and tragic—is
followed, in a more differentiated mode of experience, by the philosopher, the lover of the god's wisdom. By way of translation, the
term *prophet* was transferred to the *nabi*, the Israelite speaker of
God's word, more especially to the solitary *nebiim* who historically followed the collective "bands of prophets." Besides the principal types, there are unique representatives of truth like Moses

and Christ, the "servants of God." There are, furthermore, the metaphysicians and theologians who cast the truth of experience into the form of concepts and propositions. And finally there are the mystics. This is the representative personnel of existential truth in history that the imaginator must eclipse if he wants to eclipse reality. In order to achieve this purpose, he must project the image of a representative who believably can take over the function of the historical representatives to be eclipsed.

With the task set in these terms, the range of feasible solutions is rather narrow. First of all, we see now the reason why the projecting of the contracted self must of necessity assume the form of a philosophy of history: The truth of existence has in First Reality the dimension of history, and the imaginator, if he wants to eclipse the truth of existence, must produce an imaginary history from which he can emerge as something like a "seal of the prophets," as the prophet to end all prophetism. History and its truth of existence must die if the imaginator is to live as the founder of the ageless age. But that is not enough. There will be no ageless age long enough to fill even the few years of a *Tausendjähriges Reich*, unless the imaginator can produce a homunculus who will pass phenotypical muster as a representative of truth. This, however, is a feat not easy to accomplish, for the homunculus must be recognizable as a proclaimer of truth by his resemblance to the real representatives while proclaiming a truth in flat contradiction to the truth of reality. One cannot simply throw out theology and metaphysics, with the prophets and philosophers in the background of these types of derivative truth, and then expect to have a new philosopher and prophet accepted. People will applaud attacks on churches that have fostered wars of religion and become unpopular because of their indifference to the necessity of social reforms, but they will become suspicious when the new Christs pop up by the dozen. Hence, the imagery of "Christs," "messiahs," and "prophets" did not fare too well, as we have seen.

The imagery of "philosophy" did better; witness the "philosophes" of the eighteenth century, partly because the imaginator's attack was linguistically directed against "church," "theology," and "metaphysics," partly because classic philosophy was too little known at the time to be sensed as an obstacle to imaginative operations. The notion of "philosophy" was hazy enough to make the homunculus in the role of the "philosopher" acceptable, especially when philosophy was qualified by a cautionary adjective, as in Comte's *philosophie positive.* Still, toward the end of the eighteenth century, when the operations multiply and become more conscious of their intent, the acceleration of the movement is accompanied by a tendency to increase the authority of "philosophy" by associating it with "science." Since the tendency is a problem neither in science nor in philosophy, but rather a question of finding symbols that will lend credibility to Second Reality, the association of terms is best suited to denote a field of phenomena as variegated as the French and German uses of "science."

The social and emotional appeal of the symbol "science" radiated from the solid success of mathematics and physics, with Newton's *Principia* in the background; a study of man in society and history was considered due for a similarly prestigious development. Saint-Simon was in search of a social science that would repeat the success of physics by being founded on an equivalent to Newton's law of gravitation. But for the historical accident that Quetelet had used the term *physique sociale* for his statistical studies and thereby had made its use inconvenient to Comte, we would have a "social physics" today instead of a "sociology." Comte's neologism, with its associative fringe of "science," "positive science," and "positive philosophy," has become one of the most effective symbols for lending the authority of truth to projects of the contracted Self and, by the same token, for eclipsing First Reality.

While the French thinkers used the association of "philosophy" with "science" primarily for the purpose of enhancing the authority of Second Realities that surround and protect the contracted Self, the German thinkers used it primarily for the purpose of raising the stature of the homunculus himself. A few book titles and programmatic formulations will illuminate the German variety of the movement.

In 1794, Fichte published his *Begriff der Wissenschaftslehre oder der sogenannten Philosophie.* The title demotes philosophy to a "so-called philosophy," while the author sprouts a halo as the man who conceives a new "message of science" or a "science that must be spread as a message." No more than a paraphrase of the title is possible in the language of common experience because the new coinages of the time belong to the symbolism of imaginary prophetism. When Hegel, then, gives to his *Phänomenologie* of 1807 the title *System der Wissenschaft. Erster Theil, die Phänomenologie des Geistes,* he goes one step further and excludes the "so-called philosophy" altogether. The omission is perhaps not caused by the economy of a title but indeed reflects Hegel's program set forth in the *Vorrede* (12): "The true shape [*Gestalt*] in which truth has existence is only the scientific system. I have proposed myself to bring philosophy nearer to the form of science—to the goal where it is able to relinquish the name *love of knowledge* [*Wissen*] and become *true knowledge.*" Philosophy in the classic sense—the erotic tension toward the wisdom that is God's, will be overcome by Hegel and be replaced by a tensionless possession of knowledge in the form of a scientific system. The program announced in the *Phänomenologie* is brought, if not to its fulfillment, at least to the first volume of fulfillment by the *Wissenschaft der Logik* of 1812. The title, though it sounds harmless enough, covers the program formulated in the *Einleitung* (31): "Objective thinking is the contents of pure science . . . Logic is to be conceived as the system of pure reason, as the realm of pure thought. *This realm is Truth as it is, without veils, in and for itself.* One can say therefore justly that this contents is the *presentation* [or representation, *Darstellung*] *of God as he exists in his eternal essence* [*Wesen*] *before the creation of nature and a finite mind* [*Geist*]." The italics are Hegel's, and the passages italicized draw, as does the language of the Logos in the *Einleitung* in general, allusively on the Logos chapter in the Gospel of Saint John. Before creation, *en arche,* there was the Logos, and the Logos was with God, and God was the Logos. This pre-creational God in his eternal existence and essence presents himself now, through the Logos that has become incarnate in Hegel's thought, as the Truth without veils in the *Science of Logic.* "In the Christian religion God has revealed Himself, that is, he has let man know what He is, so that He would be no longer something hidden or secret; this possibility to know God is imposed on us as a duty." The evolution of the thinking mind (*Geist*) that has commenced with this revelation of the divine Being (*Wesen*) must at last reach the stage where "what previously has been presented to the feeling and imagining [*vorstellend*] mind [*Geist*], will be conceived in Thought" (*Phil. d.*

148

Gesch.). Hegel's homunculus has become the Second Person of the Trinity; the Science of Logic is the project of a revelation that is meant to eclipse Christ, the Gospel, and Theology.

The French and German varieties of phenotypical prophetism reflect, as has been frequently observed, the difference of Catholic and Protestant traditions in the background. The "Catholic" Comte wanted to become the founder and pontiff of a Church beyond the Church; the "Protestant" Hegel wanted to become the Christ beyond Christ. Such differences of tradition, reaching into the varieties of deformation, however, must not obscure the problem that Comte and Hegel had in common: They both had developed a contracted Self; they both engaged in the projection of Second Realities that would protectively surround the contracted Self; and they both were in search of symbols that would endow their enterprise with the socially effective images of authority. This search marks a distinct phase in the process of deformation. The imaginators become aware of what they are doing, and they want to do it competently. They want to replace the truth of existence with the truth of the contracted Self; and they know they are in competition with the representatives of truth in history. Hence, the contracted Self must be equipped with an image of existence that can hold its own against the noetic and pneumatic luminosity of existence; the Self must establish its identity against the identity of man in existential tension. Although the honest dishonesty in Schiller's operation still had the charms of exuberance and transparency, the "systems of science," especially Hegel's, have a speculative polish that even today compels admiration.

Hegel's *Science of Logic* will illuminate the point. The work eclipses not only the "Christian religion" in the sense of the Gospel and theology, but "metaphysics" as well. The new system "will take the place of the *ci-devant* metaphysics," in its whole range of ontology, and of the metaphysics of "the soul, the world, and God" (*WdL*, 46f.). There had been philosophy in the past, but hitherto it "had not found its method." This method has now been found by Hegel and presented in the system. It still is capable of "perfections" and "elaborations" in detail, but in spite of minor possible flaws, "I know that it is the only true one." Hegel can be sure of its truth because the method is not something different (*Unterschiedenes*) from its object and contents. "For it is the contents in itself, the *dialectics it has in itself*, which moves it on [*fortbewegt*]. It is clear that no presentations can be considered scientific, which do not move by this method, in accordance with its simple rhythm, as it is the movement of the matter [*Sache*] itself" (*W. d. L.*, 36).

At first reading, these passages will be baffling because they argue the truth of the "science" and its "method" in a language that derives its own validity as conceptual language from the science whose truth it wants to establish. As soon, however, as the "circularity" (Hegel's term) of a science whose truth depends on a language invented for the purpose of proving it true is understood as the principle of a self-sustaining operation, the "matter" (*Sache*) becomes clear indeed—though not in the sense intended by Hegel. God and man, as well as the existential tension of which philosophy is the noetic exegesis, have disappeared. They are replaced by an imaginary entity variously named Logos, Reason, *absoluter Geist, absolute Idee,* and *Begriff,* which unfolds itself by a movement called dialectical. The names just enumerated, it must be stressed, do not denote a property, action, or function of God or man, or of any something with status in the reality of common experience, but must be understood as a fictional entity equipped with dialectical expansiveness. The luminosity of existence has become the clarity of a "system" whose content is a method of movement and whose movement is its content. The fictional entity is, furthermore, as much "substance" as it is "subject"; and the truth of this "insight" into the nature of the fictional entity is to be justified by actually unfolding the movement of the substance-subject in a system (*Phän.*, 19). The system thus proves itself as the one and only truth of reality by the fact of its being constructed. The imaginator, finally, protects the *perpetuum mobile* of his self-contained and self-moving System of Science against confrontation with reality by interpreting the representatives of existential truth as the forerunners of the truth that has come to the clarity of its consciousness in his System. Both Faith and Reason had to be slapped down. We have seen how Hegel disposed of Christ by arrogating the full revelation of the pre-creational Logos to himself. Aristotle had to suffer the same fate. The *Enzyklopädie der Philosophischen Wissenschaften* closes triumphantly with a passage from Aristotle's *Metaphysics* which, if properly misunderstood, will suggest a future development of philosophy in the direction of Hegel's Reason, just as the Gospel of Saint John, if properly misunderstood, will suggest a future revelation by Hegel's Logos. Theology and Metaphysics, Faith and Reason, Christianity and Philosophy, Christ and Aristotle thus had been eliminated as competitors in proclaiming the truth of reality. From now on, a man had to be either a Hegelian or run the risk of being classified as *faule Existenz*, as a piece of rotten existence that had dropped out of the self-moving reason-reality of history.

In the history of deformation, one must distinguish between the primary process and the secondary movements that attach themselves to phases of the primary process.

The primary process runs its course from the exuberant projecting of the eighteenth century to the self-analysis and despair of the twentieth. It has an intelligible sequence of phases as the major thinkers who engage in the operation of eclipsing reality explore its possibilities in various directions and, as the limits become visible, move from the happy unconsciousness of its implications to the unhappy consciousness of the nihilistic impasse. As far as in the social process of literary communication men of a minor intellectual stature are influenced in their thinking by one or another of the major imaginators, or by several of them in combination, the primary process engenders a multitude of secondary movements. Hence, as the history of deformation unfolds in time, successive crosscuts will reveal increasingly complicated manifolds of deformation phenomena, for the later crosscuts will contain not only the primary phase of the moment but also the growing sediment of secondary deformation in the wake of the earlier phases. By our own time in the latter part of the twentieth century, this sediment of secondary effects has grown socially to such proportions that it is apt to obscure the phase that the primary process has reached. If we apply criteria of social success and noise on the public scene, there never was a period of deformation as atrocious as the present one; if we apply the criteria of active intelligence in penetrating the problems of existence, we must say that the primary process has come to its end with the realization of the nihilistic impasse into which the eclipse of reality has led. That is not to say that the secondary effects have become unimportant because, on the primary level, the problems of existence have moved beyond the spell of the contracted Self. On the contrary, as far as the order, or rather disorder, of society as a whole is concerned, the secondary effects determine an intellectual climate of such force that it can be, and frequently is, mistaken by the unwary for the "age" to which they must conform if they want to be up-to-date "modern men." Nevertheless, however impressive the social forces of the "age" may be, the philosopher must judge the intellectual climate by the criteria of existence in truth and recognize it for what it is: the secondary, epigonal, stagnant, and obsolescent aftermath of a primary process that has run its course and belongs to the past.

There has been more than one occasion for incidental reference to the distinction of the primary process from its secondary effects. I shall now introduce the issue as a formal part of the analysis, because the structure of the secondary effects is a variation on the structure of imaginative projecting. Moreover, it must be introduced at this juncture, before we proceed to further phases on the primary level, because the perfection of projecting to a System of Science has induced a corresponding perfection in the structure of secondary deformation. To be sure, there are secondary movements more immediately attaching to the systems that can be discerned as an independent strand of neo-Positivisms and neo-Hegelianisms in the twentieth-century jungle of deformation imagery, but there are more subtle effects that have entered as a kind of common denominator into the secondary movements attaching more immediately to later phases of the primary process, such as the various Marxisms or the proliferations of psychoanalysis and existentialism. I shall attempt to describe this perfected structure of the secondary effects by distinguishing between 1) the effects intended by the authors of the Systems, 2) the general blocking effect of the Systems, and 3) the specific effects attaching to parts of the Systems.

1. The great imaginators constructed and published their systems in order to communicate an ultimate truth about man's existence in society and history to mankind at large. About the intended social effect—*i.e.*, the transformation of mankind into a Comtean or Hegelian church—not much is to be said beyond the obvious: Neither has such a transformation occurred during the last century, nor is it likely to occur in the future. The *Fondateur de la Religion*

de l'Humanité has become the founder of Sociology, and his place in the history of French thought, both revolutionary and restorative, is being established by scholarly treatises, such as the great work of Henri Gouhier. The pre-creational Logos incarnate, in his turn, has become a German philosopher who can be ranked, according to the preferences of the historians, as the modern successor to Aristotle or to Saint Augustine. That is to say, both of the imperatorical imaginators have suffered the humiliation of being demoted to figures in the very history of philosophy that they had meant to conclude and to transcend. Hegel has not even escaped the insult of being spoken of, on occasion, as a "metaphysician."

Both Comte and Hegel, however, are beginning to be recognized as the representatives of a revolt against the state of degeneration to which the truth of existence had sunk in the dogmatic theology and metaphysics of the eighteenth century. This revolt is still going on, and though we do not know what socially acceptable form the truth of existence will find once the reality of common experience has been regained, we know that the firm ground will not be gained by a return to the dogmatisms that provoked the revolt. The place of the Systems of Science in the history, not of "ideas" or "philosophy," but of a spiritual revolt that has managed to eclipse the reality it wanted to gain is by far not yet ultimately clear.

2. The ambiguity of a revolt that claims achievement of what it has not achieved has entailed ambiguous effects. The effect overtly intended, it is true, did not follow; the new saviors were rejected. If the rejection of Hegel's epiphany proved less sensational than Comte's, this must be attributed to the obscurity of his allusive language, which confined the understanding of its implications to a comparatively small circle of disciples and adherents, as well as to the fact that no women were involved. Nevertheless, the soteriological embarrassment caused by the authors of the systems did not completely frustrate their imaginative construction of a new truth, for the factor of legitimacy in a revolt against degenerative dogmatisms had what I call the general blocking effect.

By this term I want to denote the effect, which any "new truth" in history can have, of pushing an older truth below the horizon of awareness established by the "new truth." The truth of philosophy, for instance, frequently blocks out, even to good philosophers, the truth of the myth from which it has emerged, so that the history of philosophy becomes a self-contained unit beginning with the pre-Socratics; the larger horizon of a truth of existence that can be expressed in the languages of either the myth or of noetic consciousness has disappeared. The same effect can be observed with regard to revelatory truth: There are excellent Christian thinkers who display a surprisingly haphazard knowledge of either classic philosophy or the myth. There are, furthermore, the modern national "blocks," such as Descartes and Pascal for some French, Hobbes and Locke for some English, Leibniz and Kant for some German thinkers.

It is this class of phenomena to which the blocking effect generated by the Systems of Science belongs. Comte and Hegel intended their systems to establish the truth that would be the ultimate truth for the future of mankind in history. This intention continued and perfected the Enlightenment conception of d'Alembert and Diderot that the *Encyclopédie Française* should be the sum of relevant knowledge: What had not been received from the past into the *Encyclopédie* was not worth knowing; what was to be discovered in the future had to assume the form of supplementary volumes to the *Encyclopédie*. In the Systems, this Enlightenment *hybris* received its constructivist polish. Comte was so convinced of being the possessor of ultimate truth that he engaged in diplomatic correspondence with the purpose of bringing Russian Orthodoxy, Islam, and the Catholic Church into the Positivist fold; and I have quoted Hegel to the effect that, setting aside minor imperfections, his Science and its Method was the only true one. The momentum of the Enlightenment revolt had built up to a formidable "new truth" that, though it neither did nor could succeed as a truth, could and did succeed negatively as a "block" that pushed below the horizon of awareness not only the degenerative dogmatisms of the eighteenth century but all representative expressions of existential truth in the history of mankind. Since the project of a Second Reality—barring the overlapping with sectors of First Reality—is not a truth in the reality of common experience, the Systems generated the twilightish phenomenon of a new authority of truth without substantive contents, which repeats, on the level of secondary deformation, the twilight of honest dishonesty characteristic of primary deformation. The "new truth" thus has the secondary effect of legitimating ignorance with regard to the truth of existence, be it expressed in the languages of Myth, Philosophy, Revelation, or Mysticism. It has established what I shall call the authority of ignorance.

This effect has become socially pervasive because the groups of "intellectuals" suffering from secondary deformation are solidly entrenched in the educational institutions from the universities down, as well as in the so-called mass media of communication. By virtue of this entrenchment they exert a social influence out of proportion to their actual numbers. In the Western societies of the twentieth century, there has developed as a consequence a highly diversified field of "opinions" deriving from the successive phases in the primary process of deformation. This field, furthermore, has a definite unity of structure, because the opinions, in spite of their conflicts and internecine struggles, have in common the claim to be respected as "truth," which derives from the blocking effect of the Systems. The right to be ignorant of the reality and truth of common experience has become, in the twentieth century, the most remarkable and characteristic institution of Western societies. The institution is firmly established and recognized, has entered public consciousness, and has even been elevated to something like a principle of social order by the self-interpretation of Western societies as "pluralistic societies." The intellectual climate deriving its character from the authority of ignorance has achieved a certain degree of stability that repeats, on the level of secondary deformation, the compulsiveness of imaginative projecting.

Nevertheless, the stability of the climate is precarious. Believing in the derivative imagery of "opinions" is just as much a disorder of existence as projecting on the grand scale, and the derivative imagery is just as much exposed to attrition through friction with First Reality as are the projects of the great imaginators. Disillusionment with this or that ideology, escapist conversion from one to the other, or cynicism with regard to all of them are common phenomena. If, on the one hand, a man is divorced from reality by "opinions" and experiences his contracted life as unendurable, or if, on the other hand, he cannot return to existence in truth because the habituation of disordered existence has become so strong that his spiritual energy cannot break it, or because even the access to the knowledge of truth is barred by the social pressure bearing down on him from the authority of ignorance institutionalized in the educational establishments, the mass media, and the public opinion more immediately surrounding him, then he has to fall back on the resources of his animal vitality if he wants to gain a mode of life he can experience as real. His life may then assume such behavioral forms as libertinism, hedonism, the cult of violence, destructiveness, vandalism, or outright criminality. If even his animal vitality should fail him, he may sink even lower—for instance, into the stupor of television watching—or he may take to drugs in order to "turn on" an existence that has been turned off beyond hope, or he may find the way out into a clinical neurosis. The phenomena adumbrated, common in our time, must be understood as severe forms of existential disintegration under the pressure of a social environment in which the truth of reality has been successfully eclipsed by the authority of ignorance.

3. Existence as a man and existence as a homunculus, as well as their expressions through philosophy and projecting, are in conflict with one another. Philosophy is the exegesis of man's existence in tension toward the divine ground; noetic reason is the language in which the partners in the truth of reality communicate; and the science of man's existence in society and history is a continuous discourse on the questions of existential order on all levels of being, ranging from the spiritual to the material. Projecting a Second Reality has the purpose of eclipsing the reality of existential tension; if projecting is perfected to a System of Science, the truth is revealed once and for all; and since no further inquiry concerning the order of existence is necessary, the discourse has come to its close.

A man's true self wants to lead the life of reason and engage in rational discourse; a man's contracted self is supposed to shut up. When in a spiritually disordered society the Second Reality of a System is accepted as a "scientifically" legitimate exposition of truth, the conflict becomes acute and requires a compromise solution. A man may have lost his identity of existence to such a degree that his desire to know will pounce upon the "truth" of the System as the answer to the questions that have disturbed him; but his true self may not be inclined to lose its identity completely and will want to continue the discourse on the problems that are its very own. The compromise will find the forms we have discussed. The "religious" Comte and the Logos-Hegel are rejected; the claim of the imaginary messiah to have spoken the word to end all words is unbearable; the discourse must go on. But the negative claim of the System to have scientifically demonstrated that all representative expressions of existential truth in the history of mankind, whatever relevance they may have had in their time, are irrelevant for the new age, will be gladly accepted because it permits the assuaging of anxiety by removing, with a show of legitimacy, the expressions of existential tension to one of the more or less deep cellars of the unconscious. That man's consciousness is elastic enough to accomodate both a true and a contracted self, as well as to develop the intricate nuances of semiconsciousness and unconsciousness that will keep them apart and in balance at least for some time, I have previously indicated by referring to instances of such co-existence.

With the rules of the game fixed in this manner, the discourse on man's existence in society and history continues in spite of the Systems, though it can no longer be rational because the critical center of rational discourse—*i.e.*, the luminosity of existence—has been suppressed. The pneumopathology of the sciences of man, society, and history in the wake of the Systems, however, is a vast issue to be more fully treated in a later part of this study. For the present purpose it will suffice to recall some well-known phenomena under their conventional headings of "scientisms" and "historicisms."

Since the exegesis of existential tension in the language of philosophy falls under the taboo of the blocking effect, the problems of existence, as they continue to be real, must be "explained" by means of the various "reductionist" devices in terms of social or historical causation, or of causation by phenomena on the psychological, physiological, and inorganic levels of being. The devices, however, cannot be standardized once and for all because, just like the projects on the level of the primary process, they are exposed to attrition by contact with First Reality and must be "revised." The more primitive "scientistic" reductions, for instance, though they continue well into the present, tend to be superseded by the critically refined escapes from the problems of existence into logical neo-positivism and language analysis. Bernard Lonergan has spoken of these developments as "a conceptualist extrinsicism for which concepts have neither dates nor developments and truth is so objective that it gets along without a mind" ("The Dehellenization of Dogma," *Theological Studies*, Vol. 28 [1967], 350). For the tensions on the "historicist" side, I refer to the ambiguous structure of Dilthey's "*Geisteswissenschaften*," and their offshoots in the "history of ideas" and "comparative religion." On the one hand, these historical sciences are devices that permit a scholar to record the representative expressions of existential truth in history while not obliging him to enter into the experiences that have engendered the symbols; on the other hand, the cumulative weight of this conscientious work makes ever more burning the question why so much labor should be invested in the exploration of symbolisms which by the rule of the Systems of Science are irrelevant to the "new age." At the time of this writing, the situation is still in the suspense of its ambiguity: There is more than one scholar on the verge of the breakthrough to a recognition of philosophy as the controlling center of the historical sciences, such as, for instance, Mircea Eliade; but then again, there occur such throwbacks to Hegel's system as the debate about "demythologization" or the "God-is-dead" movement. There seems to be hardly a doubt that the intellectual climate created by the secondary effects of the Systems will be a strong force in our society for a long time to come; but there also is no doubt that symptoms of corrosion become noticeable.

The "religious" Comte was rejected, the "intellectual" Comte was accepted. We remember the charges of madness in the psychiatric sense leveled against the "religious" part of his work and Comte's insistence on the unity of his project: Either the whole work was sane, or the whole work was insane. I have eliminated the issue of psychopathological sanity or insanity by treating the whole work as presenting a problem in the pneumopathology of projecting; and I have, furthermore, extended this treatment to the "scientisms" that attach themselves to the work of the "intellectual" Comte. We must return, in conclusion, to the question of the difference between pneumopathological and psychiatric phenomena, for recent developments of an "existential" psychology have given to the conception of madness a form that would bring even the "intellectual" Comte, who hitherto has escaped the charge—and together with him the scientisms attaching as effects to his projecting—to a psychiatrist's attention.

I shall first give some examples of scientistic behavior that might arouse the misgivings of an existential psychologist. In his work *Fads and Foibles in Modern Sociology and Related Sciences* (1956), Pitirim Sorokin has collected and criticized, to the extent of three hundred pages, curiosities of the social sciences that do not seem to be rarities but rather their normal fare. From his collection I select the following definitions concerning man, his mind, and his consciousness. An organism is

> a movable mathematical point in time-space, in reference to which matter-energy moves in such a way that a physical situation exists in which work is expended in order to preserve a physical system from a final gravitational and electromagnetic equilibrium with the rest of the universe.

A man is

> both a mechanical system . . . and a semantic self.

The mind of man is

> an organism's selection of particular kinds of material operations to perform upon particular kinds of matter-energy in order to minimize the organism's own probable work.

Consciousness is

> a complex integration and succession of bodily activities which are closely related to or involve the verbal and gestural mechanisms, and hence most frequently come to social expression.

Finally and roundly:

> Consciousness is an electron-proton aggregation.

From the context of Sorokin's work it is clear beyond a doubt that the secondary imaginators who have projected these fragments of Second Realities are professors at this or that university, enjoying the reputation of scientists of particular acumen. Moreover, again from the context, it is clear that the definitions are not marginal metaphorical excrescences but purport to tender relevant information on an area of reality, presumably to be verified or falsified by the rules so dear to the heart of social scientists who believe they know something about physics.

And now for the existential psychologist. In R. D. Laing's 1964 preface to the Pelican edition of his *Divided Self* (1959), we find the following programmatic passage: "In the context of our present pervasive madness that we call normality, sanity, freedom, all our frames of reference are ambiguous and equivocal. . . . A man who says that men are machines may be a great scientist. A man who says he *is* a machine is 'depersonalized' in psychiatric jargon." The application to the samples of scientistic behavior given in the preceding paragraph is obvious: if a man says "Consciousness is an electron-proton aggregation," he is a respected sociologist; if a man says "My consciousness is an electron-proton aggregation" and consistently refuses to take responsibility for the activity of electrons and protons, he is a psychiatric case. Laing seems to be inclined to classify both cases under the head of "madness." And yet we have the feeling that there is some difference between them, even though it may be difficult to formulate it with precision. Before coming to a decision, let us have a look at two further cases that will show the range of the problem.

In the *Divided Self* (148), Laing reports the following case:

A young man of twenty-two was regarded by his parents and friends as entirely "normal." While on holiday by the sea, he took a boat out to sea. He was picked up some hours later, having drifted far from the land. He resisted being rescued, saying that he had lost God, and had set out on the ocean to find him. This incident marked the onset of a manifest neurosis that required his hospitalization for many months.

On the same page of the *Divided Self* he reports the second case:

A man in his fifties who never before had any "nervous" trouble, at least not to his wife's knowledge, and who had seemed to her, up to the acute onset of the psychosis, to be his "usual self," went with his wife and children on a picnic beside a river, on a hot summer's afternoon. After the meal, he undressed completely, although there were other picnickers in view, and entered the water. This was perhaps no more than unusual. Having waded waist deep, he threw the water over himself. He now refused to come out, saying that he was baptizing himself for his sins, which were that he had never loved his wife or his children, and that he would not leave the water until he was cleansed. He eventually was dragged from the river by the police and admitted to a mental hospital.

Laing reports the two cases as examples for the onset of a psychosis "out of a blue sky." Although it is unreasonable to assume that he has not seen the parallelism, he does not elaborate on the importance of the cases as the psychotic variants of the spiritually diseased imaginator's phantasies of the "death of God" and of "self-salvation." Again one would have to say: If Hegel proclaims the death of God in his *Phänomenologie* or if Nietzsche, in his *Gay Science*, lets his "Madman" search for God with a lantern in the market place, they are great thinkers. If the unhappy young man who has lost God goes searching for him in a boat on the ocean, he "requires hospitalization for many months." And the same goes for Comte's, Hegel's, and Nietzsche's self-salvation in contrast to the unhappy family father who pours water over his head to cleanse himself from his sins.

Laing is keenly sensitive for the "madness" surrounding us in our society, but he tends, as I have said, to blur the lines that separate a spiritual disorder from a neurosis. One of the reasons, perhaps, is that he tapped existentialism at the level of Kierkegaard and Sartre, neither of whom achieved ultimate clarity on this point; the classical problems of the philosopher's existence and of noetic luminosity do not seem to have entered his horizon, as his later work *The Politics of Experience* (1967) shows. Nevertheless, though I cannot at this juncture give a complete answer to the question of the dividing line because a number of factors must be taken into account which have not yet become thematic in our analysis, at least a partial answer is possible on the basis of the cases furnished by Laing. Laing himself gives a valuable hint in the right direction when he says: "I am quite sure that a good number of 'cures' of psychotics consist in the fact that a patient has decided, for one reason or another, once more to *play at being sane.*" Sanity is a play. The man is really insane, but he plays at being sane. If we transfer this observation to our analysis of the imaginator's existential disorder, we may say that the imaginator will stay on the side of sanity in the psychiatric sense as long as he can sustain his play of honest dishonesty. The exasperating dishonesty of the Second Realities is the factor of play that holds the imaginator's personality together;

if he were to believe seriously in what he says, his personality would fall apart and he would become a neurotic case. As long as the Second Reality carries the index of "bad faith," as long as it remains a play at insanity, we have to speak of a spiritual disorder; when the Second Reality acquires the index of "good faith," the play will change over into an honest psychosis.

4

❦

The Moving Soul

I. Margenau's Fancy

The theories of Einstein and Minkowski have brought new precision to the concept of simultaneity. In Henry Margenau's *Nature of Physical Reality* (1950), we find on this point the following reflections:

> It is seen that the concept of simultaneity has lost its universal character; events simultaneous to one observer may not be simultaneous to another. . . .
> Hard-boiled classicists sometimes insist that the change in our attitude toward simultaneity has been brought about *only* by the recognition that light, the fastest of all signals, travels with a finite velocity and that, if a signal capable of infinite velocity were found, universal simultaneity could be restored. All this we must grant. But if our critic goes on to a conclusion which makes the restricted version of simultaneity into a mere stopgap forced upon us by our in-

---

"The Moving Soul," completed in 1969, is found in Box 75, Folder 2, Voegelin Papers, Hoover Institution Archives. Folders 2 through 4 also include correspondence concerning the piece.

ability to find the proper signal of infinite velocity—which after all is available to *thought*—then we must object. For he is now talking like the little girl who wondered whether her wings, if she had any, would be white or blue. Universal simultaneity is a perfectly respectable construct, but apparently not a valid one.

According to relativity theory the idea of simultaneity has not lost its meaning but has become somewhat more complex. . . . Indeed it provides amusing opportunities for fanciful reflections based on science. One which seems not to have been exploited as evidence for immortality is the fact that a soul, if it moved away from the body at the time of death with the speed of light, would observe the last dying moment as an eternity of bliss or of agony. (pp. 152–53)

II. The Thought Experiment

Margenau's remark about "amusing opportunities for fanciful reflections based on science" was made facetiously, to be sure. Nevertheless, the challenge should be taken up, not as a matter of amusement, but in the form of a thought experiment that will explore the relations between the cognition of physical reality, the spatiotemporal structure of the universe, and the velocities of light and the observer.

A

To this purpose we assume a man in an earth position O with the space-time coordinates (s, t), who is able to split off from his soul S a double Sm. With regard to the disembodied double Sm we make the following assumptions:

1. Sm is able to move away from the man in the spatiotemporal position O (s, t) at will, at any velocity it desires.
2. Sm is equipped with the faculty of experiencing physical reality, in Margenau's sense, which ranges from the spontaneity of immediate sense perception to the reflective production of constructs, and includes memory.
3. Sm is equipped only with the faculty of experiencing physical reality in Margenau's sense, but not with the faculty of experiencing existential tension and of developing the constructs peculiar to this area of experience.
4. The self of Sm is constituted by the awareness of experiencing in the sense defined. If the stream of experience should cease, the self of Sm would black out.

B

We assume *Sm* to be moving at various finite velocities. Since the velocity of light *c* is finite, the following relations between the experience of *Sm* and the events at the position of *S* at *O* (*s, t*) can be imagined:

1. If *Sm* remains stationary, hovering near the man from whose *S* it has split off, the physical events will roll off for it in the same manner as for *S*.
2. If *Sm* moves away from *S* in a straight line, with a velocity $v<c$, it will observe the future events experienced by *s* in slow motion. The motion will become slower as *v* increases, and will approach zero as the velocity of *Sm* approaches *c*.
3. If *Sm* moves with the velocity $v=c$ (Margenau's fancy), it will observe in permanence (Margenau's eternity) the events experienced by *S* at the time *Sm* left the position *O* (*s, t*).
4. If *Sm* moves with a finite velocity $v>c$, it will catch up with light rays that have emanated from the position *O* (*s, t*) prior to its departure from the point of origin at which it has split off from *S*. *Sm*, thus, will observe events from the point of origin *O* (*s, t*) rolling backward in time. The movement of the events rolling backward in time will become faster as the velocity of *Sm* increases beyond *c*.

C

We assume *Sm* to move with infinite velocity in a Newtonian universe—space is isotropic and homogeneous; space and time are independent of one another, so that motion does not affect the time scale. Time "of itself, and from its own nature, flows equally without regard to anything external" (Newton). The space and time dimensions are assumed to extend from the point of origin *O* (*s, t*) in uniform infinity.

Under these assumptions, *Sm* will outrace all light rays that have emanated from the position *O* (*s, t*) prior to the departure of *Sm*. With regard to space, *Sm* will be simultaneously present at all points of the space line along which it races. With regard to time, *Sm* will experience the events at the point of origin as rolling backward into the past with infinite velocity.

The simultaneous presence of *Sm* at all points of its course must neither be translated into an instantaneous view of a spatially infinite universe, nor into an instantaneous view, *sub specie eternitatis*, of all events rolling off in infinite time. Such translations would hypostatize the universe and transform the experiencing *Sm* into a subject of cognition outside this entity. They would be incompatible with our assumption of *Sm* as moving and experiencing within the universe of physical reality.

Under the assumption that the experience of physical reality is a process within the process of the universe, there will result certain aporiae if the observer *Sm* of physical reality moves with infinite velocity. These aporiae can be made explicit by imagining variations of the time and space dimensions of the universe in which *Sm* moves:

1. If the time dimension is imagined to be finite (if, in mythical language, the world has a "beginning"), *Sm* will run out of experiences when it reaches the limit of time. It will suffer a blackout of experience.

2. The same reflection applies if the universe is imagined to be spatially finite.

3. As far as the experience of physical reality is concerned, finiteness of time abolishes infinity of space and, inversely, finiteness of space abolishes infinity of time. An *Sm* that moves with infinite velocity can continue to experience physical reality only if the universe is infinite with regard to both space and time.

4. If *Sm* moves with infinite velocity along its course, it will be simultaneously present at all of its points. Hence, if either the time or the space of the universe are imagined to be finite, *Sm* would suffer the blackout of experience simultaneously with its start from the point O (s, t). Its self would cease to be aware of itself as experiencing. As we have assumed the awareness of experiencing physical reality to be the sole constituent of *Sm*'s self, the physical reality of a finite universe cannot be experienced by an observer moving with infinite velocity.

5. If both space and time are infinite, *Sm* will have experienced physical reality up to the point O (s, t) in the same manner as S. At the moment at which it splits off from S, it will experience a universe that up to O (s, t) moves in the time direction experienced by S and at the point O (s, t) will reverse itself and roll backward in the opposite time direction.

D

We assume *Sm* to move with infinite velocity in uniform, infinite time but in a universe whose space curves back into itself, so that

Sm will perform an infinite number of circuits on a universe line through the space point from which it has started. Under these assumptions, the following set of aporiae will result:

1. The light rays emanating from the point O with the spatial coordinates s move with the finite velocity c and will complete their circuit on the space curve in the finite time span T. The space curve running back into O can accomodate, in linear succession, no more than the light waves that have emanated from O during a sector of its past of the length T. Since we have assumed the time dimension to be uniformly infinite, the space curve will be filled with an infinite number of such sectors T. At every point of the space curve there is to be found a bundle of events that at the point O were distant from one another by the time span T. *Sm* moving with infinite velocity from O (s, t) will experience as contemporaneous, at every point of the space curve, an infinity of events that at the point O occurred with time coordinates differing by the magnitude T. The experience of physical reality will have become an infinite muddle.

2. The light rays emanating from O will reach the same spatial point at the time $t+T$. The series of coordinates $t+T$ covers in infinity the time coordinate t of O. Under our assumption, *Sm* moving with infinite velocity will be simultaneously present at the infinite series of local times of the point O. We run into the aporiae of simultaneous presence at different points of time.

3. In order to avoid these aporiae, one could imagine the following variations of our initial assumptions:
   a) In a curved universe, the velocity of light emanating from a point O diminishes, with increasing distance from O, in such a manner that a light ray emanating from O can never reach the point O again. In this case the velocity c would not be a constant.
   b) A curved universe expands with such speed that light at the constant velocity c can never reach its starting point again.
   c) In both cases, an *Sm* moving with infinite velocity would outrace all light rays that have emanated from O and suffer the blackout of experience.
   The variations *a* and *b* are closely related to Poincaré's conception of a limited universe in which the space-time distances contract, unconscious to the observer, in such a manner that the limit can never be reached.

4. As an alternative to the variations under Point 3 one could imagine the following construction: The points of the type O (s, t) are intra-universal. In addition to the intra-universal three space coordinates represented by s and the fourth coordinate t, one could imagine a fifth coordinate u on which the universe as a whole moves; this movement *Mu* could not be experienced intra-

universally. *Mu* could be imagined as a translation of the intra-universal structure along the coordinate *u* of such a nature that a movement starting from any point in the universe of our experience *Ue* would, on completion of the space curve, arrive intra-universally at *O*, but at another point of the coordinate *u*, in a universe *Un* beyond experience from any point in *Ue*. This construction, however, just like the variations under Point 3 or Poincaré's conception, carries us beyond the experience of physical reality.

III. Conclusions

(1) *The Aporiae of the Physical Universe*

(1.1) The aporetic propositions advanced under II. C and D are the analytical equivalent, for the case of modern physics, to Kant's Antinomies of Reason under the assumptions of Newtonian physics.

(1.2) Aporetic propositions will arise if we speculate on the "universe" and try to construct its structure in terms of finite or infinite space and time dimensions. The variety of recent constructs is surveyed by Margenau in his Chapter 7.12, "Are Time and Space Infinite?" He arrives at the net result: "On this, perhaps the most interesting question of all, present science is unfortunately noncommittal." All the constructs surveyed by Margenau seem to be variants of the construct I have suggested under II, D (4): they try to resolve the problem of the infinite by introducing an additional coordinate of the universe beyond the range of experience. This resolution must remain an intellectual game because it cannot be empirically validated.

(1.3) Constructs concerning the structure of the physical universe as a whole cannot be empirically validated. Why, then, do physicists engage again and again in their construction? The only possible answer to this question seems to be that physicists are men who as human beings feel obliged to develop an image of the universe. They feel obliged to engage in the creation of a mytho-speculative symbol that will satisfy our desire to know the structure of the universe in which we live.

(1.4) In constructing the observer *Sm*, I have taken care to equip *Sm* with the faculty of experiencing physical reality but to withhold from it the experience of existential tension as well as the faculty of developing symbols that express existential tension. Hence, *Sm* will suffer a blackout of experience or land in a spatio-temporal muddle, but it will not construct a universe. The physicist who constructs the structure of the universe is not satisfied with his role as an observer of physical reality but exerts his prerogative as man to create symbols expressive of existential tension.

(1.5) Physics, if understood as an empirical science of physical reality, does not furnish the means for the meaningful construction of mytho-speculative symbols. By going through the aporetic propositions, I hope to have shown that from physics follows nothing but physics.

(1.6) Still, the term *universe* can be meaningfully used with regard to the experience of physical reality if it denotes the context of the experience, and the term *context* is properly defined in the following manner:

(a) An experience of physical reality refers to a reality in a spatio-temporal context of indefinite finiteness.
(b) An experience of physical reality is an event in a universal process with the structure of indefinite finiteness.

(2) *Sense Perception and the Speed of Light*

(2.1) The older aporiae of the infinite attach to the assumption of the universe as a spatiotemporal entity; the twentieth-century aporiae attach to the assumption of an observer of physical reality, as well as to the manner in which the observer's experience is affected by the relation between the speed of light and the velocity of the observer's movement.

(2.2) This relation between our experience of physical reality and the speed of light deserves more attention than it usually receives.

Let us assume light to move not at the velocity c but at the more leisurely pace of 1 mile per hour. In this case, a person approaching us at a walking speed of 3 miles per hour would be upon us before we can visually observe his approach. We would have a haptic experience of his presence, followed by the spectacle of his approach in reverse, with his position at the moment when he entered our visual horizon seen last. Under this assumption, our experience of physical reality, based on what is lightly called sense perception, would be vastly different from the one that we have now that light moves with the velocity c.

(2.3) In order to have the kind of "sense perception" with which we are familiar, light must move with a velocity sufficiently large to give it practical simultaneity at all points of man's pragmatic range. Only with light moving at high velocity can we have the instantaneous experience of reality that we have.

(3) The Instantaneous Presence of the Cosmos

(3.1) In *Metaphysics* I.1, Aristotle proclaims the desire to know to be the nature of man and then goes on to praise sight as the noblest of senses, because it makes knowledge possible. This passage should not be read as an eighteenth-century declaration of "sense perception" as the basis of our experience of reality but as an intuition of the spontaneous and instantaneous presence of the cosmos through sight and light. Not from "sense perception" but from the visual presence of the cosmos does Aristotle's desire to know ascend to the understanding of the Nous.

(3.2) That the reality surrounding us is the intelligible whole of a cosmos cannot be derived from the experience of physical reality. Rather, the conception of the intelligible whole articulates the impact of the cosmos on the eye, as in the Xenophantic exclamation, reported by Aristotle, "Looking up at the expanse of the Heaven 'The One, he said, is the God.'" And because the One of spontaneous presence is the God, the cosmic One must partake of divine eternity.

(3.3) The idea of a universe with an infinite time dimension is the demythologized version of the divine as distinguished from the human mode of existence. This statement for the specific instance is meant to stand for the general rule that the symbolisms of the cosmos as an intelligible whole, as divine Being from eternity, or as a divine creation with a beginning and an end, arise as articulations of experiences of participation in the divine ground of all being, not as constructs based on, and to be validated empirically by, sense perception.

(4) *Space and Time—The Historical Cosmos*

(4.1) The space line traveled by *Sm* is a time line on which the past of *O* (s, t) rolls backward.

(4.2) A point *P*, distant 1000 light-years from *O* (s, t), will be the point of events which, in local time of *O* (s, t) have occurred 1000 years ago, but are experienced at *P* (s, t) as present.

(4.3) In order to experience the events which, in local time, are contemporaneous with *O* (s, t), *Sm* would have to wait at *P* for 1000 years.

(4.4) *O* is as many years ahead in time of *P*, as *P* is light-years distant from *O*.

(4.5) In order to make the events at *P* contemporary with the events at *O*, either the spatial distance between *P* and *O* would have to collapse or the velocity of light would have to become infinite.

(4.6) An event at *P*, experienced at *O* as present, is a historical event that has happened in the past of *O*.

(4.7) A contemporaneous universe is not a possible object of experience.

(4.8) What is experienced as simultaneous with the presence of the observer at *O* (s, t) is not contemporaneous with him.

(4.9) What is present in the instantaneous "look at the Heaven" is the cosmos in historical existence.

(4.10) The cosmos as a spatial structure of contemporary mass entities and events is a construct based on the model of space and time experience within the human pragmatic range.

(5) *Time Direction—Localized Memory—The Primary Experience of the Cosmos*

(5.1) We assume *Sm* to have traveled with infinite velocity from *O* to *P*, 1000 light-years distant. We call the event *P* (s, t) at the arrival of *Sm* simultaneous with *O* (s, t). Having arrived at the position *P*, *Sm* will have to wait 1000 years in order to experience as present in the local time of *P* the events at *O* (s, t) from which it has started. Since we have equipped *Sm* with memory, the events at *O* (s, t) will have rolled backward while *Sm* traveled to *P*, and now they will roll forward in the time direction again, now that *Sm* has come to rest at *P*.

(5.2) Conclusion: under the assumption of an observer *Sm*, moving with infinite velocity from one position in the universe to another, the universe has no time direction.

(5.3) Time direction in the universe is incompatible with simultaneity of observation.

(5.4) If we deprive *Sm* of its memory upon its arrival at *P*, the events at *O* (*s, t*) will roll off with time direction, as observed from *P*.

(5.5) Conclusion: the universe has time direction only for a spatially localized memory.

(5.6) The spontaneous and instantaneous presence of the cosmos in the "look at the Heaven" is possible only for an observer in a position from which one can "look at the Heaven."

(5.7) The "experience of physical reality" (perception, constructs, memory) is bound to the primary experience of the cosmos in the "look at the Heaven."

(5.8) There is no "physical universe" independent of the perspectival primary experience of the cosmos.

5

The Beginning and the Beyond

A Meditation on Truth

Divine reality is being revealed to man in two fundamental modes of experience: in the experience of divine creativity in the cosmos; and in the experience of divine ordering presence in the soul.

The two modes are always structures in man's consciousness of divine reality, but they are not always conscious in the form of reflected knowledge. The experience is the area of reality where the revelatory appeal from the divine side meets with the questing response from the human side, and reflective meditation on the response is preceded by millennia of less reflected response in the form of cosmological symbolization. Only late in history, when man becomes aware of himself, of his spirit and intellect, as an active partner in the cognition of divine reality, will the two modes be discerned and adequately symbolized. Only when the response becomes luminous to itself as a quest for the divine ground, and when the quest becomes an act of reflective questioning, will man find himself moving either in the direction of divine creativity toward a Beginning of things, or in the direction of the ordering presence within his soul toward a divine Beyond as its source.

The symbols of the Beginning and the Beyond indicate the directions in which man finds himself moving when he attempts to locate the divine ground as a something in relation to the things of this world in which it is present, though it is not one of them. They are directional indices, not abstract concepts. I am describing the movement by the contemplative phrase of man finding himself moving, because man does not actively choose these directions in

"The Beginning and the Beyond," completed in its present form by about 1977, is found in Box 81, Folder 5, Voegelin Papers, Hoover Institution Archives. Related draft pages mentioned in the Editorial Note may also be found here.

preference to others that would be equally possible. In fact, when the response becomes a questing movement, the directions are prescribed by the structure of the reality in which man finds himself situated as its part. In his search of the divine ground, man can do no more than move either in the time dimension of the cosmos or through the hierarchy of being from inorganic matter to his own questioning existence, in order to find it either in an event preceding the present state of things or in a place higher than the known hierarchy of things. Hence, when the response becomes reflectively conscious as a quest, the experience reveals a truth not only about divine reality but also about the structure of the cosmos in which it occurs. Beside the structures of appeal-response, the structures of cosmic lasting in time and of the hierarchy of being are a further area of reality that becomes visible through the movements toward the Beginning and the Beyond.

The symbols of the Beginning and the Beyond, thus, express the dynamics of the experience in all of its aspects. They articulate, first of all, the divine reality that draws man into the quest; they express furthermore the structure of consciousness in its questing tension toward the divine ground of things and of itself; and they finally bring into view the structure of reality that channels both the divine drawing and the human questing. This superb precision in articulating the structure of the experience has endowed the two symbols with their millennial durability ever since they were found in antiquity.

Site: Man the Questioner

As he moves in either of the two directions, man the questioner will find himself both frustrated and illumined. As he moves back on the time line, he will discover the regress to be indefinite. He will not find a divine beginning in time. The ground he is seeking is to be found, not in the things of the cosmos and their time dimension, but in the mystery of a creative beginning of the cosmos in a time out of time. Still, when the seeker makes the discovery, he will not abandon the directional index but use it analogically to symbolize the divinely-creative beginning of a reality that has a time dimension after all. The creational Beginning as an analogical symbol will denote therefore not a beginning in the time dimension of the world, but a beginning in the analogical time of a creation story. The time out of time, as I called it, is the Time of the Tale, of the cosmogonic myth in the bewildering variety of its manifestations in history. By the analogous Beginning, the cosmogonic myth expresses the experience of a lasting cosmos permeated by the divine mystery of its existence, and articulates the truth of a cosmos that is not altogether of this world. The reality of things, it appears, cannot be fully understood in terms of the world and its time; for the things are circumfused by an ambience of mystery that can be understood only in terms of the Myth. Since the divine Beginning, though experienced as real, is not an event in the time of the world, the imaginative creation story is the symbolism necessary for its expression. Moreover, the adequacy of the symbolism to the experience points to the miracle of a mythical imagination that can produce the adequate Tale. We are touching on the problem, to be treated more explicitly later, of an imagination and a language that is itself perhaps not altogether of this world.

When in his quest of the ground man moves not on the time line but ascends over the hierarchy of being, his search will go through the same kind of frustration and illumination. The finest early explorations of the movement in this second direction are certain dialogues of the Upanishads. The *Brihadaranyaka Upanishad* (III, 6), for instance, lets the Brahmanic sage be driven by his questioning partner in the dialogue through the hierarchy of the elements up to the sky, further on through the sun, the moon, and the stars, and still further on through the hierarchy of the traditional gods, until the Brahman is reached as the origin of the hierarchy of being. And what is the Brahman? It is not a further knowable thing; it rather is the reality at which the questioning has to stop, not because the movement has been futile, but because this reality, by its position beyond the knowable hierarchy of things, reveals itself as the answer to the questioning ascent. Making due allowance for the lesser degree of differentiation in the Upanishad, this dialogical movement through the questioning process in the *Brihadaranyaka* arrives at the same result as the monological analysis of internal reflection by Saint Augustine in *De vera religione* (XXXIX, 72). The Augustinian analysis culminates in the insight that the super-reflective truth, when reached by the reflective ascent, illuminates the questioning as a response to the movement of divine presence in the soul. The questioning has reached intelligibly its end when the hierarchy of being is exhausted while the *intentio animi* reaches further out toward its Beyond. The super-reflective truth-reality authenticates the reflective ascent as the divinely moved search, while the structure of questioning consciousness, as it out-questions the knowable, becomes the criterion of the truth truly found. As in the movement on the time line toward the Beginning we had to note the remarkable adequacy of imaginative symbolization to a cosmos that is experienced as not altogether of this world, so now we must note the remarkable structure of a question that leads to the Beyond of the world because it is not altogether of the world in which it is asked.

The truth is one, but the language in which the truth becomes articulate is not always the same. The two modes of experience just adumbrated move historically from compactness to differentiation, and the symbols expressing them change accordingly. Moreover, the two modes affect each other in the process of history. The revelatory discovery of the oneness of divine reality in the direction of the Beyond, for instance, can make a plurality of divine forces in the direction of the Beginning intolerable—though not necessarily so, as the coexistence of the divine Beyond with the intracosmic gods in Plato, Aristotle, and Plotinus shows. The experience and symbolization of the two modes thus has a historical dimension. In fact, the Beginning and the Beyond, though truly indicating the two directions, are symbols with historical dates attached to them. The literary documents that have endowed the two indices with their historical effectiveness in Western civilization to this day are the Book of Genesis and Plato's *Republic*. The cosmogony of Genesis, probably to be dated in the sixth century B.C., lets the heavens and earth be created by God in the Beginning; while Plato, in the fourth century B.C., lets the existence and essence of things, as well as their knowability, originate in the Beyond of both the knower and the known, in the Agathon. Although the directional indices have a long prehistory, embedded in more compact forms of symbolization, the *bereshit* of Genesis and the *epekeina* of the *Republic* have become the representative expressions of the experiential modes. As it becomes articulate in language, the truth of divine reality definitely has a historical dimension.

These preliminary remarks intimate the character of the following reflections as a meditation on the experience of divine reality and its differentiation in history, furthermore on the language in which the experience becomes articulate, and finally on the truth of the language as the truth of divine reality. There will be three parts to the reflections. In a first part, I shall concentrate on the problem of language as it presents itself in the Ecumenic Age when the symbols of the Beginning and the Beyond make their appearance. In the second part, I shall enter into the problem of the fully conscious meditation *de veritate* as it was developed by Aquinas in the *Summa contra gentiles*, with special attention to the historical consciousness of the Saint. And in the third part, I shall consider some problems of a meditation on truth in the present historical situation.

I. Truth and Language

I shall begin from the Beginning, from the cosmos as it impresses itself on man by the splendor of its existence, by the movements of the starry heavens, by the intelligibility of its order, and by its lasting as the habitat of man. The man who receives the impression, in his turn, is endowed with an intellect both questioning and imaginative. He can respond to the impression by recognizing the divine mystery of a reality in which he is a knowing partner, though it is not of his making. In this experience of the cosmos, neither the impression nor the reception of reality is dully factual. It rather is alive with the meaning of a spiritual event, for the impression is revelatory of the divine mystery, while the reception responds to the revelatory component by cognition of faith. This is the experience to which Saint Paul refers in Rom. 1 : 18–23, when he chides his contemporaries for not recognizing the truth of God revealed in the cosmos. From heaven itself, he says, the wrath of God is revealed against the ungodly who suppress the truth of God it reveals; for what can be known about God he has made manifest to them through the cosmos. "Ever since the creation of the cosmos the invisibles of God, his everlasting power and divinity, are seen to be known in the things that have been made." They are inexcusable who do not honor the God whom they know but, claiming wisdom, become fools as they substitute images of perishable men and animals for the imperishable glory of God. This Pauline outburst is of special value because it not only describes the experience but also intimates the historical clash between his own more differentiated experience and the compact symbolization of divine creativity through intracosmic gods in his cultural environment.

An experience that is structured in the manner just adumbrated cannot be adequately described in terms of object and subject, with reality playing the role of the object and man that of the subject of cognition. It rather is to be described as a process within a reality that comprehends both the cosmos with its divine mystery and the man with his mind in which the mystery becomes cognitively luminous. Within that comprehensive reality, the experience is luminous to itself as a divine-human movement and countermovement, as a movement of revelatory appeal from the divine side and a countermovement of apperceptive and imaginative response from the human side. Both appeal and response belong to the one reality that becomes luminous in the experience. The specific area of reality in which the process occurs, thus, is neither divine nor human, neither transcendent nor immanent, but rather has the character of an In-Between reality. Plato, when he analyzed the experience, for the case of the erotic tension toward the divine ground, has indeed developed the language of the In-Between reality, of the *metaxy*, as the symbolism that will most adequately express the ontological character of the area. Aristotle, who has to deal with the same problem, prefers to speak of it as the area of divine-human mutual participation, as the metaleptic reality. Both Plato and Aristotle agree to let the term *psyche* denote the site of the process.

There would be no record of such experiences if the process did not break forth into self-exegesis by means of language symbols engendered in the course of the event. Since this articulation of the experience through language, through the word, is part of the process itself, since it belongs ontologically to the Metaxy, it must not be treated as if it were a separate, world-immanent act outside the experience. In the contemporary climate of opinion, however, the reifications of the type just intimated have become so much an accepted habit that it is almost impossible to present the central problem of a philosophy of language without arousing bewilderment. A brief statement concerning the distortion of reality caused by such hypostases will therefore be appropriate.

The experience in the Metaxy is the source of our insights concerning the partners to the encounter, as well as concerning the encounter itself. This source will be eclipsed, if the partners and their encounter are reified into entities independent of the source. Neither must the divine partner be hypostatized into an object, nor the human partner into a subject, of cognition; nor must the encounter itself, with its movements and counter-movements in the Metaxy of the psyche, be hypostatically transformed into the world-immanent experience of a hypostatic human subject; nor must the insights be transformed into a description of the hypostatized experience of the hypostatized subject by means of language symbols conveniently at hand for the purpose. For hypostatic constructions of this type would destroy the dynamics of movement and counter-movement in the event of reality becoming luminous; and, the dynamics destroyed, they would leave the component parts of the experience, which become visible and articulate on the occasion of the event, as a wasteland of static objects. The consciousness that goes through the process of becoming luminous for itself in the Metaxy would be replaced by an immanent consciousness of man that experiences a transcendent object. On this immanent consciousness there would then be superimposed a reflecting conciousness that articulates the experience by means of a pre-existent language. A construction of this type would establish a massive block of immanent subjectivity that separates from each other, on the one side, a hypostatized divine reality and, on the other side, a hypostatized language. The construction would effectively remove the articulating language from the Metaxy and break its dynamic connection with the movement and countermovement it expresses.

Hypostatizing constructions are generally inadmissible for theoretical reasons. They distort the reality that we want to explore. In the present case, furthermore, they are incompatible with the history of language as we know it empirically, as well as with the self-understanding of the men who have the experiences. For as far back as the written records go—that is, to about 3000 B.C.—the key symbols of exegesis arise on the occasion of the experience either as neologisms or as new meanings attached to older symbols as their carriers. There is no such thing as a pre-existent language that can be applied to the movement of appeal-response; there is only the language that arises from the Metaxy of the process in its course. Moreover, the hypostasis of language is in open conflict with the insight into its metaleptic dynamics on the part of the spiritualists who suffer the experiences. The men whose utterances emerge from the divine-human encounter are well aware that the language erupting in them is as much divine as it is human. When the event occurs in very compact form in a tribal society, as in the case of the Rig-Veda, the divine-human Metaxy may not even yet have differentiated, so that the utterance has, in the consciousness of the speaker, still the pre-personal sacrality of the divinely mysterious reality breaking forth into self-illumination through truth in language. The hymn to *Vac, i.e.,* to Speech (X, 125), represents this pre-personal experience of the comprehensive reality becoming luminous in the word; and the compactness of this early experience dominates the further development of Hinduism so strongly that it forces the form of a Vedic commentary on the far-reaching differentiations of consciousness in the Upanishads. In the case of Israelite prophecy, on the other hand, the Metaxy has differentiated so far in the pneumatic direction that God and man have become personalized as the partners in the divine-human encounter. Hence, the encounter assumes the form of a divine "call," while the man who responds to it is constituted by the call as the *nabi,* as the speaker of the calling God, as his prophet. As a consequence, the prophetic utterance can be understood both as the human word of the speaker and as the word of the God spoken through his prophet. This word of God, though, must not be misunderstood in a literalist fashion as an acoustic phenomenon emanating from God and received as an auditory experience by the prophet. The word, as it emerges from the Metaxy, need not be "heard"; it also can be "seen," as in Amos 1 : 1 or in Isa. 2 : 1 and 13 : 1; or vision and word can blend in the tale of a dialogue between God and the prophet, as in the visions of Amos 7; or the word can directly assume the form a divine-human dialogue, as in Jeremiah 12. Any tale or imagery will do, so long as it conveys the awareness that the word is not an utterance of immanent man but emerges from the intangible point of the divine-human encounter in the Metaxy.

The prophetic personalization of the encounter differentiates one segment of the integral experience of reality, but it does not invalidate the truth of the prepersonal, comprehensive reality contained in the compact experience of the Vedic type. Differentiation of a segment does not abolish the truth of reality experienced compactly; there is no simple succession in which a historically later truth makes an earlier one obsolete. On the contrary, in postexilic Judaism the prophets fade out and give way to such new types of spiritualists as the apocalyptic visionary and the scribe of the Wisdom literature, while the prepersonal reality asserts itself in the emergence of a new symbolic form to be superimposed over the former prophetic word of God. I am speaking of the creation of Scripture and of the Scriptural word of God. The details of this symbolism and its creation are rather complex: I must confine myself here to a formulation of the general issue.

Scripture

Scripture is a stratum of meaning superimposed on a body of Israelite and Judaic literature by the organizers of the Book of the Torah, the Prophets, and the Writings. The organization of the Torah, in the narrower sense of the Pentateuchal Torah, begins in the sixth century B.C. and is substantially completed in the first half of the fourth century B.C.; the process of extending the symbolism of Scripture to the Prophets and the Writings, however, as well as the debates about the sources to be included, continue into the second century A.D. The principle of the symbolism is formulated in Pirke Aboth 1: "Moses received the Torah from Sinai and committed it to Joshua, and Joshua to the elders, and the elders to the Prophets; and the Prophets committed it to the men of the Great Synagogue." The line of transmitters then is continued from Simeon the just, one of the "remnants of the Great Synagogue," down to Hillel and Shammai, ca. 30 B.C. to A.D. 10. By a remarkable feat of mythical imagination, a literary document assembled and organized in the postexilic period is construed to have been engendered by a divine-human encounter in the Mosaic period. The construction intends to protect the spiritual insights gained in the course of Israelite history against the pressure of competing wisdoms in the ecumenic-imperial society that now has become the politically and culturally powerful environment surrounding the small Judaic enclave. It tries to achieve this purpose by endowing the insights with the superior sacrality of a unique divine outburst in reality that reveals once and for all the mystery of divine creativity in the cosmos as well as in man's existence in society and history.

The protective device cannot be simply dismissed as a clever invention. It could be a plausible act of mythopoesis, and remain historically effective for two thousand years, because it could mobilize the experience of the comprehensive, prepersonal reality breaking forth into self-illuminating truth. The breaking forth does in fact not occur as a single manifestation of truth in history but assumes the form of an open historical field of major and minor divine-human encounters, widely dispersed in time and space over the societies who together are mankind in history. Nevertheless, in spite of the pluralistic historical form, what breaks forth in this field is the one truth of the one reality. The experience of the one truth breaking forth from the one reality is the authenticating motive in the mythopoetic concentration of a social field of historically related encounters, such as the Israelite, into one revelatory event.

The result of this mythopoetic feat is, in the Israelite case, an oddly ambiguous symbolism. On the one hand, the Scriptural word of God freezes the literary records of real encounters and their historical circumstances into an impersonal block of truth that originates in the mythopoetic consciousness of priests in the sixth century B.C., with the structure of the block approaching the prepersonal compactness of Speech in the Vedic type. On the other hand, since the differentiation of prophetic personalism cannot be reversed, the block cannot be allowed to emerge anonymously as an event of self-illumination from prepersonal reality but must be attributed pseudepigraphically to Moses as the recipient of divine communication. Beyond the present case of an attribution to Moses, this tension between the one truth and the historical manifold of its manifestation must be acknowledged as the general motive in the rise of a pseudepigraphic literature in Judaism.

The historical consequences of the mythopoetic ambiguity are well known. Like the Veda in Hinduism, Scripture becomes in Judaism and Christianity the sacred starting point of a tradition into which later revelatory events, however much they modify the insights gained in the earlier encounters, must be fitted by the methods of commentary and interpretation. There develops the rich variety of methods that we know as the Midrashic allegoresis, the philosophical allegoresis of a Philo, or the Christian-philosophical allegoresis of the Patres. Parallel in time with the congealing of the word into the pseudo-compactness of Scripture, however, the prophetic insight into the illumination of consciousness as a personal encounter between God and the prophet remains at work and deepens to the insight into the universal presence of divine reality as the source of illumination in every man. This is the insight that breaks forth, after centuries of incubation, in the epiphany of Christ.

The finest analytical formulation of the insight, and of its revelation through the epiphany, is given in Colossians 2: The Christ is the mystery of God in reality; in him are hidden all the treasures of wisdom and knowledge; for in him the divine reality, the *theotes*, is present in its whole fulness (*pan to pleroma*); and by responding to this maximal fulness through faith, all men will achieve the fulness of their own existence (*pepleromenoi*). This symbolism of the pleromatic presence of divine reality in man, and of its maximal presence in Christ, is engendered, if I understand its motivation correctly, by the visionary component in the experience. At least it appears to be Saint Paul's intent to clarify the problem of this component when he carefully distinguishes between the God who sends the vision and the vision itself. There is, first, the God who, as the pleromatic partner in the encounter, sends the vision to him, the man Paul, who by his responsiveness to the pleromatic irruption becomes the Apostle; and there is, second, the vision itself of the man who by the maximal presence of the *pleroma* has become the Resurrected, who by his visionary appearance as the Resurrected assures that reality is engaged in the immortalizing process of transfiguration, and who by his visionary appearance in the historical event of the Pauline encounter with God is revealed as the Christ. The vision is for Saint Paul the source of the insight into the immortalizing presence of the word, not in Scripture but in man.

But then again, this anti-Scriptural epiphany of the word in the flesh has to submit to Scripture when a collection of early Christian writings is canonized as the New Testament, complementing as the new Scripture the older one that now becomes the Old Testament, with all the attendant problems of verbal inspiration and literalist deformation, of allegoresis and prefiguration. The organization of the second Scripture had the same pragmatic motives as that of the first one: It was a protective device against the competing wisdoms in the surrounding ecumenic-imperial society, especially against the Gnostic movements within Christianity. Moreover, the protection of insights gained had to be expanded beyond the Scriptural canonization of basic writings to the development of a theology that mobilized for the defense of truth the arms of the intellectually superior and for that reason most serious competitor, of Hellenistic-Roman philosophy.

I have traced the consciousness of language through a number of representative cases in the period of the great differentiations. The variants of consciousness reach from the Vedic outburst of the comprehensive reality into self-illuminating speech, to the emergence of the word from the Metaxy of the psyche, further to its emergence from the personal encounter of the prophet with God and its imaginative transformation into the ambiguous word of Scripture, and finally to the epiphany of Christ with its insight into man as the acting, suffering, and ultimately victorious partner in a process in which reality becomes luminous for its divine mystery through the truth of language. Although the variants cover a wide range on the scale of compactness and differentiation, the spiritualists who go through the experience all agree on the sacrality of a language in which the truth of divine reality becomes articulate. The experience and the language of truth belong together as parts of a process that derives its sacrality from the flux of divine presence in it. It will now be possible to give precision to some of the insights implied in the process as it presents itself empirically.

The most serious obstacle to a proper understanding of the experience, as I have intimated, is the penchant to hypostatize. The object in the world of sense perception has become so forcefully the model of "things" that it intrudes itself inadvertently into the understanding of experiences that are not concerned with objects but with the mystery of a reality in which the objects of the external world are to be found among other "things." The experience of divine reality, it is true, occurs in the psyche of a man who is solidly rooted by his body in the external world, but the psyche itself exists in the Metaxy, in the tension toward the divine ground of being. It is the sensorium for divine reality and the site of its luminous presence. Even more, it is the site in which the comprehensive reality becomes luminous to itself and engenders the language in which we speak of a reality that comprehends both an external world and the mystery of its Beginning and Beyond, as well as the metaleptic psyche in which the experience occurs and engenders its language. In the experience, not only the truth of divine reality becomes luminous but, at the same time, the truth of the world in which the experience occurs. There is no "external" or "immanent" world unless it is recognized as such by its relation to something that is "internal" or "transcendent." Such terms as *immanent* and *transcendent, external* and *internal, this world* and *the other world*, and so forth, do not denote objects or their properties but are the language indices arising from the Metaxy in the event of its becoming luminous for the comprehensive reality, its structure and dynamics. The terms are exegetic, not descriptive. They indicate the movements of the soul when, in the Metaxy of consciousness, it explores the experience of divine reality and tries to find the language that will articulate its exegetic movements. Hence, the language and its truth engendered by the event do not refer to an outside object, but are the language and truth of reality as it becomes luminous in man's consciousness. On another occasion I have concentrated this problem in the statement: The fact of revelation is its content.

Since the experience has no content but itself, the miracle of reality breaking forth into the language of its truth will move into the center of attention when consciousness differentiates sufficiently to become luminous for its own movements. The language of truth about reality tends historically to be recognized as the truth of language in reality. An important phase in this process is represented by the cosmogony of Genesis. The creation story lets the cosmos, with its hierarchy of being from the inorganic universe, through vegetable and animal life, to man, be spoken into existence by God. Reality is a story spoken in the creative language of God; and in one of its figures, in man who is created in the image of God, reality responds to the mystery of the creative word with the truth of the creation story. Or inversely, from the human side, divine reality must be symbolized analogically as the creative word of God because the experience engenders for its expression the imaginative word of the cosmogonic myth. Reality is an act of divine mythopoesis that becomes luminous for its truth when it evokes the responsive myth from man's experience. This perfect correlation between the language of truth and the truth of language in reality that is the distinguishing mark of the creation story was not achieved in a day. As the story in its present form has to be dated in the sixth century B.C., the perfection has been long in the making, for the efforts to symbolize divine creativity in a non-material manner through the word that creates *ex nihilo* go back to the Egyptian *Theology of Memphis* in the third millennium B.C. Even the cosmogony of Genesis still bears traces of these millennial efforts inasmuch as a Babylonian Tiamat appears to be a pregiven reality when the creational work begins.

The experience of divine reality in the mode of cosmic creativity requires the cosmogonic myth for its expression. But the change of symbols used in the myth from the compact imagery of elemental, physiological, sexual, or materially demiurgic creativity to the symbolism of the creative word occurs historically under the pressure of man's consciousness differentiating in the direction of the Beyond. This pressure is strongly present in Israelite-Judaic history, thanks to the early break with the cosmological myth proper through the experience of the Thornbush Episode (Exodus 3). The God who reveals himself as the I-am to Moses is incompatible with the intracosmic gods of the earlier myth. Nevertheless, the effect of the experience, which moves an Etienne Gilson to characterize all Christian metaphysics as the metaphysics of Exodus, is oddly ambiguous, because the human side of the experience—the movement of consciousness toward the Beyond—is not fully differentiated. The accent in the divine-human encounter falls heavily on the revelatory irruption, so heavily that the divine command appears as a burden imposed on a hesitant Moses rather than as an insight sought. The massively commanding irruption from the Beyond leaves little emotional room for the seeker's ascent toward the super-reflective truth that will assuage the unrest of his search. The word from the Beyond is present, crushing all hesitations and doubts. This heavy accent on the divine irruption in the experience remains a constant in Israelite-Judaic history and prevents the full differentiation of the two modes of the Beginning and the Beyond. Even in the Gospel of John, the word that is present in Christ has to be the word of the Beginning that now has become flesh, causing the later difficulties of theological construction that could only partially be overcome by the introduction of philosophy and the development of mysticism.

The differentiation of the Beyond as the answer to the quest for the divine ground of being has been achieved by the classic philosophers, by Plato and Aristotle. In the present context I shall only recall the language engendered in the exegesis of the experience. It is the language of questioning, searching, and seeking in a state of unrest caused by ignorance concerning the divine ground and the meaning of existence. In this state of unrest, man experiences himself as moved from the ground and drawn into the search; he wants to escape from his ignorance and finds himself turned in the right direction by the tensional experiences of faith, hope, and love toward the divine ground; and he gains the desired knowledge when the search becomes luminous as a response to the movement of divine presence in the soul, when he becomes conscious of his search as not merely a human effort but as the event of a divine-human encounter in the Metaxy. The ground that is sought is the divine presence that moves the search. As in the Israelite experience of the Beginning, the luminosity of the encounter with the Beyond then becomes articulate in the insight into the word as both divine and human. Man is engaged in the search with the divinest part of his soul, with the *nous;* the language employed in the articulation of the search is noetic language; and the ground that moves the search, when it is found, is the divine Nous. The language of noetic philosophy is the language that emerges from the response to the divine movement; it has revelatory character. In Plato's theology of history, the Nous reveals himself as the third god after Kronos and Zeus. Hence, the noetic quest of the ground is more than a merely human effort at cognition with merely human means; it is a process in the divine-human Metaxy of the psyche; and to be engaged in this process means to be existentially engaged in the growth from human mortality to divine immortality. The action of noetic philosophizing is the transfiguring action of immortalizing, of *athanatizein.* The accent in this experience of transfiguring immortalization falls on the search, not on the assurance of transfiguration through the overwhelming divine presence, as it does in the Israelite-Judaic case. Nevertheless, the revelatory consciousness is present in the noetic quest and becomes articulate in such

Platonic symbols as the *periagoge*, the conversion of the prisoner in the Cave who is forced to turn around and to begin his ascent toward the light, or in the myth of the divine Puppetplayer in the *Laws*, who pulls the Golden Cord of Reason, or in the gift of the gods brought by Prometheus "together with a fire exceeding bright" in *Philebus* 16–17.

II. On Meditation

The inquiry has evoked the manifold of experiences from which the problems of truth and language arise in history. But what is this inquiry itself? Is it a historiographic study? or is it an act of philosophizing? or perhaps of theologizing?

There is no unequivocal answer to such questions. If there were, they would not have to be asked. We are confronted with the situation, peculiar to the twentieth century A.D., of having no generally accepted language, or literary form, for dealing with the fundamental problems of truth and language raised by our present state of knowledge concerning the historical manifold. It will be necessary, therefore, to reflect on the inquiry, in order to establish the legitimacy of its method and the criteria of its truth. Denoting for the moment its nature by the neutral term *reflection*, we must now reflect on reflection and its function in the process of a reality that lets its truth become articulate in time.

Cognitive Reflection

The reflections on the historical field of experiences and symbolization cannot be brought under the head of a "history of ideas," nor can they be classified as an exercise in "comparative religion," for they do considerably more than tender information on the doxographic level. The reflections, in order to evoke the field, had to enter into the In-Between reality, into the divine movement and counter-movement, and into the meaning of the language symbols arising from the Metaxy as the articulators of its truth. They had to accept the symbols as the carriers of a truth that could, and should, be made further intelligible by a reflective inquiry into their meaning.

The procedure implies a number of assumptions. First of all, the meaning is assumed not to be tied to the symbols so tightly that it can be conveyed only by strictly repetitive adherence to their language; it rather is assumed to be translatable, without distortion, into the language of reflective analysis. This assumption, then, can be sustained only if one assumes the original symbols to contain, however compactly veiled, a rational structure that can be made intelligible through reflection. Moreoever, since neither the original nor the reflective symbols refer to an object outside of the metaleptic experience from which they emerge, there is no external criterion by which the truth of the one or the other, or the truthfulness of transition from one to the other, can be measured; the procedure thus assumes the criterion of truthful transmission from the first to the second set of symbols to be internal to the process itself. And finally, since the criterion of truth is internal to the process, the reflective inquiry is assumed to belong to the same human-divine Metaxy as the symbols submitted to inquiry. While the original symbols contain a rational structure that can be further articulated through reflection, the reflective acts of cognition can be true only if they participate in the divine reality that participated in the emergence of the symbols. The reflection, thus, assumes a reality engaged in becoming cognitively luminous. Reflection is not an external act of cognition directed toward the process as its object, but part of a process that internally has cognitive structure.

This property of the process, of having a cognitive structure internal to itself, has consequences for the conceptual work of reflection. Since no reflection on the Metaxy can be true unless it is conducted from a position within the metaleptic truth-reality, neither the events of experience and symbolization, nor the process of the events as a whole, can become objects of analytical conceptualization for an external subject of cognition. However abstract the concepts may become when the mind of man explores its own consciousness in response to the divine appeal, the analysis remains a concrete event within the process. However compact or differentiated the events may be, they all are concerned, in equal concreteness, with the mystery of divine presence in reality. As a consequence, the concrete-abstract events of reflection are related to one another, not as objects and subjects of cognition, but as partners in the common quest of the truth that becomes luminous in the process. If the concreteness that the earlier events have as divine-human encounters is deformed into a concreteness of immanent objects, to be made a possession of knowledge by a later event of world-immanent reflection, the very structure to be explored will be destroyed. The past of the process will become a dead past if its structure does not continue into the present of the reflection; and the present will become a dead present if the reflection does not participate in the mystery of divine presence in reality. If the metaleptic structure of reality is lost, the result will not be a minor theoretical error but an existential deformation that becomes manifest in the God-is-dead syndrome, together with the major misconstructions of reality it entails.

The metaleptic structure thus pervades all the strata of the process from experience to symbolization, and from the less to the more reflected symbolisms. The In-Between of the divine-human encounter extends into the In-Between of its exegetic symbolization; the In-Between of symbolization extends into the concrete-abstract structure of reflective consciousness; the concrete-abstract structure of reflection extends into the tension between the finality of the mystery of divine presence and the non-finality of its experience and symbolization in the ongoing process; and the tension of reflective consciousness extends into the very conception of a self-illuminating process inasmuch as this symbolism does not arise from the observation of an external object but within the process from acts of reflection that relate present insights to earlier ones. This pervasiveness ultimately affects the language of truth itself, for none of the languages articulating the truth is final, even though each of them partakes of the finality of insight into the divine truth it articulates. And what is final about the present language can be established only by relating it to the finality of the divine mystery present in the earlier experiences and their language, thus accepting the non-finality of its position in the process. If the consciousness of this metaleptic balance in the language of truth is not preserved, the reflective acts will derail into either an absolute finality or an absolute non-finality, as they did in the eighteenth and nineteenth centuries A.D. The phantasy of absolute finality can produce the conception of a system like the Hegelian, which claims to be the ultimate transformation of revelation into a dialectical "system of science"; and the phantasy of absolute non-finality can become the basis of a relativism that infers from the historical manifold of different and conflicting languages the non-truth of every language.

Fides Quaerens Intellectum: Saint Anselm

If this analysis be now applied to itself, the difficulties of finding the adequate language for an act of reflection in the twentieth century A.D. will become apparent.

The preceding analysis of the cognitive structure had to be formulated with the degree of abstraction required by its time-position in the present when the enlargement of the ecumenic horizon to globality, and of the temporal horizon by the archeological millennia, has brought the historical manifold of the process into fuller view than ever before. We can no longer use, without critical examination, concepts that have proved highly satisfactory within spatially and temporally more limited horizons of the past, if they are not abstract enough to apply to the manifold that fills the horizon of the twentieth century. At the same time, however, the earlier reflective concepts cannot be simply ignored, because then we would lose the *ratio essendi* of the present reflection together with its position in the process. The historical dimension of reflection must be faced. I have taken special care, therefore, to conduct the analysis in such a manner that its abstractness would not hide its close relation to Saint Anselm of Canterbury's language, in the Augustinian tradition, of the *fides quaerens intellectum* and the correlative *credo ut intelligam*. The present reflection is consciously an expansion of the *fides quaerens intellectum* beyond Anselm's Christian horizon to the manifold of non- and pre-Christian theophanic events, as well as to such order as can be discerned in the revelatory process.

But if the two reflections are indeed as closely related in my consciousness as they are, why did I not use the language of the Scholastic thinkers? Why did I engage in an abstrusely abstract reflection, if all that was intended was a generalization of the traditional problems of faith and reason?

The elegant formulations of the eleventh century A.D. could not be simply taken over, because the historical dimension of the process indeed affects the language of truth in a number of ways. There is to be noted, first, the inertness of history, which endows the striking formulation achieved by a great thinker with an extraordinary durability. More frequently, this inertness will let the prestige of a phrase outlast its usefulness, but sometimes, as in the Anselmian case, it can obscure the validity of an analysis for a range of instances wider than the one for which it was originally intended. Anselm's *fides* and *credere* were concretely applied to the Creed of the Church; and the firm tie of his questing analysis to the Creed has never been seriously broken in Western consciousness. Through the burden of its medieval-Christian context, the prestige of the phrase has become an obstacle to recognizing the profoundness of an analysis that will illumine a much larger historical horizon than the one of its own time. Hence, though both the Anselmian and the present reflections are informed by the same tension between divine appeal and human quest, the separation of the *fides quaerens intellectum* from the concrete case of the Creedal faith, and its generalization to a structural insight that will also apply to such events of questing symbolization as a Taoist speculation, or a Platonic dialogue, or the bronzes of Alasha Hoyuk, or to Stone Age petroglyphs, would have met with considerable resistance unless it had been carefully prepared.

A straightforward generalization of Anselm's insight is handicapped, second, by the lack of consensus concerning its content. From the beginning, the great debate aroused by the *Proslogion* concentrated on the syllogistic merits and demerits of the argument that later came to be called the ontological proof for the existence of God, while the experiential context in which the argument was supposed to make sense was neglected. A long succession of critics, from Gaunilo and Thomas, through Descartes, Spinoza, Locke, Leibniz, Kant, and Hegel, has established the association of Anselm's name with the ontological proof so firmly that the *fides* behind the quest has practically faded away. The full import of the Anselmian insight has been recovered only in the twentieth century by such studies as Karl Barth's *Fides Quaerens Intellectum* (1931), which prepared its author for the revision of his *Dogmatik*, or by Etienne Gilson's remarkable chapters on *philosophia Christiana* in his Gifford Lectures *L'Esprit de la philosophie médiévale*, of the same year. The inertness that has kept the analysis of the *Proslogion* bound to the Christian *fides* has also preserved the mutilation of the analysis through the preoccupation with the ontological proof. Only when the structure of appeal-response in the experience of divine reality has been sufficiently clarified can the Anselmian analysis be disentangled from the handicapping effects of limitation and mutilation.

Most important, finally, there must be noted what Karl Barth has called the "divine simplicity" of Anselm's thinking. Although a search for the better understanding of the *fides* by means of the philosopher's reason implies a critical distance to the symbolism explored, no such distance is to be sensed in the Anselmian reflections. The finality of the Creed is absolute. Even more, the same simplicity extends to the instruments of inquiry; the validity of the philosophical concepts employed in the so-called ontological proof is taken for granted. There is no attempt to establish, or question, the truth of the concepts in the light of the experiences that have engendered them. Hence, the Anselmian language cannot be taken over *telquel*, because it lacks the stratum of reflection that is our present concern. The implications of Anselm's analysis, which affect the meaning of philosophy and theology, have yet to be made explicit.

Saint Anselm's Prayer

Our first concern must be with Anselm's insight into the In-Between reality of the divine-human encounter.

In the *Proslogion*, the insight is overwhelmingly present through the form of the prayer Anselm has given to his work. For the *Proslogion* is not a treatise about God and his existence, but a prayer of love by the creature to the Creator to grant a more perfect vision of His divinity. To the God who has revealed Himself to his faith as the Creator, Anselm now prays to reveal Himself as the reality toward which he, the creature, finds himself directed by his questing mind, by his *ratio: Ostende Te Quaerenti!* Questing reason is given to the image of God to reach as far out toward the creative original as the creaturely imperfection of his humanity after the Fall will permit. The unquestioned faith in the Creator-God of the Beginning is now to be raised to a higher luminosity through the quest in the present. This Prayer, it should be noted, does not pray for an object or event in the external world; the action of the quest, successfully carried out in the argument of the *Proslogion*, is

193

both the action of the Prayer and its fulfillment. In his Prayer we are moving with Anselm, within his faith, toward the limit of its understanding.

And limited the understanding is indeed. For even when understood by reason, faith is still not the vision, the *species*, of God Himself; on the contrary, the limit set to man's cognition by faith becomes even more poignantly conscious when understood. And yet, the understanding achieved by the quest is so much more than unreflected faith that on occasion, in the preface to *De Fide Trinitatis*, Anselm can speak of the understanding possible in this life as a *medium inter fidem et speciem*, as something between plain faith and the vision granted through grace in death.[1] The *medium*, the In-Between, thus appears as a concept after all, though restricted in its meaning to the movement of reason, from the Christian *fides*, in the direction of the Beyond; the Anselmian *medium* thus denotes only a part of the *medium* in which the lover of God moves toward the beatific vision. By this restriction, we may say, Anselm acknowledges the process in which metaleptic consciousness acquires a new luminosity when reason articulates itself through reflection—*i.e.*, the process that had been experienced and analyzed by Plato in the transition from myth to philosophy; and at the same time he brings the eschatological dynamics of the noetic quest into the sharper focus that becomes possible when the lower stratum of the medium is not the myth but the Christian *fides*. We have to come back to the historical issues involved in these distinctions.

For the present, we must stress the character of the restriction as an insight into the stratification of the Metaxy rather than as an attempt to establish reason as an independent source of knowledge concerning divine reality, a misunderstanding still to be found in the classification of Anselm as a "rationalist." Not Anselm's reason is in quest of understanding but his faith. The labor of the mind will not arrive at the understanding of anything unless the some-

1. Voegelin refers here to the work bearing the full title *De Fide Trinitatis et de Incarnatione Verbi* to be found in Migne, *Patrologia Latina*. The exact text reads: "Denique quoniam inter fidem et speciem intellectum, quem in hac vita capimus, esse medium intelligo . . ." This passage can be translated: "Finally, since I know that the understanding we gain in this life is a middle-stage [*medium*] in between faith and vision [*inter fidem et speciem*] . . ." (Migne, *PL*, Vol. CLVIII, 261A; editors' translation).

thing to be understood is already present, even though in the form of an intellectually less satisfactory response to the divine appeal. Without the *fides*, there is no Creator to whom the creature can pray that He may let Himself be seen also by the questing reason that is given to the image of God. Moreover, while the quest raises the *fides* to the level of the noetic *medium*, it penetrates the mystery of divine reality no more than faith itself. When the quest has found the Creator of the Creed to be indeed the God of the quest, Anselm must admit that the God found by reason is not yet the God whom the seeker experienced as present in the formation and re-formation of his existence. He continues his Prayer: "Speak to my desirous soul what you are other than what it has seen, that it may clearly see what it desires." And the insight of reason is then surmounted by the further insight: "O Lord, you are not only that than which a greater cannot be thought, but you are also greater than what can be thought" (XIV–XV).

Behind the quest, and behind the *fides* that quest is supposed to understand, there now becomes visible the true source of the Anselmian effort in the living desire of the soul to move toward the divine light. The divine reality lets the light of its perfection fall into the soul; the illumination of the soul arouses the awareness of man's existence as a state of imperfection; and this awareness provokes the human movement in response to the divine appeal. The illumination, as Saint Augustine names this experience, has for Anselm indeed the character of an appeal, and even of a counsel and promise, for in order to express the experience of illumination he quotes John 16:24: "Ask, and you will receive, that your joy may be full." The Johannine words of the Christ, and of the Spirit that counsels in his name, which are meant to be understood in their context, express the divine movement to which Anselm responds with the joyful counter-movement of his quest (XXVI). Hence, the latter part of the *Proslogion* consistently praises the divine light in the analogical language of perfection.

The Prayer is a movement of the soul. Anselm moves from the first person of the Trinity to the second and third persons, from the Creator to the Christ and the paracletic Spirit, from the mortal imperfection of the creature to its immortal perfection in the beatific vision, from existence in the time of creation to existence in the eternity of the Beyond. For Anselm, thus, the trinitarian Creed is more than the letter of a doctrine to be believed, it has to be lived through as the true symbolization of a reality that moves from creation to salvation; and Anselm can live it through, and can enact the drama of the Trinity in the drama of the Prayer, because the quest of his reason is the proper response to the intelligible movement in the *fides*. There is reason in the Creed. The Prayer is a *meditatio de ratione fidei*, as he formulates the nature of the quest in the first title of the *Monologion*. The praying quest responds to the appeal of reason in the *fides*; the *Proslogion* is the *fides* in action, in pursuit of its own reason. Saint Anselm, we must conclude therefore, clearly understood the cognitive structure as internal to the Metaxy.

Ontology

The Prayer is a tightly woven, internally cognitive reflection. If the famous argument, the so-called ontological proof, is isolated from this context, and if it is treated as if it were a piece of doctrine to be tested for its syllogistic impeccability, the meaning of both argument and context will be destroyed. Nevertheless, the mutilating treatment persists historically, and such persistence suggests a problem of secular range in the language of truth that is somehow connected with the form the insight into the cognitive structure has assumed in Anselm's analysis. Before the argument can be presented in its original form, the mutilating symbolism must be removed, but it must be removed in such a manner that the historical connection of the distortion with Anselm's fundamental problem of reflection will not be lost. Both requirements can be fulfilled by the recall of certain philological data concerning the symbol *ontological proof*, as well as the language surrounding it.

The questionable symbol occurs nowhere in the work of Anselm. Hence, the attribution of an ontological proof, without thorough justification of the terminology, violates the elementary rule that a thinker's language takes precedence of the interpreter's. A change of language is permitted only if the interpreter can show the thinker's analysis to have a defect that requires the new language for its emendation. Such a demonstration, however, has never been attempted, as far as I know. Still, one cannot flatly state that there is no ontological proof in the *Proslogion*. The denial, to be sure, would come closer to the truth than the affirmation, but it would ignore the existential, social, and historical complications of the issue that come to light as soon as one considers the parts of the composite symbol separately. For the phrase is composed of a noun and an adjective, and the problems are different for the component parts. As far as the noun is concerned, Anselm himself speaks of his *argumentum* as a proof, a *probatio*—not in the *Proslogion*, however, but in his answer to Gaunilo. And that, as we shall see presently, is a point of some importance. As far as the adjective is concerned, its use has no basis in the *argumentum* at all; its application is a bad anachronism. For the term *ontology* is a neologism of the seventeenth century. It appears for the first time in Clauberg's *Metaphysica* (1646) and finds acceptance among philosophers through its use, in the eighteenth century, by Leibniz, Wolff, and Kant. The *Meditations* of Descartes are not yet encumbered by the term, and that is perhaps the reason why they still could be real meditations, close to Anselm's quest, which Descartes did not know, in their reliance on the tension of perfection-imperfection for the dynamics of the questing movement. In the *Critique of Pure Reason*, then, Kant applies the symbol "ontological proof" to the Cartesian *Meditations* as a term already in general use.

The data just given point to an area of discourse that moves rather on the fringe of exact experiential analysis; and the further pursuit of the data shows this area, as well as the obscure cause of its inexactness, to be a matter of long standing in the history of reflective analysis. For the term *ontology*, meaning a "science of being," was devised as a more precise synonym for *metaphysics*; this latter term had been introduced by Saint Thomas into the Western languages in order to denote the conceptual area of the *transcendentia*. Saint Thomas had taken it over from the Arab philosophers; the Arabs in their turn had, for the same purpose of denoting a science of being, formed the word *metaphysics* by deforming the Aristotelian title *meta ta physica*; and this title, affixed to the Aristotelian "first philosophy" or "theology," was no more than a general pointer to the area of philosophical concepts beyond the categories that apply to physical phenomena.

The philological data suggest a problem of reflection that had not been sufficiently clarified by Aristotle in his confrontation with the myth and then had become acute in the Islamic and

Christian confrontations with the symbols of a revealed *fides*. It appears that the successive phases in this millennial process must be understood as attempts to establish, in their respective historical situations, the cognitive function of the quest in relation to the divine revelatory movement. The appearance of the term *ontology* in particular marks a phase in the Western effort to extricate philosophy from its bondage to a dogma that had degenerated, in the wake of the Reformation disputes about a true theology, to the conception of an autonomous doctrine. This effort was necessary, and it is still necessary today, but in the eighteenth and nineteenth centuries it miscarried with unfortunate consequences. Although ever since Locke one of the declared purposes of the effort was the recovery of experience, the experiential basis of symbolic language, "metaphysical" or "theological," was in fact not recovered. On the contrary, the effort threw out, together with the degenerative doctrinism of the *fides*, the *ratio fidei* that had been Anselm's concern, without regaining even the erotic tension toward the divine ground that had been the moving force in the noetic quest of Plato and Aristotle. As a result, far from recovering the reason of the quest, the effort set "reason" free to become the instrument for "rationalizing" the ideological irrationality of doctrinalizing experiences of alienation.

Considering the historical situations and their differences, we have to conclude therefore that it is definitely anachronistic to speak of the Anselmian argument as "ontological." Whether the argument is a proof or not, there can be no doubt about the adjectives to be used with the noun, if such use proves necessary: Since Anselm is quite articulate about Spirit and Reason as the motive forces of his quest, the adjectives to be combined with the noun will have to be *pneumatic* and *noetic*.

Folly and Theology

But in what sense can the term *proof* be connected with a noetic quest in response to the movement of the Spirit at all? The key to the answer is given in the fact that the term does not occur in the *Proslogion* itself but only in the discussion with Gaunilo. There is no reason why it should be used in the *Proslogion*, because the existence of God is not in question when a believer explores the rational structure of his faith. In his answer, however, Anselm must use it because Gaunilo acts the role of the fool, of the *insipiens*, who says "There is no God" and assumes that the explorer of faith is engaged in a "proof" for the assertion that God exists. The noetic reflection of the spiritualist acquires the character of an affirmative proposition concerning the existence of God only when confronted by the *insipiens* who advances the negative proposition that God does not exist. The symbolism of the noetic quest threatens to derail into a quarrel about proof or non-proof of a proposition when the fool enters the discussion. The existence of God can become doubtful because, without a doubt, the fool exists.

The fool cannot be dismissed lightly. The folly of responding to the divine appeal by denial or evasion is just as much a human possibility as the positive response. As a potentiality it is present in every man, including the believer; and in certain historical situations its actualization can become a massive social force. But who, or what, is a fool?

The philological situation is clear. When Anselm and Gaunilo speak of the *insipiens*, their language draws on Psalm 13 (14) in the translation of the Vulgate: "The fool [*insipiens*] says in his heart 'There is no God.'" The *nabal* of the Hebrew text is translated by the Vulgate as *insipiens* and further translated, by both the Standard Version and the Jerusalem Bible, as *fool*. This last translation is perhaps not the best, for the English word *fool* derives from the Latin *follis*, meaning a bellows or windbag, and has retained from its origin an aura of windbaggery, silliness, lack or weakness of judgment, that will neither suggest the fundamental corruption of existence, nor the spectrum of corruptive symptoms, intended by *nabal*. The fool of the Psalm is certainly not a man wanting in intellectual acumen or worldly judgment. Such alternative translations as the impious, the profane, the reckless, or the worthless man, which all have been tried and all have their merits, show the difficulty of rendering the richness of meaning peculiar to a symbol as compact as *nabal*. However, because a more satisfactory translation, better fitting contemporary usage, seems to me impossible, I shall retain the established "fool" and take care only to make its meaning clear.

In Psalm 13 (14), the *nabal* signifies the mass phenomenon of men who do evil rather than good because they do not "seek after

God" and his justice, who "eat my people as they eat bread" because they do not believe in divine sanction for acts of unrighteousness. The personal contempt for God will manifest itself in ruthless conduct toward the weaker man and create general disorder in society. The situation envisaged by the Psalm seems to be the same as the contempt for God and his prophets characterized by Jer. 5 : 12ff. and, as early as the eighth century B.C., by Isaiah 32. In these Israelite contexts, the contempt, the *nebala*, does not necessarily denote as differentiated a phenomenon as dogmatic atheism, but rather a state of spiritual dullness that will permit the indulgence of greed, sex, and power without fear of divine judgment. The contemptuous folly, it is true, can rise to the radical "there is no God," but the phrase does not appear to be experienced as a noetic challenge. The fool stands against the revealed God, he does not stand against a *fides quaerens intellectum*. This further component, characteristic of the Anselm-Ganuilo debate, must be sought rather in the philosophers' tradition that has entered Christian theology. It is Plato who describes the phenomenon of existential foolishness, as well as the challenge it presents to the noetic quest, for the case of Sophistic folly, the *anoia*, in *Republic* [Book] II and *Laws* [Book] X.

In Greek society, the potentiality of responding to the divine appeal by rejecting it has expressed itself in a series of negative propositions that circumspectly cover the whole range of the experience. In both the *Republic* (365b–e) and the *Laws* (888), Plato presents these propositions as a triadic set:

1. It seems that no gods exist;
2. Even if they do exist, they do not care about men;
3. Even if they care, they can be propitiated by gifts.

Although Plato does not give a specific source for the set but refers to it only as in general use in his intellectual environment, it probably is a Sophistic school product, for it has the same structure as the set of propositions preserved in Gorgias' essay *On Being:*

1. Nothing exists;
2. If anything exists, it is incomprehensible;
3. If it is comprehensible, it is incommunicable.

The sets suggest that, in the Sophistic schools, the contempt for the gods had grown into a general loss of experiential contact with cosmic-divine reality. The triadic patterns of negative propositions appear to have developed as an expression for the resultant contraction of man's existence. The mass acceptance of this pattern aroused Plato so strongly as a challenge to his noetic quest of the divine ground that he devoted the entire Book X of the *Laws* to its refutation. The details of the refutation, resulting in the positive propositions that the gods exist, that they do care about man, and that they cannot be made accomplices in human criminality by offering them bribes from the profits of crime, are not our present concern. But we must consider his analysis of the noetic challenge and the language developed for its articulation.

The Sophistic argument for the negative triads apparently rested on a radical denial of divine reality experienced as present in either the order of the cosmos or the soul of man. In order to be plausible in the Hellenic culture of the fourth century B.C., the denial had to be couched in the form of a countermyth to the symbolization of divine order in reality by the cosmogonic myth of the Hesiodian type. The form actually assumed by the argument apparently was a cosmogony in which the gods of the myth were replaced by the elements in the material sense as the "oldest" creative reality. At any rate, Plato considers the negative triads invalidated in principle, if he can refute the assumption that all reality originates in the movement of material elements. Against this assumption he argues: There is no self-moving matter; all material movements are caused by movements of other matter; the patterned network of cause and effect must be caused in its turn by a movement that originates outside the network; and the only reality we know to be self-moving is the Psyche. Hence, in a genetic construction of Being, the elements cannot function as the "oldest" reality; only the divine Psyche, as experienced by the human psyche, can be "oldest" in the sense of the self-movement in which all ordered movement in the world originates. The argument sounds quite modern in its recourse to the reality of the psyche, and of its experiences, against constructions that express the loss of reality and the contraction of the self—though the modern constructors do not have to deform a Hesiodian myth for their purpose but must replace the divine ground of Being by an item from the world-immanent hierarchy of being as the ultimate "ground" of all reality. But it is neither modern nor ancient; it rather is the argument that will recur whenever the quest of divine reality has to be resumed in a situation in which the "rationalization" of contracted existence, the existence of the fool, has become a mass phenomenon. The argument, of course, is not a "proof" in the sense of a logical demonstration, of an *apodeixis*, but only in the sense of an *epideixis*, of a pointing to an area of reality that the constructor of the negative propositions has chosen to overlook, or to ignore, or refuses to perceive. One cannot prove reality by a syllogism; one can only point to it and invite the doubter to look. The more or less deliberate confusion of the two meanings of the word *proof* is still a standard trick employed by the negators in the contemporary ideological debates; and it plays an important role in the genesis of the "proofs" for the existence of God ever since the time of Anselm.

That the negative propositions are not a philosopher's statement concerning a structure in reality but express an existential deformation is the insight gained by Plato. The Sophistic folly, the *anoia*, is not merely an analytical error; it is a *nosos*, a disease of the psyche, requiring the psychological therapy that he grants in the *Laws* to the extent of five years. In *Republic* II, he further develops the language that will describe the existential disease inasmuch as he distinguishes between the falsehood in words and the falsehood, or lie (*pseudos*), in the soul itself. The "ignorance within the soul" (*en te psyche agnoia*) is "truly the falsehood" (*alethos pseudos*), while the falsehood in words is only "the after-rising image" (*hysteron gegonon eidolon*). The false words, therefore, are not an "unmixed falsehood," as is the "essential falsehood" (*to men de te onti pseudos*) in the soul. The verbal falsehood, the "rationalization," we may say, is the form of truth in which the diseased soul expresses itself (*Republic*, 382). As the distinctions show, Plato is struggling to find the analytical language that will fit the case under observation, but he has by far not completed the task of developing the concepts of a "pneumopathology," as Schelling has called this discipline. Plato does not yet have, for instance, a concept like the *agnoia ptoiodes*, the "scary ignorance" of Chrysippus that has become the "anxiety" of the moderns; nor does he have the Chrysippian *apostrophe*, denoting the inversion of the movement, the *epistrophe*, that leads the prisoner in the Cave up to the light; nor Cicero's characterization of the existential disease, of the *morbus animi*, as an *aspernatio rationis*, a rejection of reason. Still, he has seen the crucial point that the negative propositions are the syndrome of a disease that affects man's humanity and destroys the order of society.

In the analysis of the disease and its syndrome, Plato created a neologism of world-historic consequences: when dealing with the propositional sets he used, as far as we know for the first time in the history of philosophy, the term *theology*. In the *Republic*, Plato speaks of the negative propositions as *typoi peri theologias*, as types of theology (379a), and opposes to them the positive counter-propositions as true types. Both types, the negative as well as the positive, are theologies, because they both express a human response to the divine appeal; they both are, in Plato's language, the verbal mimesis respectively of man's existence in truth or falsehood. Not the existence of God is at stake, but the existence of man; not the propositions stand against each other, but the response and the nonresponse to the divine appeal; the propositions have no autonomous truth. The truth of the positive propositions is neither self-evident nor a matter of logical proof; they would be just as empty as the negative ones if they were not backed by the reality of the divine-human movement and countermovement in the soul of the proponent; and Plato provides this truth by his magnificent analysis and symbolization of the experiences. Hence, the verbal mimesis of the positive type, because it has no truth of its own, can be no more than a first line of defense or persuasion in a social confrontation with the verbal mimesis of the negative type. Even more, the positive propositions derive an essential part of their meaning from their character as a defense against the negative propositions. As a consequence, the two types of theology together represent the verbal mimesis of the human tension between the potentialities of response or non-response to divine presence in personal, social, and historical existence. If the fool's part in the positive propositions is forgotten, there is always the danger of derailing into the foolishness of believing their truth to be ultimate. But that assumption of ultimacy would make them indeed as empty of the experiential truth in the background as the fools pretend them to be.

The Historical Situation of Saint Anselm

Plato's analysis of folly and its verbal expression is not the last word in the matter, but it must be kept in mind as the first word that is still valid, when now we turn to the complexities of the historical situation in which Saint Anselm had to advance his argument.

Anselm did not have to face the folly of Sophists who discard the experiences of divine reality together with the gods of a Myth that has lost its credibility. He does not have to create philosophy as the analysis of the tension toward the divine ground in the experiences of ignorance, unrest, and search, of love, hope, and faith, of justice, of death and immortality; neither does he have to discover man's noetic existence as bounded by the divine reality of Apeiron and Nous; nor does he have to create a philosopher's myth that will symbolize the divine ambiance of man's existence more adequately than the people's myth, the Homeric, or the tragedians' myth. Philosophy is part of his cultural heritage through its absorption into Christian theologizing by the Patres, in particular by Saint Augustine; and the intracosmic gods of the Myth have given way to the Creator- and Savior-God of Revelation. Although man's potentiality to prove himself a fool has not disappeared, the historical situation in which it is to be actualized, or its actualization to be averted, has fundamentally changed. The Benedictine brethren for whom Saint Anselm elaborates in writing the problems that form the subject of their oral debates are not nonbelievers. On the contrary, they want to believe; but, like Saint Anselm himself, they also want to know the reason why. They are young, intelligent, and alert; and they do not like to have their concerned questioning cut off and rejected by being referred to layers of authoritative texts. They do not accept the doctrine of the Creed without discussion; and they make it a condition of the dialogue that Saint Anselm will not support the Creed by biblical quotations instead of reason. Anselm's situation resembles closely that of Plato in his Socratic dialogues with the young; and we have no difficulty in recognizing our own situation in the discussion with our students. The inherited symbols, it appears, cannot rely for their personal and social acceptance on "tradition" alone. Their truth emerges from the divine-human movements and counter-movements in the mysterious flux of divine presence that we call history; and whenever the divinely created reason of man moves historically toward a better understanding of its own structure and its function in the creation of symbols, the symbols inherited must go back to the test of the encounter in order to prove that they truly represent the divine appeal to man's questing response. That is what happens at the beginning of the great movement of Scholastic philosophy. Anselm sets himself the task of "proving" to his brethren that the revealed God of the Creed is also the God for whom they search by their reason.

One has to be clear about Anselm's situation if one wants to avoid the later misunderstanding of his problem. No more than Plato does Saint Anselm want to prove the existence of God. Such an attempt would make him captive to the foolishness of the fool. He wants to discover the structure in human reason that permits the questing response of man to understand the *ratio* in the symbols of Faith. A search of this type presupposes a number of factors in the seeker's situation: 1) a trust in the existence of the unknown structure, a sort of anticipatory knowing of the unknown; 2) an awareness that its knowledge is missing, either because it is lost or because it never has been found before; 3) a state of the intellectual means that will permit the discovery if sufficient effort is put into the work; and 4) a pressure in the historical situation that arouses the awareness of the problem and makes the search impelling.

Taking the last point—the situational pressure—first, there obviously was enough of it to move Saint Anselm to his enterprise. The disorder that tends to actualize the potential of folly, as well as the counter-action, can be characterized by the metaphor of an arteriosclerosis, both intellectual and spiritual, of the cultural heritage, vividly sensed in the eleventh century, at the beginning of the great flowering of a Western-Christian civilization. The fool lurks under the surface of existential order, ready to spring into action whenever major events disturb the social and historical order or when a weakness in the culture of reason offers the opportunity to draw the reality of divine order into doubt on principle. And the age of Scholasticism is marked by a good deal of disturbance indeed, for it is the age of rising towns and national kingdoms, of new religious orders, of the struggle between Imperium and Sacerdotium, and above all of the Crusades. One should be aware that the First

Crusade falls in the lifetime of Saint Anselm, and the last one still in the lifetime of Saint Thomas. It is the age that abandons the Augustinian conception of history after Christ as a time of waiting for the Second Coming, as a *saeculum senescens*, and through such thinkers as Joachim of Flora and Otto of Freising creates the vision of a new spiritual age in the history of mankind, carried by the spiritualism of the new orders. Disturbances of this magnitude will move their contemporaries to re-examine the fundamentals of existential order and to question the adequacy of their expression by the traditional symbols. Saint Anselm is quite outspoken about the pressure under which he is put by the disconcerting questions of his brethren, about his effort to find an appropriate answer, and his near despair of ever finding it.

The answer to the questions was not at hand in the philosophical tradition; the argument of the *Proslogion* had yet to be discovered. In his effort at finding it, however, as well as of making it as adequate as possible, Anselm was handicapped by an intellectual weakness in the tradition that went back to classic philosophy. Although his argument is not marred by the defect that later thinkers discerned in an "ontological proof" that Anselm never attempted, it suffers from the inherited lack of clarity about intentionality as a structure in consciousness. The vagueness about the problem of intentionality causes the uncertainties surrounding the use of the terms *esse* and *existere*, of Being and Existence, that plague Saint Anselm in his debate with Gaunilo and are at the root of the later misunderstandings. The problems of this class were not new in his time—I have touched on the related problems in Plato's struggle with the Sophists—but they acquired a new acuteness in the confrontation of Reason with the doctrine of Faith. In fact, they will hardly ever become obsolete, because they are inherent to the ambiguous structure of philosophizing as an act of reflection on reality from a position within the reality on which the philosopher reflects. We must clarify this fundamental weakness if we want to understand the degree of clarity that Saint Anselm has achieved in the matter.

Being and Intentionality

As an event within reality, the consciousness of man is structured by the experiences of birth and death, apeirontic depth and noetic height, mortality and immortality, of an external world and divine presence, of creation and salvation, of the Beginning and the Beyond. At the same time, however, the reality in which the event occurs moves into the position of an object in relation to the consciousness of man; we are conscious of something, of the object intended by the act of consciousness, and we refer to the object by means of the symbols engendered in our experience of reality. Consciousness has, among other structures, the structure of intentionality. As a consequence, there is always the possibility of philosophy derailing into propositions about things when second-rate thinkers destroy the complexity of the event by reducing consciousness to the relation between "thought" and "object-of-thought." The structure of intentionality can become the model of consciousness so intensely that the thinker will ignore the divine-cosmic Whole in which his act of consciousness occurs as a participatory event. When this happens, reality will be reduced to a catalogue of items duly comprising gods and men, animals, plants, and physical objects, all to be subsumed under the head of "being things" (ta onta); the vast range of human knowledge, rooted in the metaleptic experiences, will be reduced to its intentionalist sector of knowledge about objects—to "information," if I may use a contemporary slogan; and correspondingly, language will be reduced to its intentionalist sector of "referents" and propositional statements. I shall refer to this phenomenon and its symptoms as the intentionalist reduction. It should be noted that with the reduction of consciousness to its intentionality we touch upon the deeper, structural causes of the previously discussed tendency to hypostatize the poles of the existential tension into autonomous entities.

The intentionalist reduction works havoc among the plurality of meanings in which the term *being* must be used, if one insists on using it indiscriminately to cover all the points on which an analysis of consciousness must touch. Obviously, the "being of the Whole" in which the "being things" participate is not the mode of being of the participating things. The "being things," furthermore, do not all have the same mode of being, for the divine mode of being, to mention only the difference of our immediate concern, is not the physical mode. When a Parmenides, for instance, has his vision of divine Being and expresses it by the exclamatory *Is!*, the reality of the external world diminishes to the status of *doxa*, of appearance or illusion; and inversely, when a thinker accepts the physical mode of being as the model of reality, he may arrive at the conclusion that God, who indeed does not exist in the manner of a physical object, does "not exist." And to make the muddle of "being" complete, one cannot avoid acknowledging that the intentionality of consciousness, though real without a doubt, is not one of the "being things" intended; for the intentionality of the act belongs to the In-Between of participation, to the luminosity of consciousness in the Platonic sense of the Metaxy.[2]

As these remarks suggest, the several modes and meanings of "being" will not make sense unless two conditions are fulfilled. In the first place, the aggregate of meanings must not be fragmentized. The several meanings will make sense only if they are understood as integral parts of the analytical complex articulated and symbolized by the Greek philosophers as Being when they discovered structure in reality as the object to be explored by the questing *nous* of man. Only when the cognitive powers of *nous* and *logos* become articulate consciousness will the mythically compact "things past, present, and to come" of the Homeric age give way to the differentiated symbols of *kosmos, to pan, to on, ta onta,* and *aletheia,* which denote the various aspects of the complex. Being

---

2. At this point in an earlier draft of some of the pages of this section, Voegelin included the following lines, which he did not keep in his last draft:

Among the modern attempts to cope with this problem there should be remembered the great line that runs from the Cartesian *cogitare* and the Kantian *apriori* to Edmund Husserl's "phaenomenological reduction" of the act to the structures of Noesis and Noema, or to William James's construction, in his phase of Radical Empiricism, of a "pure experience" that neither belongs to consciousness nor to the external world. These attempts are of fundamental importance because they are moved by the awareness, and have preserved it for us, that the "subject-of-thought" must not be "psychologized" or "physiologized," while the "object-of-thought" in the sense of Husserl's Noema is not the "being thing" to which it refers. Nevertheless, important as these attempts are, they still have to carry the historical burden of defense or offense against the various aspects of a medieval "metaphysics" or modern "ontology," as well as against the variegated derailments of a "science of being." They have not yet penetrated to the multi-layered structure of an experience that is, at the same time, the process in which reality becomes luminous to itself in consciousness. They are not sufficiently clear about the distinctions of "being" I have just made; nor are they clear about the complex of analysis in which they have to be made as a whole that will disappear from sight if one tries to approach it from a "position" taken in any one of its interdependent parts.

as structured reality, and questing Reason as the instrument of its exploration, are correlatives. Even if the correlation is acknowledged, however, and the integrality of the complex is respected, one still can make nonsense of the great discovery of structure in reality and its intelligibility, of Being and Reason, unless the second condition is fulfilled: The discovery must not be misunderstood as dissolving or replacing the divinely-mysterious reality in which the structure of Being and its discovery as intelligible to the mind of man occurs, or as making superfluous the symbolization of the mystery through Myth and Revelation. No exploration of structure in Being can answer the two fundamental questions concerning existence and essence, formulated by Leibniz: Why is there something, why not nothing? and Why is the something as it is?

Gilson

In his discussion of Thomas' *Deus est ipsum esse per suam essentiam*, Etienne Gilson has brought the point of potential derailment to attention. In the Thomist conception of reality, the *actus purus* of divine existence is absolute, while all other existence is creaturely contingent on the existence of the creator-god. In this "enchanted universe," as Gilson calls it, all being things attest by their act of existence the existence of God. Nevertheless, while accepting the Thomist conception, Gilson believes that, by its "technical nudity," the language of Being obstructs rather than facilitates the entrance to this divinely enchanted world. The truth that enchants him so strongly that he would "not care to live in any other universe" will not be enchantingly transmitted by perfect metaphysical concepts but requires, for its convincing expression, the vision of a "sacred world impregnated in its most intimate fibers by the presence of a God whose sovereign existence saves it forever from nothingness." What "enchants" is not the conceptual work of the saint but the sacredness of a creation that bears testimony to the divine omnipresence. If in this manner, however, metaphysics is relegated to second place, we must ask by what criterion the Thomasic vision can be judged more "enchanting" than any other experience of divine presence in the cosmos, such as, for instance, the Platonic? Gilson is sure of his answer to this question. With a slightly contemptuous touch he writes: "That is a beautiful thought that all is full of gods: Thales the Milesian had it, and

Plato has borrowed it from him; but now all is full of God." And then he leaves it to the reader to draw the conclusions from a confrontation he supposes to be convincing by its mere statement (*Le Thomisme* [5th ed., 1948], 146ff.).

Gilson is dismayed by an exuberant language of Being that tends to obscure the experience of the divine-cosmic reality it is supposed to make intelligible. The dynamics of the human quest threatens to overpower the divine appeal; and the one truth of reality, as it emerges from the Metaxy, is in danger of dissociating into the two verities of Faith and Reason. One can sense in the work of Thomas the possibility of the science of Being sliding over, as it did in the modern centuries, into an autonomous source of truth. Reacting to this tendency, Gilson wants to shift the dynamics of appeal-response back to where it belongs—*i.e.*, to the revelatory, theophanic pole of the existential tension. The enchantment of the quest derives from the enchantment with the reality of which the quest is a part. However, when he attempts to restore to the truth of reality a balance he feels endangered by the preponderant conceptualization in terms of Being, Gilson lets his compensatory language overcompensate. The "visions" of Thales-Plato and Saint Thomas tend to appear as autonomous entities of a revelatory character, not touched by any involvement with the Reason of the human quest. Such a conception, however, would hypostatically lean over as far to the side of the theophanic appeal as the exuberant language of Being leans over to the side of the human quest. Hence, while I agree with the observations and sentiments of Gilson, I am not sure that the conclusions I now shall draw would be his, if he had cared to make them explicit.

Gilson's response to a correctly sensed flaw in the Thomasic perfection has to be ambiguous because it relies on a conventional language that is becoming obsolete in our historical situation. The dichotomies of Faith and Reason, Religion and Philosophy, Theology and Metaphysics can no longer be used as ultimate terms of reference when we have to deal with experiences of divine reality with their rich diversification in the ethnic cultures of antiquity, with their interpretation in the cultures of the ecumenic empires, with the transition of consciousness from the truth of the intracosmic gods to the truth of the divine Beyond, and with the contemporary expansion of the horizon to the global ecumene. We can no longer ignore that the symbols of "Faith" express the responsive quest of man just as much as the revelatory appeal, and that the symbols of "Philosophy" express the revelatory appeal just as much as the responsive quest. We must further acknowledge that the medieval tension between Faith and Reason derives from the origins of these symbols in the two different ethnic cultures of Israel and Hellas, that in the consciousness of Israelite prophets and Hellenic philosophers the differentiating experience of the divine Beyond was respectively focused on the revelatory appeal and the human quest, and that the two types of consciousness had to face new problems when the political events of the Ecumenic Age cut them loose from their moorings in the ethnic cultures and forced their confrontation under the multicivilizational conditions of an ecumenic empire.

If the various structures in the personal, social, and historical process of consciousness are taken into account, one can no longer speak of the Platonic-Aristotelian exploration of Being as "philosophy" in the topical sense. The reflective action of the Hellenic thinkers is a quest by concrete human beings in response to a divine appeal from the Beyond of the soul; and the appeal is so outspoken as to its source that it becomes word in the very symbol of the Beyond. But who is this "god" who does not speak from Olympus but from somewhere beyond the cosmos? The philosophers' effort to answer this question has to struggle with the traditional *fides* in the intracosmic gods who are present "in all things" from the Beginning. If the personal gods are intracosmic, can the "god" beyond the intracosmic gods be personal too? And if the appeal from the One Beyond should emanate from a One personal god, would this revelation not condemn the hitherto personal gods to nondivinity? The questions of this class do not arise merely from the problem of conventional "anthropomorphism," though that is also a factor in the situation, as we know from the pre-Socratic struggle with the issue, in particular from Xenophanes. They have their deeper reason in the conflict between a God of the Beyond who orders the psyche of man by attracting it toward Himself and a God of the Beginning who creates an order so imperfect that it requires a special effort of revelation and response to extract man from the disorder of reality. Can the savior-god of the soul be the same god, or the same type of god, as the god who has created the reality from which salvation is necessary? These questions cannot be reduced to the Gilsonian alternative of a Pagan cosmos "full of gods" and a Christian cosmos "full of God," for they arise within "Paganism" itself when the One of divine reality reveals itself from the Beyond by appealing to the responsive soul. The same questions, it should be noted, arise in the revelatory evolution of Israel, when the One God of the Chosen People has to cope with the "other gods" of the other nations, until the "other gods" develop into "false gods" and finally into "no-gods." The Israelite case is especially illuminating for the dynamics of the movement, because the very Yahweh who, by the strength of his spiritual Oneness, pressures the other gods into nondivinity retains so much of the character of the "other gods" from whom he separates that he becomes the victim of the more radically spiritualized divinity of the Gnostic thinkers. For in the Gnostic psychodrama of divine reality, resulting in the libidinous creation of the world, the Israelite creator-god is assigned the role of the daemon whose work must be undone, with the knowing help of man, by the penumatic God of the Beyond who reveals himself through Christ as his messenger.[3] Whatever the "Christian" answers will be, the problem is definitely pre-Christian and "Pagan."

Plato's Myth of the Phaedrus

Within the "Pagan" context of Hellenic philosophy, the language of Being arises in the transition from the truth of the cosmos and its gods to the truth of the soul in existential tension toward the Beyond. It is engendered by the experience of a conflict between the compact *fides* of the cosmological myth and the new, more differ-

---

3. At this point in an earlier draft, Voegelin added the following lines:

In the case of the classic philosophers, the divine Beyond does not reveal itself as the one personal God, but remains in an impersonal anonymity by which it is distinguished from the intracosmic, divine personalities. That this cannot be the whole story of the Beyond, however, Plato acknowledges by his creation of the philosopher's myths that tell the "stories" of a divine reality that reveals itself from the Beyond. Still, while he knows that the divine ambiance of the psyche, once it has become conscious of its tension toward the Beyond, cannot be sufficiently expressed by the analytical language of Being, and that the "more" that is required cannot be supplied by the older myth, the language of his own myth remains in debt to the symbolization of the intracosmic gods; it never becomes as radically "revelatory" as the symbols that emerge from

entiated *fides* of a divine reality beyond the cosmos. At least that is how Plato experienced and symbolized the event. In the Myth of the *Phaedrus*, he ranks the Olympian gods together with their human followers as the beings within the cosmos who are endowed with souls and therefore are concerned with their immortality. The Olympians, who already enjoy the status of immortals, have only to preserve it by appropriate action, while the human souls who desire immortality have yet to rise to it by an effort that is, in various degrees, handicapped by their mortal bodies whose passions drag them down. Neither the preserving actions of the gods, however, nor the desirous efforts of their human attendants can achieve their goal through processes within the cosmos. For the source of immortality is the extracosmic divine reality beyond the heaven (*exo tou ouranou*) that surrounds the cosmos, and the intracosmic beings who have souls must rise to this source by means of the noetic "wings" that enable them to ascend to the truth of the Beyond. This ascent of the souls is not everyday business. Ordinarily, so Plato lets the Myth tell us, the gods and their followers will attend to their intracosmic affairs, and only on festive occasions will they rise to the superheavenly region (*hyperouranios topos*). And there, from the roof of the cosmos, they will contemplate the *ousia ontos ousa* that is visible only to the *nous*, the guide of the soul.

Although the overall meaning of the Myth is clear, the interpretation in detail is beset with various difficulties that have their center in the linguistic problems previously touched upon. Our modern philosophical idioms suffer so strongly from the millennial overlaying of the original language of Myth and Philosophy with the meanings of Metaphysics that simple idiomatic renderings of the original meanings have become next to impossible.

---

the spiritual crisis of the Ecumenic Age in its later, Judaeo-Christian phase. In the Platonic myth, the Being of the Beyond can become the Demiurge of the cosmos and the Puppetplayer who draws the soul toward its immortality, but it does not become the radically transmundane Creator *ex nihilo* nor the Savior who enters the world to incarnate himself in its suffering. The personnel of the Platonic "true" or "likely" stories does not have the divine authority of either the intracosmic gods or of the radically revealed God. The revelatory authority that radiates from the Platonic "stories" nevertheless to this day derives from the imaginative elaboration, in the familiar language of the intracosmic myth, of the divine appeal to which the philosophers responded by their inquiry concerning the structure of reality in the language of Being. The symbolism of Being becomes, and remains, the authoritative language of the new *fides*.

Such conventional translations of the *ousia ontos ousa*, for instance, as "the essence" (Jowett), or as "true being" (Hackforth), or as the "truly existing essence" (Fowler), though certainly the best one can do idiomatically, will not do justice to a phrase that would have to be rendered literally as "Being-beingly-being"; and even a Latinization such as "reality-really-real" is questionable because it injects too much of thinghood, of *res*, into something that Plato tried to symbolize as not one of the "things" like the Olympian gods and their followers. In its context of the "story," the phrase is a mythical symbol; it does not occur as the predicate in a metaphysical proposition about the nature of God, and consequently does not anticipate, in perhaps a less perfect form, the Thomasic *Deus est ipsum esse per suam essentiam*. The immortalizing Being of the Myth is not the personal God of the Israelite-Christian revelation who overwhelms by his pneumatic inrush into the soul; it is precisely not the Person that in later speculation can become, as *Deus*, the subject of metaphysical predications, but rather remains in the impersonal remoteness of a transcosmic "region" that "never has been hymned worthily by a poet inside the cosmos, and never will be" (*Phaedrus*, 247c).

But how is the precise meaning of such a symbolism as the *ousia ontos ousa* to be ascertained if the Latin-Christian metaphysics of essence and existence is not admissible as the language of interpretation? The key to the answer is given in Plato's remark on the difficulty of worthily praising the unknown God of the Beyond from the intracosmic position. The very transition from the gods of the cosmological myth to the unknown god to whose appeal man responds with meditative reflection is the experience in search of a language. The millennial proportions of the problem will come into better view if one remembers that Plato, though his symbolization is analytically superior to earlier responses, is not the first thinker in history to experience the situation in which it becomes acute. In fact, the same observation on the difficulty of "worthily" responding to the appeal of the unknown is to be found in the Egyptian *Amon Hymns* of Dynasty XIX, after Akh-en-Aton, about the time of Moses. In these hymns, the meditating thinker attempts to rise above the intracosmic gods to an understanding of the divine reality that is at the origin of all reality, including the gods. In the course of his reflection, Amon becomes "the divine god who came into being by himself," "who came into being at the beginning, so that his mysterious nature is unknown." The *Hymns* have the pragmatic purpose of elevating the Amon of Thebes against rival divinities to the rank of the imperial *summus deus*, and the meditation is therefore closely bound to the theogonic type of mytho-speculation by which conventionally the rank of *summus deus* is established; it does not yet reflect on the manner in which the very act of responsive meditation affects the symbolism of the cosmological substratum. Precisely because of this limit, however, which the pragmatic purpose sets to a fuller analytical development of the response, the *Hymns* bring to light the peculiar problem of the "transition" from cosmological to existential truth that occupies Plato. For the god whose mysterious nature is unknown carries the name of the known god Amon; and this well-known member of the Egyptian pantheon becomes unknown when the meditative response to his appeal tries to differentiate his divine reality from that of the known intracosmic gods. The known god becomes unknown when the appeal of his reality awakens in man the response of meditation. The source of the linguistic difficulty thus appears to be the meditative process itself.

This is indeed the problem in the *Phaedrus*. When the meditation reaches the luminosity of self-reflection, the quest of the unknown god is enriched by the awareness of the hitherto unknown man who now discovers himself as the knower of the unknown. And this new awareness becomes manifest in the creation of the language symbols for its expression.

There now appears, first of all, the verb *anakyptein* as the symbol that is meant to express the "rising" or "raising" of the soul to the fulfillment of the self-reflective response. Plato can speak of the "rising" of man's vision above the things, including the gods, that we now speak of as "being" (*einai*), to the being that is "truly" or "beingly" being (*to on ontos*, 249c). The verb recommends itself because it can function in both the senses of man's existential growth into his own response to the unknown, and of an external rising or straightening up when the growth is told as an event in a mythical tale. One can encounter it therefore in such widely different stories of man's immortalizing growth as the Myth of the *Phaedo*, where the process is described as the "rising" of man above the waters to their surface and a view of the upper world

(*Phaedo*, 109d), or in the Apocalyptic Discourse attributed by Luke to Jesus, where the faithful are enjoined to "raise their heads" when the Second Coming assures them that their redemption is near (Luke 21:28).

Since in the *Phaedrus* that substratum of the meditation is still the cosmological *fides*, Plato has then to find the language symbols that will describe the effect of the "rise" on both the Olympian and the human souls. As far as the gods are concerned, their knowing (*theou dianoia*, 247d) is unencumbered by the diversions of mortality and can derive its nurture purely from the *nous* of the Beyond; their nearness to the "truly being" makes the "gods truly divine" (*theos on theios*, 249c). In this respect Plato moves still close to the *Amon Hymns*, where the cosmological gods, engaged like the Olympians in contemplating the true divinity beyond themselves, "boast of (Amon), to magnify themselves through his beauty, according as he is divine." What is new is the concern with the souls of the human beings. The Platonic mortals not only can follow the immortal gods by their *fides*, but in following they can "rise" with them meditatively to the source of divine immortality beyond the gods. This miracle of the human "rise," which has become personal, social, and historical reality in the Socratic meditation as well as in Plato's own, requires an "explanation" in terms of the Myth. How can the hitherto unknown reality make itself sufficiently known to move man's soul into meditative action, at least in the rare cases of the "philosophers"—of the men who are stricken by the "fourth mania" (249d)? Plato's answer to the mystery of the revelatory appeal is the myth of Anamnesis. The appeal experienced here and now is to be understood as the "memory" (*mneme*, 250a) that the souls retain of their mythical "rise." However, though all men are equally drawn into the "rise," the "memory" retained will vary with the ability and willingness that have gone into the mythical vision; and the various degrees of achievement result in the wide amplitude of characters among the human souls, ranging from the "philosopher" to the "tyrant" (248d–e). In the optimal case, that of the "philosopher" who makes the right use of these memories, the soul will be "always initiated into the fullest of mysteries." This last phrase—in Greek, *teleous aei teletas teloumenos*—presents difficulties of idiomatic translations similar to those of *ousia ontos ousa*. Literally, it would have to be rendered as something like "fulfillment-fully-fulfilled." As in the case of the superheavenly "being," however, *to on ontos* could serve as a shorter synonym, so now Plato uses *teleos ontos* as a more succinct symbol, parallel with the more elaborate one. The man whose soul has achieved the existential status of the "philosopher" will be "truly fulfilled," or perfect (*teleos ontos, 249c*).

The Myth leaves no doubt about the source and meaning of its language. The phrases that resist idiomatic translation emerge as the exegetic symbols from a divine-human encounter, specifically from a meditative "rise" toward the Beyond of the cosmos, the *epekeina tes ousias* of *Republic,* 509b; they arise from the event of the "rise" as the articulation of its structure in language. They are definitely not subjects or predicates in "metaphysical" propositions about a previously known object-of-thought, such as a Scholastic "Deus." On the contrary, the symbols comprehend in their meaning the ambiguity of an unknown that becomes known as the unknown, of a noetic quest that knows where the unknown is to be found. This ambiguity permeates all the analytically distinguishable parts of the noetic encounter:

1. The experience of the "rise" itself, which hitherto had not been experienced and now requires for the expression of its revelatory component the symbolism of the anamnetic myth;

2. The "transcendent" pole of the quest, the Beyond, which is "colorless, formless, and impalpable," but nevertheless "visible" to the mind (*nous*), and inasmuch as it can be characterized in these terms is denotable by language; and

3. The human pole of the movement, the man who discovers himself as the noetic man when he is anamnetically initiated into the "perfection" of the "philosopher's" questing existence (*Phaedrus,* 247c).

Transcendence

Even this reminder of the internally cognitive structure of the experiential process, however, will not dissolve all the difficulties a "modern mind" has in understanding the event. The principal source of confusion is again the change in the meaning of a leading language symbol. I have deliberately spoken of the Beyond as the "transcendent" pole of the experience in order to bring the problem arising from the "modern" use, or misuse, of the term *transcendence* to attention. For in today's conventional usage we let "transcendent" refer to a divine reality beyond the reality of a de-divinized "world," while in Platonic usage the Beyond symbolizes the goal of a meditative act that transcends the divinely permeated reality of the "cosmos." Moreover, between the Platonic and modern usages there interposes itself the Christian act of transcendence in which the world, though no longer "full of gods," is far from being de-divinized, but "full of God," as Gilson formulates it. Hence, the indiscriminate language of "transcendent reality" tends to obscure the problem of the Beyond in several respects. In the first place, there is no "transcendent reality" other than the Beyond experienced in the "rise." If it is torn out of the experiential context, it suffers the intentionalist reduction to an object in whose existence one can believe or not; the experienced *fides*, we may say, leaves a fideistic belief as its sediment. Grammatically, the reduction manifests itself in the tendency to separate the participle *transcendent* from the act of transcendence and to transform it into a fideistic attribute of the reality that becomes "visible" in the act. Since the phrase favors the intentionalist reduction, it furthermore obscures the historical process in which the modes of the "rise" change from the Platonic to the Christian experience of the Beyond, and creates an atmosphere of general vagueness in which an otherwise solid commentator can speak of the famous passage in *Republic*, 509b, as a piece of "transcendental rhetoric." Finally and decisively, the phrase obscures both the content of the Platonic experience and the analytical insight arising from it exegesis. The experience becomes unrecognizable as an advance of the *cognitio fidei* from the intracosmic *fides* to the *fides* of the Beyond, while the philosopher's understanding of the divine-human encounter in the noetic act as the moving force in the historical advance is altogether eclipsed by the intentionalist reduction of the result.

The Parousia of the Beyond

In the meditative event, the Beyond is analytically inseparable from the act in which it becomes "visible," as well as from the language symbols by which the act and its result will be expressed. With these critical observations in mind, the verb *transcend* can now be applied to certain problems in the Platonic language of Being without, I hope, provoking new misunderstandings. By his meditative act, Plato does not transcend the "cosmos," or the "world," as if they were given objects, but engages within reality in a movement that will let a compact, and therefore comparatively opaque, image of Being become transparent for the truth of the Beyond. As a cognitive event, the act is a man's exodus, in response to a divine appeal, from opaque into luminous Being, conducted within a process of reality that lets both images of Being, as well as the exodus movement from one to the other, become historically manifest. Hence, if the cognitive act of transcendence be not fragmentized by the intentionalist reduction, but understood in its integrality, the language of Being arising from the act will intelligibly tend to develop as many aggregates of meaning as there are phases in the process when they become articulate in the reflective consciousness of the man who experiences the event. In Plato's case, the three principal aggregates are:

1. The image of Being before the event;
2. The image of Being after the event;
3. The image of the Being in which an illuminating event of this kind can occur.

These images, as well as the relations between them, create the problems peculiar to an integral language of Being.

The intracosmic *fides* is Plato's image of Being before the event. It is the firm starting point for his act of transcendence and retains a primary claim to the symbol Being. When the divine reality of the Beyond becomes "visible" in the meditative act as the goal of the quest, the claim of this newly differentiated something to the name of Being in the traditional sense will appear doubtful. In a first attempt to establish the relation of the new something to the intracosmic symbolism, it will therefore be characterized as "non-Being" (*ouk ousias ontos tou agathou*), as a something "beyond-Being" (*epekeina tes ousias, Republic,* 509b). This first attempt, however, cannot be the last word. For the act of transcendence occurs within the very Being that is symbolized by the image before the event; it is an inquiry concerning the noetic adequacy of the intracosmic image, conducted within the same Being that had allowed the image now under inquiry to emerge as its adequate symbolization. The new image, in order to be recognizable as more adequate, must be an image of Being, not of "non-being"; and if it is recognizably more adequate, it will have to become in its turn the standard by which the earlier one is to be measured. This inversion of the standard occurs indeed in Plato; it dominates the language of the *Phaedrus;* but it leads to new complications in the language of Being. For the divine reality that reveals itself in the act, though it is "beyond-being," is not "non-being" but has now become "truly-being"; and as it is the source of immortality for the gods and men who "rise" to it, it even is the divinity "truly-divine." The newly discovered Beyond requires a language of intensification that characterizes it as both Being and non-Being in relation to the image of Being before the event. But if the Beyond is now the "being-beingly-being," what happens to the Being of the intracosmic image? Will it now in its turn have to become "non-being", or will the image have to be declared simply wrong? Neither the one nor the other course is adopted by Plato. The Being of the cosmos remains the Being that it was, because the Beyond was present in it even before its presence revealed itself in the act of transcendence; and the image before the event is not wrong but is now recognized as opaque, because it was not yet luminous for the dependence of the cosmos, including the gods, on the presence of the divine Beyond. By its movement toward the Beyond, the act of transcendence has discovered a hierarchical structure in Being. Hence, the image after the event, though it becomes the new truth of Being, does not simply replace the earlier one but makes it noetically luminous for the hierarchy of being compactly contained in it. Plato's act of transcendence is truly an intracosmic *fides quaerens intellectum;* and when the noetic understanding, the *intellectus,* is achieved, the emerging image is the standard of truth, for the time being, in the historical process of the *cognitio fidei.*

The image after the event is a new measure of truth, because it has differentiated the previously compact structure of a hierarchy in Being and found the language symbols that will articulate the structure. But what is the nature of this hierarchy, and what are the language symbols articulating it? I have spoken of this hierarchy as a dependence of the cosmos on the presence of the Beyond; and in choosing this formula, I have tried to render as exactly as possible the meaning of Plato's rather dense language in *Republic,* 509b. In this passage, Plato characterizes the relationship by the verbs *pa-*

reinai and *proseinai*. They mean literally that the cosmos derives its Being from its participation in the Beyond, and that the Beyond, if the cosmos is to participate in it, must be present as a participant in its Being. If now one uses the noun that belongs to the verb *pareinai* in order to facilitate the expression, one arrives at the formulation: the Being of the cosmos derives its existence and essence (*to einai te kai ten ousian*) from the presence, from the *parousia*, of the divine Beyond. Precisely this insight into the Parousia of the Beyond creates the difficulties in the Platonic language of Being. For the Beyond, while it is the creative presence in the cosmos, is not quite of its Being. In the famous passage under discussion, it is still "non-being" because it surpasses (*hyperechontos*) all cosmic Being "by its rank and power." In fact, in this passage it is related to Being by hardly more than one of the punning assonances in which Plato sometimes likes to indulge, *i.e.*, by the assonance of *ouk ontos* and *hyperechontos*. The divine reality that reveals its presence in the meditative act is both within Being as its creative core and outside of Being in some Beyond of it.

The paradox of the within-without of Being cannot be resolved on the level of doctrinaire metaphysics. Whatever the merits of a debate about the location of the Idea *in re, ante rem,* or *post rem,* or the value of classifying Plato's "position" by concepts of modern ontology such as pantheism, transcendentalism, or panentheism, the language of propositional metaphysics has no function where a philosopher is concerned with articulating and symbolizing his experience of divine reality. The paradox must be understood on the terms of the experience from which it arises. There is no Beyond lying around somewhere, to be or not to be included in somebody's "system"; there is no differentiated insight concerning the Beyond and its presence in the cosmos at all, as long as there is no experience of its immortalizing presence in the act of meditation. Plato's image of Being before the event is dominated by the Anaximandrian symbolism of the Apeiron. The things (*ta onta*) emerge from the Apeiron and return to it; they exist under the law of *genesis* and *phthora*, of Becoming and Perishing. When the presence of the Beyond is experienced in the noetic act, there reveals itself a Being that is neither the Apeiron nor one of the cosmic things but the immortally divine reality that will redeem its followers from their

Apeirontic fate. The Beyond is indeed beyond the cosmos because the participation in its *parousia* permits the soul of man to "rise" from intracosmic mortality to transcosmic immortality. In this sense of overcoming the fate of the cosmos, the Parousia of the Beyond symbolizes an eschatological experience in Plato. The image of Being after the event has to struggle with problems of a hierarchy in Being because it has to absorb the eschatological insight gained in the meditative act. The cosmos that is full of gods is at the same time, though still not "full of God" in the Christian sense, at least full of the eminent (*hyperechontos*) Being of the Beyond.

The issue will now have become sufficiently clear. The noetic act of exploring the structure of Being does not abolish the Being it explores, nor does it create an alternative truth to the truth of the cosmological *fides*. The philosopher, if he wants to be intelligible, must continue to speak of reality in the pre-analytical language of the *fides* from which he started. There is still the cosmos with its mystery of Becoming and Perishing, there are still gods and men, and there is still the world of matter, plants, animals, and artifacts external to the body in which the consciousness of man is rooted. The noetic act, as a *fides quaerens intellectum*, does not destroy the *fides* it tries to understand. Nevertheless, something has happened that affects the truth of the cosmological *fides*. For the noetic act has reflectively discovered itself as the response to an appeal from the immortal, and immortalizing, divine reality "beyond" the cosmos. Moreover, in discovering itself, it has revealed the Parousia of the Beyond as the sustaining core of all cosmic Being. Hence, the act is a revelation of divine reality as the "eminent Being" beyond the cosmos and, at the same time, the reflective discovery of the human *nous* as the responsive agent that can discern which of the symbolizations of divine reality truly symbolizes the "truly divine." That is not to say that the consequences of this divine-human epiphany in the noetic act were realized all at once in the context of Platonic-Aristotelian philosophizing. On the contrary, the manner in which the standard of meditative truth affects not only the cosmological but every unreflected *fides* in quest of its own understanding is a matter of the millennial history in which we still participate today. A few observations on this problem will at least suggest its dimensions.

Immortality and the Gods

In the context of Plato's *fides quaerens intellectum*, the problem becomes tangible in certain questions that impose themselves but must be left open. They concern the fate of the intracosmic gods once the meditative act has become noetically reflective.

If in the noetic act the Beyond reveals itself as Being in the eminent sense, the "things" of the cosmos, including the gods, will have from now on to occupy the inferior rank of derivative or contingent Being. That is no more than the logic that the insight requires. But since the noetic act articulates an experience of divine reality, and since the Beyond is not a further member of the Olympian society but reveals itself as the One that is "truly divine," one would expect the revelatory insight to affect the Olympians more harshly. If the presence of the Beyond in the philosopher's act is supposed to reveal its presence in all of the cosmic "things," why should the Parousia of Being not dethrone the intracosmic gods completely and transform them into no-gods? Plato, however, dismisses the intracosmic gods no more than do the Egyptian authors of the *Amon Hymns,* or the Upanishadic mediators on the rise toward the Brahman, or the kshatriya author of the *Bhagavad Gita,* or, centuries after Plato, his Egyptian-Roman successor Plotinus. Even when the Beyond has revealed itself to the questing mind of man as the One that is truly divine, the cosmos remains full of gods. The Beyond, it appears, is not experienced as exhausting all of the divine reality of which man has compact knowledge through his cosmological *fides.*

What is this surplus of divine reality represented by the intracosmic gods even when the divine Beyond has revealed itself? Although the issue does not become fully articulate in the Platonic context, it becomes acute in the problem presented by the relation between the Beyond and the Beginning.

The meditative action, as we know, can move either in the direction of the Beyond or of the Beginning, thus raising the question whether the god of the creative Beginning is the same as the god of the Beyond. To this great question there is no unambiguous answer in Plato's work. On the one hand, the expansion of the Parousia of Being to the cosmos points in the direction of identification. On the other hand, the eminent Being on its noetic height as the One, in *Philebus,* 17a, has the creative depth of the Apeiron as its divine counterpole; and in the Myth of the *Timaeus,* the Demiurge has to impose the order of form on a pre-existent material. Obviously, the creativity of the Beginning has something to do with the surplus of divine reality that Plato does not consider exhausted by the experience of the Beyond. This observation, however, is not a final answer but raises further questions in its turn, for the Near Eastern mytho-speculation on the Beginning had become part of Hellenic intellectual culture at least since Hesiod, and by the fourth century it was well understood as a type of meditative action closely related to the noetic quest. Aristotle occasionally remarks that his quest of the *arche* of things is substantially the same quest as that of the mytho-speculative thinkers; and Plato, the master of mythical creation, could so well distinguish between the time of the cosmos and the time of the tale in which the story of the Beginning is told that Saint Augustine could fall back on him when he had to explain that there is no time before Creation. But if the relation between the two types of meditative action was so well recognized, why could it not be pursued further? Why should the issue cause hesitation and ambiguity?

For the student of the *Phaedrus* Myth, the answer is not difficult to find. It will sound unconventional, however, because it must be sought not in a Platonic "doctrine" on the level of intentionalist reductions but in the experiential conduct of the cosmological *fides quaerens intellectum.* Plato cannot simply dismiss the Olympian gods, because they represent the immortality that is to be achieved by the human psyche. The function of the immortals in Plato's *fides* is equivalent to that of the visions of the resurrected Christ in the Christian *fides.* Immortality is the experiential issue that causes the uncertainties.

Once the Beyond has revealed itself as the truly divine reality, as Being in the eminent sense, it becomes clear that the immortality of the mortals cannot mean their transformation into the eminent source of immortality. There has to be an "intermediate" immortality, accessible to at least certain "things" in the cosmos through their participation in the eminent immortality of the Beyond. The problem becomes acute in the philosopher's meditation, because the noetic act is experienced as an act of participation in the divine reality it explores. In Aristotle's language, noetic philosophizing is a practice of immortalizing, of *athanatizein* (*NE*, 1177b27ff); and for Plato it is the practice of death, *melete thanatou*, that will let the psyche in death arrive at its divine, immortal, and wise status in truth (*Phaedo*, 81a). The philosophers have differentiated, together with the noetic tension of existence, the spiritual meaning of life and death that formerly was compactly contained in the cosmological symbolization of afterlife. In *Timaeus*, 90a–b, Plato has formulated the issue:

> Now, when man abandons himself to his desires and ambitions, indulging them incontinently, all of his thoughts of necessity become mortal and as a consequence he must become mortal every bit, as far as that is possible, because he has nourished his mortal part. When on the contrary he has earnestly cultivated his love of knowledge and true wisdom, when he has primarily exercised his faculty to think immortal and divine things, he will—since in that manner he is touching the truth—become immortal of necessity, as far as it is possible for human nature to participate in immortality.

Or, to paraphrase this passage in Aristotelian language: If it is the nature of man to have Reason, to be the *zoon noun echon*, then by his nature he is conscious of being both mortal and immortal. His death is not simply a biological event; nor is he a "mortal" in the compact Homeric sense, by his mortality distinguished from the "immortal" gods; but he is immortal in his present existence inasmuch as by his noetic psyche he participates in the Beyond. Hence, when noetic participation has become fully activated and articulate in reflective consciousness, the meaning of life and death acquires the peculiar ambiguity of the existential agon, which in Hellenic thought can be traced back to Pythagoras. In the *Gorgias*, Plato lets Socrates voice this agonic ambiguity:

> Well, but in your own view, life is strange. For I tell you I should not wonder if Euripides' words were true, when he says:
>> Who knows if to live is to be dead,
>> and to be dead to live?
> and we really, it may be, are dead. In fact I once heard one of our sages say that now we are dead, and the body is our tomb.
>> (492–93)

Life will be symbolized as a tomb from which the soul can rise, by dying to the cosmos, to the life of the Beyond, when man's existence is experienced as more than life in the cosmos. The agonic ambiguity of life and death has become the classic symbolism of man's existence between the cosmos and the Beyond, of his existence in the Metaxy. Life and death have to take their meaning from each other: Man cannot die unless he is immortal, and through mortality alone can he gain life.

When the agon of existence has become luminous to the point of articulating itself in the ambiguity of life and death, the situation becomes difficult for the Olympians. The intracosmic gods, it appears, compactly represent the divine reality that is experienced as present in the cosmos. Once the immortality of the Beyond, which they formerly co-represented, has been differentiated by the noetic act, they cannot simply disappear, because no more than the Beyond has been differentiated from their compact immortality. Nevertheless, their status as "immortals" has been gravely affected. For, in the first place, their divinity and immortality become intermediate between the cosmos and the Beyond, and, second, man has become immortal, too. The moving factor in this change of status is the action of the psyche as it advances from the reflection on the gods and their beginning, to the reflection on its own reflective action as the response to the appeal from the Beyond, and ultimately to the self-reflective discovery of its theomorphic nature. An early manifestation of the movement is the Hesiodian theogony that endows, by its mytho-speculative construction, the immortality of the immortals with a beginning, a genealogy, and a history; and a first climax of insight into the theomorphic nature of the psyche is reached in the Aeschylean *Prometheus,* where a drama of the psyche is enacted by the gods as the *dramatis personae.* But precisely when the movement arrives at the self-reflective clarity of the philosopher's noetic act, it becomes also clear that the immortality of the gods compactly co-represents a movement within the cosmos toward its own immortality or, if not of the cosmos as a whole, at least of the cosmic "things" called men. From man's experience of the Metaxy of mortality-immortality, and of his movement from the one to the other, there emerges the vision of the movement coming to its end in a theomorphosis unencumbered by the cosmic imperfection of Becoming and Perishing. This perfect state, however, is neither the traditional immortality of the gods nor the newly discovered immortality of the Beyond but a symbolism that will express the phi-

losophers' experience of themselves as overcoming their own perishing, the Anaximandrian *phthora*. From the experience of cosmic
existence in the noetic Metaxy emerges the vision of transcendent
existence in a Metaxy of immortal perfection.

Analytically, from the side of the human quest, the issue of the
vision is comparatively simple. There is no difficulty in finding
such symbols as "intermediate immortality" or "theomorphic Metaxy," or to speak of a "theomorphic beyond" as distinguished from
the truly-divine Beyond, or to accept Saint Thomas' concept of *deiformitas* (*ST*, I, 12, 6) or Dante's symbolism of *trasumanar* (*Para-
diso*, I, 70) in order to articulate with sufficient adequacy the truth
of this intermediate realm revealed by the Parousia of the Beyond
in the noetic act. Beyond this point, however, the problems of symbolization become highly complex, because the *cognitio intellectus*, the noetic range of cognition, is limited. The noetic inquiry
can arrive at insights concerning the noetic component in all
human experience and symbolization of reality; it can achieve the
self-reflective understanding of its own action as the noetic response to the divine appeal; it can create the symbols of a "theomorphic beyond" or of a *deiformitas*, expressing the experience of
immortalizing perfection; and in doing all this it can develop even
the criteria by which the visions of the "theomorphic beyond" will
have to be judged adequate or inadequate to the insights into the
noetic structure of man's existence. But it cannot provide the *cognitio fidei* of the visions in which the noetic structure is no more
than a component. "Imaginative vision," emerging from reality in
response to the appeal of reality, is the comprehensive event of
experience and symbolization. The philosopher's meditation can
operate only within the comprehensive vision and make it self-
reflectively luminous for man's existence in tension toward the Beyond. Hence, imaginative vision and noesis are not independent,
rival, or alternative sources of knowledge and truth but interacting
forces in the historical process of an imaginative vision that has
noetic structure.

The Interaction of Vision and Noesis

The interaction between the comprehensive vision and its noetic
component is a constant problem in the history of Western thought,
but its treatment has remained curiously fuzzy to this day. The

analysis that would have been required has always stopped short of penetrating the topical symbols that obscured the analytical issue with their stress on the aspect that was emotionally most exciting at the historical moment. The term *myth*, for instance, can still be used indiscriminately for all manifestations of the cosmological mode of experience in spite of their diversification into distinct historical types of interaction, such as the interaction of vision and noesis in the creation of theogony, cosmogony, anthropogony, and historiogenesis. I have called the symbolisms of this type "mytho-speculative" because they result from a noetic speculation on the Beginning within the medium of the cosmological myth, without however breaking through to self-reflection and the differentiated experience of the Beyond. "Mytho-speculation" is not simply a "myth" but a well-documented type of interaction in several civilizations in the same sense in which the *Phaedrus* is the document of the self-reflective interaction between noesis and the cosmological vision of reality that Plato has called "philosophy." Moreover, mythospeculation does not disappear when the comprehensive vision changes from the cosmological myth to the existential vision of divine reality as the God who is One, without however developing the symbolism of the Beyond through noetic philosophizing, as it does in the Israelite-Judaic ethnic culture. On the contrary, the speculative myth of the Beginning comes to its classic perfection in Genesis. And yet the reasons why the speculation on the Beginning should survive its origin in the context of the intracosmic myth and come to perfection within an increasingly self-conscious vision of the divine Beyond have never been fully clarified; they rather have been obscured by severing it from its visionary origin and bringing it under the general head of "revelation"—obscured, because the symbolism of "revelation" itself is in need of some clarification. For the Muses of Hesiod breathe into the poet the "divine voice" that now will speak through him the story of the *Theogony.* Is mytho-speculation perhaps revelatory, even when it occurs in the pre-revelatory medium of the intracosmic myth? It certainly is revelatory in the consciousness of Hesiod, just as a prophet's utterances are revelatory in the consciousness of an Isaiah or Jeremiah, or as "philosophy" is revelatory in the anamnetic consciousness of Plato.

And finally, there is the problem presented by the Platonic experiences and their symbolization through the "myth"—through the myth of the anamnetic "rise" toward the Beyond, of the prisoner in the Cave who is forced to turn around toward the light, of the God who pulls the human puppets by his cords, of the Judgment of the Dead, of the Islands of the Blessed and the Tartarus as the places of reward and punishment for the good and bad souls, of the Demiurge and his creation of the cosmos, of the Brotherhood of Man, and of the three ages of history governed in succession by Kronos, Zeus, and Nous. What are these "likely" or "true" stories that conventionally we call "myths"? They certainly do not belong to the rich store of the anonymous people's myth, nor to the myths of the Homeric epics, nor are they Hesiodian mytho-speculations, nor are they the tragedians' myths. They are again a symbolism *sui generis.* In Plato's own conception, they are visions of the divine ambiance that will be compatible with his noetic vision of the philosopher's existence. The *opsis,* the vision, is Plato's technical term for the experiential process in which the order of reality is seen, becomes reflectively known, and finds its appropriate language symbols. The "vision" in this comprehensive sense, which includes the noetic vision, appears in the key-passages of *Timaeus* 47 as the *opsis* of the order in the cosmos, and in *Republic,* 507–509, as the *opsis* of the Agathon that creates the order in the soul of man. Moreover, Plato is careful about precluding subjectivist misunderstandings. The "vision" is not somebody's fancy but the imaginative power of response to the reality seen; and the reality seen is the cause (*aition*) of this power (*dynamis*). The passage sounds as if Plato had anticipated the possibility of garbling the meaning of "vision" by a modern "projection psychology." Against such mutilation by diseased minds he stresses the visionary power of the imaginative response as caused by an *epirryton,* by an inrush or influx of the divine light (*Republic,* 508b). Plato's self-analysis of his experience thus leaves no doubt about the revelatory character of the comprehensive vision; it is conceptually clear about the interaction of the noetic quest and the vision in the imaginative creation of a new type of "mythical" symbols.

The few instances selected from the vast historical field of experience and symbolization will be sufficient to make the general issue clear. The symbols of the past, whatever their analytical value may have been at the time of their genesis, cannot be used unquestioned as analytical concepts in our present historical situation. Their critical value as instruments of historical interpretation must be reexamined; and since this reexamination extends to our common language of "philosophy," "being," "theology," "religion," "myth," "reason," "revelation," and so forth, a considerable upheaval in the conventional use of these symbols is to be expected. Still, we do not need an entirely new universe of symbols. Emerging as we are from the distortions of history through the dogmatisms of theology, ontology, the methodologies and ideologies, we discover the new language needed to be for the most part the old language of experiential analysis that has been buried under the doctrinal deformations. To the old language of the Beginning and the Beyond, the *fides quaerens intellectum*, the presence of the divine reality, the divine appeal, and the human response, the divine-human movement and countermovement, the human quest and the noetic pull from the Beyond, the Parousia of the Beyond, the existence in the Metaxy, the existential agon of man in the Metaxy of mortality and immortality, we now must add the vision as the comprehensive mode of man's cognitive participation in reality.

On Vision

Vision in the Platonic sense is an event in the cognitive process of reality. As an event, it has neither a subject nor an object of cognition. To speak of the vision as a Platonic act of cognition and of the reality seen as its object would deform the event by intentionalist reduction. Besides, such language would flatly contradict its careful description as a divine-human encounter by the Plato who experienced it. The partners to the encounter must not be converted into the grammatical subjects of such statements as "Plato thinks . . ." or "God reveals . . ."; a Platonic *opsis* is neither a Cartesian *cogito* nor a revealed doctrine. Faced by this difficulty, one might then feel tempted to make "reality" the grammatical subject and to predicate of it the process of becoming luminous in the vision. In fact, I have used this proposition more than once myself, in order to avoid hypostatizing the partners to the encounter. But its use would be a misuse if it were to suggest "reality" as a something about which propositions can be advanced short of the experiences analyzed. For as soon as we ask further what this "reality" that now has become the grammatical subject "really" is, we can only say that it is as what it appears when it becomes luminous for itself in the visionary event. Again, the transformation of the term into the subject of a defining proposition leads only back to the insight of the vision itself.

I have touched on this problem previously in the section on "Folly and Theology." Plato's positive "type of theology" derived its validity from the defense of truth against the negative type of the Sophists, but the truth defended was not to be found in the propositional "type" itself; even the positive type would have been empty without its background in the truth of experience. The "foolishness" of the negative type expands into the positive propositions if their connection with the experiential source of truth is broken by the assumption that analytical propositions make sense independent of the experience that they analyze. This specific relation between the fool's existence and the misuse of propositional language suggests the larger problem that there is something "foolish" about the conception of language as an instrument of reference to a reality outside itself. Language, it is true, has the referential character that corresponds to the intentionality of consciousness, but a propositional language "about" reality could be autonomously valid only if it were a language "beyond" reality. In order to sustain this assumption, however, one would have to ignore, or to deny, the fact that not only our consciousness of reality but also its language are constituted in such historical events as the Platonic *opsis*. In the event of the *opsis* and its language we reach the limit at which language does not merely refer to reality but is reality emerging as the luminous "word" from the divine-human encounter. The emerging word is the truth of the reality from which it emerges; it is what we call a "symbol" in the pregnant sense. And since the truth emerging is the truth of the divine Beyond and of its Parousia in the cosmos and the soul of man, the denial of its emergence is the denial of the truth itself. The restriction of language to the intentionalist component in its structure is indeed "foolish" inasmuch as it tries to establish a realm of propositional truth beyond the Beyond and its Parousia in the psyche. In the contemporary context, the restrictivist action is part of the general movement which, since Nietzsche, goes under the name of the murder of God.

The problems of vision and its language, of the truth of reality and the reality of truth, come to analytical consciousness when the experience of reality has differentiated so far that the Metaxy of the psyche and the divine-human encounter can be discerned as the site and source of reality experienced and symbolized. The newly differentiated and the earlier, more compact experiences present conflicting claims to truth; and the conflict of verities concerning divine reality and its presence in the cosmos cannot be settled on the level of argument about objects in the external world. The noetic experience of the Beyond and its Parousia in the soul of man and the cosmos does not correct an erroneous opinion about a detail in external reality, nor does it add a piece of information to a previously existing body of knowledge; it is a something that Plato calls by the technical term *vision*. And this something, this vision of the Whole of reality, of its structure and movement, is in conflict with the earlier vision of the Whole as a cosmos full of gods. The problem of the vision and its status in the cognitive process of reality becomes acute for Plato because he *has* a vision and is conscious of it as the source of the truth that he elaborates in the work of a lifetime.[4]

4. A separate page, consisting of the following short paragraph, was found by the editors, and it indicates Voegelin's intention to continue his analysis from the point at which he had left off:

The conflict of truth between the visions leads to the previously intimated difficulties of analysis and symbolism. The meaning of *being* has to be revised, a hierarchy of being has to be acknowledged, the new symbolism of Eminent Being has to be created, divine reality becomes the "truly divine" Beyond, the Olympian gods have to be reduced to a derivative status of immortality, man becomes immortal but not quite as immortal as the Beyond, and so forth.

Appendix

As the editors stated in the Editorial Note on the Texts Selected for This Volume, the first four texts were written between the time of publication of *Plato and Aristotle,* Volume III of *Order and History,* in 1957, and the appearance of Volume IV, *The Ecumenic Age,* in 1974. The editors thought that it would be worthwhile for the reader to have available Voegelin's outlines, or tables of contents, from two points during this period. The first outline dates to 1961 and was prepared for the Volume IV that had already been announced as *Empire and Christianity.* Two other outlines, from around 1970 (the letters accompanying them are dated December 12, 1969, and January 30, 1971), are for a volume that was to be called *In Search of Order* (the eventual title of Volume V, published posthumously in 1987). In these last two outlines we can see the contours of the actual Volume IV published in 1974 as well as the titles of three of the pieces published in the present volume.

We have preceded each of the three outlines with Voegelin's letters to the respective directors of the Louisiana State University Press. (The first letter is found in the Voegelin Papers, Box 23, Folder 28, while the other two are from Box 24, Folder 1.)

November 13, 1961

Dr. Donald R. Ellegood
Director
Louisiana State University Press
Baton Rouge 3, Louisiana

Dear Don:

Enclosed you will find a synopsis of Volume IV on <u>Empire and Christianity</u>.

From this synopsis you will see what the enormous difficulties of organization had been. The principal difficulty was that there are running through this volume four lines of meaning which had to be represented without making a mess of the book. These four lines are the following:

1) The structural parallelism of the various civilizational complexes—the Near-Eastern and Mediterranean, India, China—which permit to speak of the whole period as the Ecumenic Age.
2) The lines of meaning which are internal to each of these complexes.
3) The line of meaning which starts 2000 years before the Ecumenic Age, runs through it, and goes on into the present.
4) The main line of historical meaning running from the Ancient Near East through Rome and Christianity into our Western present—a line by the side of which the developments in India and China appear as side lines.

I hope I have found a solution to this interplay of meanings by giving a survey of the whole problem in Part I. Then, in Part II, I draw the internal lines of meaning in the various civilizational complexes. And beginning with Part III, I let the main line of meaning run from the Ancient Orient into Western civilization.

You will easily see from this account in which manner my conception differs from Toynbee's. In the <u>Study of History</u> Toynbee can easily proceed by taking up one structural element after another and pursue it through the various civilizations. He has no serious problems beyond this organization. I have to cope, in the first place, with a line of meaning running from Mesopotamian empires and Egypt to the present—a problem of which Toynbee can dispose by saying that the contemporary civilizations in his opinion have no visible meaning. Furthermore, I do not treat all the civilizations on the same level but accord the representative rank to the line which runs from Israel and Hellas into the West. Again Toynbee does not have to worry about this question, as he simply indulges in a happy fraternization with everybody who lives today as equals.

The lecture on <u>World Empire and the Unity of Mankind</u> which I have sent you recently was the key to the organization inasmuch as its substance will be incorporated in Part I, Chapter 1 of the present synopsis. I hope that this information will give you some comfort in your unrest about the further development of <u>Order and History</u>.

With kindest regards, I am,

Sincerely yours,

Eric Voegelin

Empire and Christianity

Part I. The Configuration of History

   Ch. 1: The Empire as Incarnation of Order
      Israel and Hellas:
        a. The Enclaves in the History of Empire
        b. The Main Line in the History of Mankind
        c. The Europocentric Structure of History
      The Phases of Empire:
        a. The Cosmological Empires—
          The Compact Myth of the Cosmos
        b. The Ecumenic Empires—
          The Truth of Existence Differentiated
          Dissociation of Power and Spirit
        c. The Orthodox Empires—
          Western, Byzantium, Islam, Hinduism, Neo-Confucian
          China
        d. The Twilight of Empire and the Apocalypse of Man

   Ch. 2: The Ecumenic Age—A Survey
      (1) The Parallel Beginnings about 800 B.C.
        Etruscans—The Hellenic Polis—The Isolation of Judah—
        Iran and India—The Eastern Chou Dynasty
      (2) The Spiritual Outbursts
        Philosophers—Prophets—Zoroaster—The Buddha-
        Confucius and Lao-tze
      (3) The Imperial Outbursts
        Persian, Macedonian, Roman—The Maurya Empire—The
        Han-Empire
      (4) The Tentative Associations of Power and Spirit
        The Achaemenid Empire and Zoroastrianism
        Rome and Imperial Theology
        The Maurya Empire and Buddhism
        The Han Empire and Confucianism
      (5) The Councils
        Rome and the Christian Councils
        Maurya and Buddhist Councils
        Han and Confucian Councils
      (6) The Emergence of New Civilizations
        Western Christian, Byzantine, Islamic, Hindu, Far Eastern
      (7) The End of the Period: The introduction of the Christian Era
        in the ninth century A.D.

Part II. Ecumenism: Imperial and Spiritual

    Ch. 1: The Near Eastern and Mediterranean Main Line
          Persia, Alexander, Rome
          Polybius: Theory of the Ecumene and of Pragmatic History
          Spiritual Ecumenism: Christianity, Mani
          Ecumenism and Universalism

    Ch. 2: Iranian Problems
          Zoroaster—The Achaemenian Inscriptions—Zurvanism—
             The Sassanian Empire

    Ch. 3: The Anthropomorphic Conception of Man in India and China
          Buddha, Confucius, Lao-tse

    Ch. 4: India
          The Emergence of an Ecumenic Civilization from Tribal Society
          Its Non-Historic Character
          The Cosmological Speculations on Space and Time
          The Stimulation of Empire from Persians and Macedonians
          The Asoka Empire and Buddhism

    Ch. 5: China
          The Ecumenic Conception on the Tribal Level
          Early Cosmological Symbolism of Rulership
          The Expansion of the Homocentric Ecumene and the Disintegra-
             tion of its Order
          The Construction of Traditional History

Part III. The Encounter with History

    Ch. 1: The Stratum of the Cosmological Myth
          Historiogenesis and the Genesis of History

    Ch. 2: Hellas
          The Truth of Philosophy and the Truth of the Myth
          Metaphysics, Metaanthropology, and Methahistory
          Alexander: The Differentiation of Intellect and Spirit
          Polis and Cosmos
          The Stoic Development

    Ch. 3: Israel
          The Exilic Reaction
          The Canonic Torah
          Apocalypse
          Sectarianism—the Qumran Texts
          Tannaitic Judiasm

    Ch. 4: Christianity
          The Apocalypse of Christ and the Gospel
          The Apostolic Apocalypse—St. Paul

December 12, 1969

Mr. Richard L. Wentworth
Director, Louisiana State University Press
Baton Rouge, Louisiana 70803

Dear Mr. Wentworth:

Your letter of November 26, by which you inquire about In Search of Order, has still gone unanswered, because I had to finish the manuscript on Henry James that is supposed to come out in the Southern Review. Now that it is finished, I immediately turn to your question and make the following suggestion:

What held up the further volumes of Order and History and practically exploded them is, as I have detailed in earlier correspondence, the vast amount of materials that had to be reworked in order to arrive at the theoretical conclusions that would have to form the skeleton for the whole work.

During the last 10 years, I have done one such study after another to be sure of my ground. A part of these studies has been published in Anamnesis. Now I have advanced far enough in the detailed studies to arrive at the following division of materials:

(1) There should be a volume entitled In Search of Order, which I can offer you now for publication as the volume that will conclude the work I had started in Order and History, though I would not consider it a fourth volume, but an independent work under the title given.

(2) I have now been able to isolate the theoretical issues and shall publish them in a volume entitled The Drama of Humanity, on which I am at work at present.

In Search of Order is what I can offer you now with definite prospects of early completion. I am enclosing what might be considered a table of contents enumerating the studies to be included. A second sheet repeats the titles with information on the state of publication or non-publication of the manuscripts, with the page numbers the manuscripts have at present. The whole volume would, in my estimate, have about 700 pages in manuscript, which would run to approximately 500 pages in print. All of these manuscripts, with the exception of the study on the Meaning of the Gospel, are finished. The only work that has yet to be done, will be stylistic revision and decisions on whether this or that page should be dropped because the problem has come up in the context of another one of the studies.

For your further information, I include the manuscript of (1) The Eclipse of Reality, (2) Equivalences of Experiences and Symbolizations in History, and (3) Henry James for your inspection. These pieces will give you an idea of the state at which the manuscripts have arrived. You will see that hardly a word has to be changed.

If you should decide that this volume is acceptable to the LSU Press, I could set to work immediately to put the finishing touch on it, and let you have the whole manuscript ready for print by the middle of 1970.

Your acceptance of <u>In Search of Order</u> would have consequences for the translation of <u>Anamnesis</u>, which you have considered. I think it would be superfluous to translate <u>Anamnesis</u>, because the present studies represent a considerable advance over this volume, besides, two of the studies that have been published in <u>Anamnesis</u>, i.e. <u>Historiogenesis</u> and <u>Mongol Orders of Submission</u> will be absorbed into <u>In Search of Order</u>. If you would decide not to publish <u>Anamnesis</u>, that would dispose of the problem which, as I take it from your letter, looks bothersome and rather hopeless.

Please, let me know what you think of this suggestion.

With all good wishes for the Holidays, I am,

Yours sincerely,

Enclosures

Eric Voegelin

IN SEARCH OF ORDER

Introduction

1. Historiogenesis   (Published in <u>Anamnesis</u>, 57 pp.)
2. Anxiety and Reason   (Unpublished manuscript, 50 pp.)
3. Ecumenic Empire   (Unpublished manuscript, 87 pp.)
4. Mongol Orders of Submission   (Published in <u>Anamnesis</u>, 44 pp.)
5. Empire and the Unity of Mankind
    (Published in <u>International Affairs</u>, 19 pp.)

*   *   *

6. History and Gnosis   (Published in <u>The Old Testament and Christian Faith</u>, 25 pp.)
7. Immortality   (Published in <u>The Harvard Theological Review</u>, 45 pp.)
8. Meaning of the Gospel   (Unpublished manuscript; lecture to be delivered at the <u>Pittsburgh Theological Seminary</u>, April, 1970, cca. 30 pp.)

*   *   *

9. Equivalences of Experience and Symbolization in History
    (Unpublished manuscript, 25 pp., will come out in the Symposium of the <u>Instituto Accademico di Roma</u> in 1970)
10. The Moving Soul   (Unpublished manuscript, 20 pp.)

*   *   *

11. The Eclipse of Reality   (Unpublished manuscript, 15 pp., to be published in the Memorial Volume for Alfred Schutz, 1970)
12. Schiller's Universal History   (Unpublished manuscript, 20 pp.)
13. On Hegel   (Unpublished manuscript, 40 pp., partially to be published in the First Conference of the <u>International Society for the Study of Time</u>, 1970)
14. On Schelling   (Unpublished manuscript, 80 pp.)
15. On Nietzsche and Pascal   (Unpublished manuscript, 61 pp.)
16. Henry James   (Unpublished manuscript, 50 pp., to be published in <u>The Southern Review</u>, 1970)

January 30, 1971

Mr. Leslie E. Phillabaum
Assistant Director and Editor
Louisiana State University Press
Baton Rouge, Louisiana 70803

Dear Mr. Phillabaum:

It was hard work, but I could finish the crucial first Chapter of Historio-genesis having 83 pp. manuscript. Please find enclosed a copy of it.

I am sending only this manuscript today, because there probably is not much sense in sending you parts which are separated by gaps. Chapter 2 on The Ecumenic Age is not yet quite finished.

For your information, I am enclosing the table of contents, as it is planned at present. Of this table there are finished for print the Chapters 3, 4, 5, 6, 7, 8, 10, 12, 14, and 15. I can send them if you want them, but for the reason given above, it will be better to wait for the gaps to be filled.

I hesitate to set a fixed date for completion, but you can see for yourself that the matter looks quite hopeful, especially since the difficulties which were inevitable in the case of Chapter 1 do not occur in the later ones.

Your editor can go to work on this Chapter 1, and that would be quite a help for me, because I could see what suggestions you possibly will have to make and could use them in finishing the further manuscript.

With best regards, I am,

Yours sincerely,

Encls.

Eric Voegelin

(Dictated but not read
by Eric Voegelin)

IN SEARCH OF ORDER

Introduction
Part I: Empire

1. Historiogenesis   (Unpublished manuscript, 83 pp.)
2. Ecumenic Age   (Unpublished manuscript, 94 pp.)
3. Conquest and Exodus   (Unpublished manuscript, 90 pp.)
4. Mongol Order of Submission
    (Published in Anamnesis, 44 pp.)
5. Empire and the Unity of Mankind
    (Published in International Affairs, 19 pp.)

Part II: The Height and the Depth

6. Immortality   (Published in The Harvard Theological Review, 45 pp.)
7. Equivalences of Experience and Symbolization in History
    (Unpublished manuscript, 25 pp.)
8. History and Gnosis   (Published in The Old Testament and Christian Faith, 25 pp.)
9. The Meaning of the Gospel
    (Published in Vol. II of Jesus and Man's Hope, 54 pp.)
10. The Moving Soul   (Unpublished manuscript, 20 pp.)

Part III: The Eclipse of Reality

11. The Eclipse of Reality   Schiller's Universal History (Published in the Memorial Volume for Alfred Schutz, 15 pp.; Unpublished manuscript, 20 pp.)
12. On Hegel   (Published in Studium Generale, 65 pp.)
13. On Schelling   (Unpublished manuscript, 80 pp.)
14. On Nietzsche and Pascal   (Unpublished manuscript, 61 pp.)
15. Henry James   (Published in the January, 1971 issue of The Southern Review, 50 pp.)

Index

Abel-Remusat: on cultural diffusion, 41
Abraham: 43; Exodus from Ur, 19
Achaemenian empire, 16
Achaemenid expansion, 37
Aditya, 96
Aeschylus: and theomorphism of soul, 27; *Prometheus*, 80, 226
Age of Reason, 92, 138
Ages of World: in Hesiod, 72
Aggregate of symbolisms: as equivalent to a philosophy of being, 72–75
Agnoia (ignorance), 102
Aition: as ground or cause, 89
Akh-en-Aton, 24, 42, 214
Alasha Hoyuk, 192
Alcibiades, 32
Aletheia (truth-reality): principal passage on in Aristotle, 109; double meaning of, 114
Alexander: 17, 56; and conquest of Persia, 19; drive for empire, 31–32; conquest marks an epoch, 37; cosmic religion, 67
Allegoresis: Midrashic, 182; philosophical, of Philo, 182; Christian philosophical, of the Patres, 182
Altizer, Thomas, xxviii*n*
Amon, 60
Amon Hymns, 214, 216, 223
Amon-Re, 69
Amphictyonic Leagues, 26
Analogy of being, 75
Anaximander, 227
Anaximandrian symbolism of the Apeiron: Plato's image of Being before the event, 221
Anima animi, 5
Anselm, Saint: xxix, xxxvi, 191–206

passim; De Fide Trinitatis et de Incarnatione Verbi, 194*n*1; *Proslogion,* analyzed, 192–206; *Monologion,* 196
Anselm-Gaunilo debate, 200
Anthropogony: classed with historiogenesis, 53; forming aggregate with theogony, cosmogony, and historiogenesis, 72–75; in Hesiodian Ages of the World, 72
Anthropomorphic conception: in China, 28
Anu, 95
Anxiety: discussed, 58, 61–63, 66–68, 70; and search of order, 70; search of ground as response to, 74; responds to diversions, 83; assuaged by acts of symbolization, 87; response provoked by non-cognitive awareness of existence out of nothing, 89; no exact equivalent in Greek language, 102; related to cosmogonic question in Aristotle, 103
Apeiron, 221
Apocalypse: as symbolic form, 14; Jewish, 59; modern equivalents of, 66; immanentist forms of, 82
Apocalypse of Abraham: discussed, 4; quoted and analyzed, 96–98; as pneumatic meditation, compared to Aristotle's noetic meditation, 104
Apocalyptic sects, 31
Aquinas, Saint Thomas: xxix, xxxvi, 177, 192, 210; concept of *deiformitas,* 227
Arche (beginning): as first cause origin, beginning, or ground, 5, 89, 107; in speculation on origins in Ionian philosophers, 52, 57; equivalents of cos-

mological and philosophical speculation on, 74; in Aristotle, 107–108

Aristotle: xxii, 131, 153, 170, 176, 178, 187, 198, 224; reception in Middle Ages, 7; cyclical time in *Problemata* discussed, 64; increase of cosmological awareness, 67; Nous and First Cause in Macrobius, 77; conception of life of reason, 77; *homonoia* in, 90; philosophic life, 92; use of term *theology*, 99, 107; *Metaphysics* texts discussed and exegesis given, 99–110; *Metaphysics* I as new symbolism to establish continuum of noetic search, 101; *Metaphysics* as lasting arsenal in defense of reason, 101–102; Platonic education, 106; *Nichomachean Ethics*, 108; *Politics*, 108; passage from *Metaphysics* cited at end of Hegel's *Enzyklopädie*, 150–51; philosophizing as *athanatizein*, 225

Arrianus: *Indika*, 18

Assyrian empire, 32

Athenian empire, 16

Athens: and transfer of authority, 48

Attunement to divine being: discovered in experience of transcendence, 21

Augustine, Saint: xxviin19, 32, 75, 139, 153, 204, 224; *amor Dei* and *amor sui*, 32; analysis of internal reflection in *De vera religione* XXXIX, 175; on illumination, 195

Augustus, 37

Axial time: core of truth in, 46

Babylon: expansion of, 17; conquest of by Persians, 17

Babylonian Prayer: "to whom it may concern," 70–71; compared to image in T. S. Eliot, 85

Barth, Karl, 192–93

Beginning: symbol indicating direction of questing movement, 173–74; conflict between God of Beginning and God of Beyond, 211

Behistun Inscription, 59

Being: in Parmenides' speculation, 2; differentiated and endowed with indices, 5; discussion of several modes and meanings of, 207, 209; language of and its aggregates of meaning, 218–20; complications in the language of, 220; new symbolism of Eminent Being, 232n4

Bergson, Henri: and open soul, 5; *Deux Sources de la morale et de la religion*, 41; opening and closing of vistas, 57

Berossus: *Babyloniaka*, 20; and historiogenesis, 56

Beyond: divine Beyond same as divine Within, 5; of the experiencing soul, 21; symbol indicating direction of questing movement, 173–74; conflict between God of Beyond and God of Beginning, 211; of the cosmos in Plato's *Republic*, 217; analytically inseparable from act in which it becomes "visible," 218; immortalizing presence in act of meditation, 221

Bhagavad Gita, 223

Bible:
—Genesis, Book of: 176, 185; and Schiller's deformation of Fall of man, 123
—Exodus: 4:22, quoted, 24; 3 (Thornbush Episode), 98, 186
—Judges: Book of, 67
—2 Samuel: 9, p. 15
—1 Kings: 2, p. 15
—Chronicles: Books of: 15
—Ezra: Book of, 15
—Nehemiah: Book of, 15
—Psalms: hybrid character of, 67–70; creator-god in, 68; 13 (14), 199
—Isaiah: 2:1, 13:1, p. 180; 32, referred to, 200
—Jeremiah: 1: 9–10, p. 49, 12, referred to, 180, 5:12ff., 200
—Amos: 1:1, p. 180; 7, referred to, 180
—Maccabees, Books of: 15
—Luke: 21:28, p. 216
—John, Gospel of: and the Word of the Beginning, 186; 16:24, p. 195
—Romans: 1:18–23, quoted and discussed, 177
—Ephesians: 4:22–24, p. 71
—Colossians: referred to, 71; 2, and *theotes*, 183
—2 Timothy: 3:17, p. 143
—Hebrews: 11:1, and formula of faith, 69

Brahman, 96

Bréton, André: *Ode à Charles Fourier*, 145

Brihadaranyaka Upanishad, 175

self-interpretation, 40; Colossians referred to, 71; old man and new man, 139; *homo dei* in 2 Tim. 3:17 opposed to Comtean *homo humanitatis*, 143; Rom. 1:18–23, quoted and discussed, 177; Colossians 2 and the *theotes*, 183

Periagoge (conversion of the prisoner in the Cave), 188

Periodization: of history, 37

Persia: conquest of Babylon, 17

Persian empire, 37

Persian Wars, 16, 26

Pharaoh: 68; as mediator of divine presence, 24

Philo, 182

Philodoxos (lover of opinion): in Plato, 105; equivalent of *philosophe*, 136

Philodoxy (love of opinion): in Plato, 30

Philomythos (lover of myth): in Aristotle, 105

Philosopher: represents truth of existence, 50; discipline of, 106

Philosophes: 146; Plato's philodoxers, 136

Philosophy: versus Sophistic thought, 3; of history, revolutionary action, 66; does not increase certainty, 69; cooperates with myth in mythospeculation, 74; equivalence to Myth, 74; as handmaid of theology, 92; superiority over myth, 93; confronts myth in Aristotle, 104

Physical reality: experience of, 166

Pindar: as prophetic poet, 145

Pirke Aboth I: quoted, 181

Plato: xxii, xxviii*n*19, xxx, xxxvi, 14, 21, 27, 29, 33, 36, 176, 187, 198, 202, 204–205, 210, 214, 220–21, 223, 229, 232; and conception of Ideas, 6; *Timaeus*, 6; conception of great cycle of civilizational order, 19; creates symbol *methexis*, 21; "attack" on Homer, attack on Sophists, 28–30; and *philodoxy*, 30; respect for people's myth in *Epinomis*, 30; opposition to Sophists, 32; time as *eikon* of eternity in *Timaeus*, 39; and transfer of authority, 48; transformation of historiogenesis, 58; increase of cosmological awareness, 67; and Idea in Macrobius, 77; cautions against depriving people of myth, 78; cautions against depriving

people of God, 80; *Kallipolis*, 92; coins term *theology*, 99; *Symposion*, 99; dialogue tradition in Aristotle, 100; *Phaedo*, 100; dialogic filiation to Aristotle, 101; *Gorgias*, 134; developed language of In-Between reality, 178; *anoia* equivalent of Israelitic *nebala*, contempt for God, 200; refutation of Sophistic triads, 201; *typoi peri theologias*, 203; myth of the *Phaedrus*, 212; philosopher's myth as story of divine reality, 212*n*3; luminosity of self-reflection in *Phaedrus*, 215; discussion of the "rise" in *Phaedrus*, 216; does not transcend the "cosmos," or the "world," 219; discussion of creativity of Beginning in *Timaeus*, 224; *Timaeus* 90a–b, *Gorgias*, quoted 225; philosophy of self-reflective interaction between noesis and cosmological vision, 228

Player of the Puppets: Platonic myth, 80, 213*n*3; cords become prison bars, 83

Pleonexia (personal power drive), 27, 32

Plotinus: xxviii*n*19, 104, 176, 223; Emanation in Macrobius, 77

Pneumopathological case: Schiller's spiritual alienation, 132

Pneumopathology: in the sciences of man in the wake of the Systems, 157; term coined by Schelling, 202

Poincaré, Jules Henri: conception of a limited universe, 167–68

Polytheism: Homeric type never developed in China, 28

Polytheistic myth: in Hellas, 27

Pompey: capture of Jerusalem, 15

Positivism: perversion of immanence, 88

Pragmatic history, 31

Prajapati, 96

Primary experience of cosmos: 58, 59, 62, 64, 67; and experiences of transcendence, 21, 22–23; as background to Homeric society of gods and men, 27; emancipation of sophists and philosophers from, 29–30; and totality of being, 30; defective forms of, 30; by experiences of transcendence, 35; break from, 43; in contemporary Western societies, 56; dominates cosmological